MW00624610

New Concepts in Latino American Cultures
A Series Edited by Licia Fiol-Matta & José Quiroga

Ciphers of History: Latin American Readings for a Cultural Age
by Enrico Mario Santí

Cosmopolitanisms and Latin America: Against the Destiny of Place
by Jacqueline Loss

Remembering Maternal Bodies: Melancholy in Latina and Latin American Women's Writing
by Benigno Trigo

The Ethics of Latin American Literary Criticism: Reading Otherwise,
edited by Erin Graff Zivin

Modernity and the Nation in Mexican Representations of Masculinity: From Sensuality to Bloodshed
by Héctor Domínguez-Ruvalcaba

White Negritude: Race, Writing, and Brazilian Cultural Identity
by Alexandra Isfahani-Hammond

Essays in Cuban Intellectual History
by Rafael Rojas

Mestiz@ Scripts, Digital Migrations, and the Territories of Writing
by Damián Baca

Confronting History and Modernity in Mexican Narrative
by Elisabeth Guerrero

Cuban Women Writers: Imagining A Matria
by Madeline Cámara Betancourt

Forthcoming Titles

Other Worlds: New Argentinian Film
by Gonzalo Aguilar

Cuba in the Special Period: Culture and Ideology in the 1990s,
edited by Ariana Hernandez-Reguant

Telling Ruins in Latin America,
edited by Michael J. Lazzara and Vicky Unruh

New Directions in Latino American Cultures
Also Edited by Licia Fiol-Matta & José Quiroga

New York Ricans from the Hip Hop Zone
by Raquel Rivera

The Famous 41: Sexuality and Social Control in Mexico, 1901,
edited by Robert McKee Irwin, Edward J. McCaughan, and Michele Rocío Nasser

Velvet Barrios: Popular Culture & Chicana/o Sexualities,
edited by Alicia Gaspar de Alba, with a foreword by Tomás Ybarra Frausto

Tongue Ties: Logo-Eroticism in Anglo-Hispanic Literature
by Gustavo Perez-Firmat

Bilingual Games: Some Literary Investigations,
edited by Doris Sommer

Jose Martí: An Introduction
by Oscar Montero

New Tendencies in Mexican Art
by Rubén Gallo

The Masters and the Slaves: Plantation Relations and Mestizaje in American Imaginaries,
edited by Alexandra Isfahani-Hammond

The Letter of Violence: Essays on Narrative and Theory
by Idelber Avelar

Intellectual History of the Caribbean
by Silvio Torres-Saillant

None of the Above: Contemporary Puerto Rican Cultures and Politics,
edited by Frances Negrón-Muntaner

Queer Latino Testimonio, Keith Haring, and Juanito Xtravaganza: Hard Tails
by Arnaldo Cruz-Malavé

The Portable Island: Cubans at Home in the World,
edited by Ruth Behar and Lucía M. Suárez

Forthcoming Titles

Violence without Guilt: Ethical Narratives from the Global South
by Hermann Herlinghaus

Puerto Ricans in America: 30 Years of Activism and Change,
edited by Xavier F. Totti and Felix V. Matos Rodriguez

Mestiz@ Scripts, Digital Migrations, and the Territories of Writing

Damián Baca

Foreword by
Linda Martín Alcoff

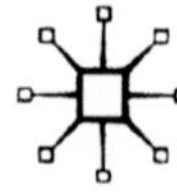

MESTIZ@ SCRIPTS, DIGITAL MIGRATIONS, AND THE TERRITORIES OF WRITING

First published in 2008 by
PALGRAVE MACMILLAN™
175 Fifth Avenue, New York, N.Y. 10010 and
Houndmills, Basingstoke, Hampshire, England RG21 6XS
Companies and representatives throughout the world.

PALGRAVE MACMILLAN is the global academic imprint of the Palgrave Macmillan division of St. Martin's Press, LLC and of Palgrave Macmillan Ltd. Macmillan® is a registered trademark in the United States, United Kingdom and other countries. Palgrave is a registered trademark in the European Union and other countries.

ISBN-13: 978–0–230–60515–2
ISBN-10: 0–230–60515–X

Library of Congress Cataloging-in-Publication Data

Baca, Damián, 1975–
Mestiz@ scripts, digital migrations, and the territories of writing / Damián Baca.
p. cm.—(New concepts in Latino American cultures series)
Includes bibliographical references and index.
ISBN 0–230–60515–X
1. Picture-writing—Mexico—History. 2. Mestizos—History. 3. Mestizos—Social life and customs. 4. Manuscripts, Mexican (Pre-Columbian) 5. Indians of Mexico—Languages—Writing. 6. Indians of Central America—Languages—Writing. 7. Culture—Semiotic models. I. Title.

F1219.3.W94B33 2008
305.868'72073—dc22 2007047316

A catalogue record for this book is available from the British Library.

Design by Newgen Imaging Systems (P) Ltd., Chennai, India.

First edition: June 2008

10 9 8 7 6 5 4 3 2 1

Printed in the United States of America.

Transferred to Digital Printing in 2010

For my maternal and paternal ancestors y familia, friends, and those who are discontent with the dominant history and pedagogy of "writing" in the Americas.

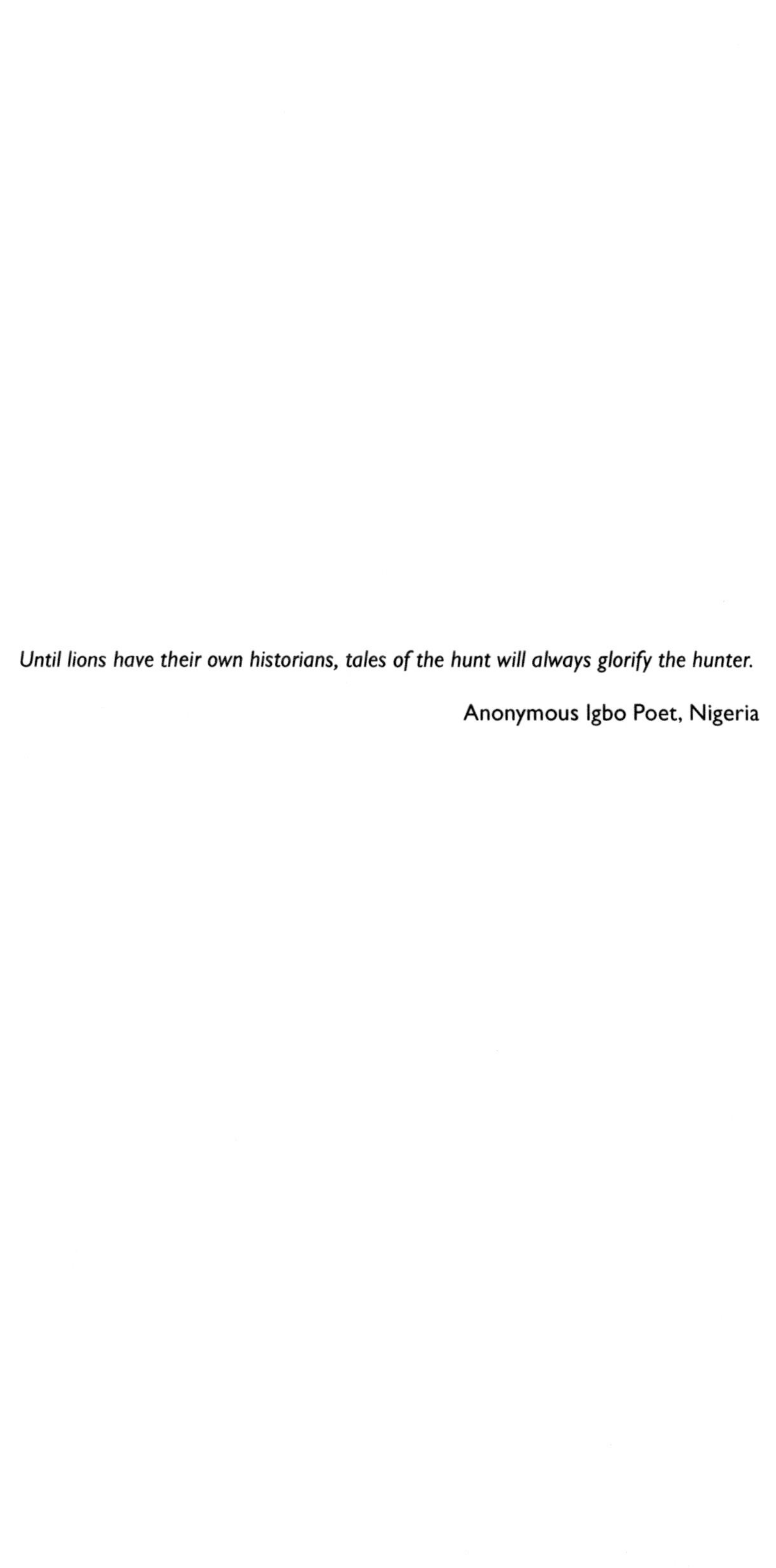

Until lions have their own historians, tales of the hunt will always glorify the hunter.

Anonymous Igbo Poet, Nigeria

Contents

Foreword by Linda Martín Alcoff xi

Preface xv

Acknowledgments xix

Pronunciation Guide and Brief Chronology: 500,000 BCE–2012 CE xxi

1 Mestiz@ Scripts and the Rhetoric of Subversion 1

2 New Consciousness/Ancient Myths 15

3 Mestiz@: A Brief History, from Mexicatl to Chican@ 33

4 Codex Scripts of Resistance: From Columbus to the Border Patrol 63

5 The Spreading of Color: Sacred Scripts and the Genesis of the Rio Grande 95

6 Crossing Borders: Gloria Anzaldúa and the Territories of English Composition 119

7 Thinking and Teaching Across Borders and Hemispheres 133

Notes 165

Glossary 185

Bibliography 195

Reading and Discussion Guide 205

Index 207

Foreword

The irony of a study in composition and rhetoric written from the perspective of Mexican American and Mesoamerican historiography will be lost on no one who knows the history of the Conquest in the Americas. Even progressive and *contemporary* analysts of the Conquest portray the conquered peoples as illiterate: the French critic Tzvetan Todorov, for example, in a widely lauded study portrayed the "absence of writing" as perhaps the most important cause of the Aztec defeat, rendering the native peoples vulnerable and defenseless before the improvisational abilities of the literate Europeans.[1] Pictographic modes of communication, he claims, are ritual-bound, incapable of improvisation, comprising an experience, not a language. This account only updates while echoing the sixteenth-century claim by Sepúlveda, as the great Jesuit apologist for the genocide, rape, and pillage of the Conquest, that the war on the Indians is justified "against [an] uncivilized people who are more barbarous than can be imagined, for they are absolutely lacking in any knowledge of letters…"[2] This key aspect of the colonial imaginary is still very much in operation today, especially in the halls of higher education that prize the alphabetic text as the sine qua non of civil societies.

Damián Baca's innovative study of New World composition and rhetorical practices provides an alternative account not only of the practices at the time of the Conquest, and before, but also of the evolution of a "gradual and cautious syncretism" that has been practiced ever since. He offers a revised history of writing in the Americas that reads both the differences and similarities that exist between the new and the old worlds. His account of ritual dances such as the *Matachines* demonstrate precisely their improvisational character, their ability to subvert the narratives of the dominant, and to communicate insurrectionary hopes in a rhetorical manner in which the message was carefully concealed, safely subtle, yet unmistakeable to its intended audience.

Postcolonial theorist Walter Mignolo has suggested that we should gain some critical distance over the currently widespread project to prove that non-Europeans had their own letters, philosophy, and art in the European style.[3] Because in the effort to prove our non-European ways equal or even identical to the Europeans', we might unwittingly eclipse the possibility of a true difference to emerge into view, a difference without analogy or equivalent, a capacity to "think otherwise." What if, he asks, the thought of the native peoples does not conform to the standards of rationality, or the criteria by which we identify philosophical discourses, among others? Shouldn't we hold open the potential of different cultures doing things differently, in such a way that genuinely new ideas might emerge, that might inspire and invigorate? Baca, I take it, is answering Mignolo's question decidedly in the affirmative. At the same time that he disputes certain fallacious ways of reading mestiz@ scripts, he is also suggesting their difference, particularly for the codices that in both style and structure expanded on the linearity of alphabetic modes of constructing meaning.

Moreover, Baca's argument, building from Gloria Anzaldúa, that there exists a fundamental syncretism in all aspects of the linguistic and rhetorical practices of the Americas makes this the central and defining feature and strategy that poses new lessons for northern cultures that continue to fetishize pure lineages, clear boundaries, and secure borders. His analyses of contemporary pictographic rhetorics, such as the 1992 exhibit *Chicano Codex: Encountering Art of the Americas*, and other expressive and performative works by artists, such as Guillermo Gómez-Peña, showcase a modern-day, politically motivated cultural syncretism still at work. Syncretism, he persuades us, is not an option; it is occurring all around us in ways we cannot understand without the tools of this expanded rhetorical analytics.

At the end of the day, Baca's own account is less rigidly oppositional than it is syncretic as well, arguing not for a return to the essence of an imagined pure past but for a revised way of understanding both rhetoric and writing in its comparative, coevolutionary context. His goal is not to segregate, but to reinscribe mestiz@ writing and rhetorical practices within expansive and inclusive frameworks of cultural history from which they have been too long absent. As Mignolo has called for, we need to reinscribe the simultaneity of local histories against the colonial temporal frameworks that divided geographies by the state of their approximation to the modernist ideal. This is insurrection at the borders, without a doubt, with the aim of supporting the processes of deassimilation that those from the south have been slowly engaging in for some time. It makes for a fascinating read, as well as the start of a more productive conversation long overdue.

LINDA MARTÍN ALCOFF

Notes

1. Tzvetan Todorov, *The Conquest of America: The Question of the Other.* Trans. Richard Howard. New York: Harper and Row, 1984. 80.
2. J. Ginés de Sepúlveda, "Del Reino y los Deberes del Rey." *Tratados politicos.* Madrid: Instituto de Estudios Politicos, 1963. 4–5.
3. See, for example, his "Dussel's Philosophy of Liberation: Ethics and the Geopolitics of Knowledge." *Thinking from the Underside of History: Enrique Dussel's Philosophy of Liberation.* Lanham, MD: Rowman and Littlefield, 2000. 27–50.

Preface

I write with the same knowledge, the same sadness, recognizing the full impact of the colonial "experiment" on the lives of Chicanos, mestizos and Native Americans. Our codices—dead leaves unwritten—lie smoldering in the ashes of disregard, censure, and erasure. The Last Generation *emerges from those ashes. I write against time, out of a sense of urgency that Chicanos are a disappearing tribe, out of a sense of this disappearance in my own familia.*

—Cherríe Moraga

This book was inspired by a timely question: how, when, and under what circumstances do Mestiz@s, this nation's largest ethnic and linguistic "minority" group, enter into world history? Not long ago, Western Europeans self-proclaimed themselves as the pinnacle of "civilization." The genesis of human progress allegedly emerges in a Europeanized ancient Greece, then migrates westward through the conquests of Rome. From Roman imperialism, civilization eventually reaches Western Europe, we are told, and navigates across the Atlantic, migrating westward yet again with Puritan colonists seeking freedom and opportunity on American Indian land. The myth of civilization imposes a vanguard narrative of thinking *from* East-to-West, and this narrative remains firmly embedded in our classrooms.

Thus, it is no surprise that Mestiz@s are imagined as making a belated entrance into the "advancement" of Western civilization. In my own field of English Composition, Mestiz@s appear only recently as unnamed linguistic "problems" in remedial or standard first-year writing seminars. After a few months when the semesters end, Mestiz@s curiously disappear from English Composition scholarship and its civilized world of the art of letters. When studying written communication, we are instructed to gaze back across the Atlantic to

Ancient Greece and Aristotle. From Aristotle to the unexplained arrival of present-day American composition instructors, writing East-to-West is sheltered by the dominant pedagogical mantle under which our minds and writing practices are disciplined.

Yet, the Americas did not exist only to belatedly join world history through Western eyes. Europe tragically viewed the region as needing "civilization" through preemptory warfare and occupation. This plight has also befallen Mestiz@ cultures. As a corrective to this East-to-West myth, I propose thinking and writing *from* contemporary Mestiz@ scripts and *from* the Indigenous land upon which our colleges and universities are built. This project, specifically the analysis of "new" histories and theories of Mestiz@ inscription practices, is not a call for recognizing our own "civilization" against the vanguard East-to-West trajectory. On the contrary, this study challenges European-centered history, provincializes alphabetic dominance, and positions Mestiz@ scripts at the center of twenty-first century writing.

Thinking and writing *from* the Americas presents teachers and students with a multitude of inscription practices unique to the Western Hemisphere, as Mesoamerican scripts are the only systems on the planet that did not emerge from Sumarian or Egyptian cultures. Moreover, the Americas are the only continent upon which an alphabetic script was so brutally and rapidly imposed upon a multitude of other highly complex, equally suitable communication systems. Today, Mestiz@ scripts adapt and revise violent, colonial narratives by strategically fusing numerous scripts, thereby migrating across the Western territories of "art" and "writing."

This book forwards a long-overdue proposal for teaching in the southwest region of the United States and beyond. First, I call for a renovation of writing practices specific to the Americas without the baggage of searching for essential reclamations of "authentic" history or nostalgia. My aim instead is to analyze historical possibilities, to develop new ways of thinking about writing today, based on material and corporeal practices that have shifted across time. In addition, I challenge educators to reinscribe Mesoamerican and Mestiz@ writing practices into the dominant intellectual frameworks of the study of written language.

Rethinking writing *from* Mesoamerican and Mestiz@ literatures advances a more constructive understanding of parallel literacies in the Americas, yet also promotes an intervention in the politics of writing instruction in the present. I am not suggesting that we treat Mesoamerican or Mestiz@ writing practices as tokenized, celebrated "alternatives" to a stabilized East-to-West narrative before which academics might remain uncritical. To the contrary, I call for a new politics of rhetorical analysis that will lead us to entirely new inquiries, such as how and in what ways are the enduring histories of Western civilization preferable to the immense plurality that remain obscured on American Indian land?

Acknowledgments

I thank the following mentors and allies for their honesty, insight, faith, and good company:

Linda Martín Alcoff, Christian Anible, Tomás Atencio, Katalina Baca, Maxine Baca-Zinn, Bernadette Marie Calafell, Davíd Carrasco, Michéle Ceballos, Albuquerque Mayor Martin J. Chávez, Pedro Cuperman, Richard Encinias, Rhina Espaillat, Linda Espinosa, Mónica Espinosa, Paul Espinosa, María Fránquiz and the NCTE Cultivating New Voices Foundation, Shearle Furnish, Sandra Gibbs, Cheryl Glenn, Roseann Dueñas Gonzáles, Juan Guerra, Guillermo Gómez-Peña and La Pocha Nostra, Rafael Jesús González, Michelle Holling, Bobbi Ciriza Houtchens, Dolores Huerta, Verónica Iglesias-Swanson, Inmaculada Lara-Bonilla, Carol Lipson, Danette Lovato-Pimentel Enterprises Inc., Violeta Luna, Scott Lyons, Apachu Maíz, Harriet Malinowitz, E.A. "Tony" Mares, Demetria Martínez, the Ronald E. McNair Postbaccalaureate Achievement Program, Jaime Armin Mejía, Teresa Meléndez, Eduardo Mendieta, Cecilia Rodríguez Milanés and the CCCC Latino Caucus, Delilah Montoya, Rob Namaste, Carrie Noland, Louise Wetherbee Phelps, Malea Powell, Cristián Roa de la Carrera, R. Joseph Rodriguez and the National Council of Teachers of English Committee on Racism and Bias in the Teaching of English, Marta Sánchez, Kyoko Sato, Eileen Schell, Roberto Sifuentes, Geneva Smitherman, Kent Swanson, Irma Svanadze, Syracuse University, Sandra Gail Teichmann, Stacey Lane Tice, Silvio Torres-Saillant, National Hispanic Cultural Center Foundation's History and Literary Arts Administrator Katie Trujillo and Director Carlos Vásquez, Frederico Vigil, Victor Villanueva, and my doctoral students in Rhetoric and Writing, Chicano-Latino studies, and American Indian studies at Michigan State University.

Pronunciation Guide and Brief Chronology: 500,000 BCE–2012 CE

Nahuatl is currently spoken by approximately 1.5 million people across Mexico, El Salvador, and the United States. There are numerous language varieties of *Nahuatl*, some of which are mutually unintelligible. *Nahuatl* may have originated in Chaco Canyon, New Mexico, and is recognized as the linguistic progenitor of Aztec, Apache, Toltec, Navajo, Shoshone, and Hopi Nation languages. Words and phrases are constructed by joining prefixes, root words, and suffixes to form an idea. Chocolate, for example, is a derivative from the compound word *chikolatl. Chikol* translates as "beater stick with twigs on one end," and *a:-tl* is "drink." *Chikolatl* is a ceremonial drink, foamed with a beater stick.

As the lingua franca of Mesoamerican commerce and trade, *Nahuatl* varieties were in significant use, from Canada through Panama. When the Aztecs founded the administrative and spiritual center of *Tenochtitlán* in 1325 ADE, *Nahuatl* was used as the official imperial language, though over 170 other languages thrived across Mesoamerica. Prior to the Spanish invasion in 1521, *Nahuatl* was recorded with pictographic scripts as a mnemonic to remind speakers and performers of memorized text. The language was inscribed on stone and Codex *papel amate*, most of which Conquistadors systematically burned during the first wave of occupation and Christianization. Spanish Franciscans translated *Nahuatl* into the Latin alphabet by "collaborating" with surviving Aztec writers under brutal and colonial circumstances. Although scholars debate over the accurate spelling of *Nahuatl* and its numerous language varieties, the following pronunciations are the accepted standard ones:

a is pronounced *ah*
e is pronounced *eh*
c is pronounced *cee*

ch is pronounced *sh*
ll is pronounced *l*
x is pronounced *sh*
hu, uh is pronounced *w*
qu is pronounced k and sometimes *qu*
z is pronounced *s*
tl is pronounced with the final "*e*" cut off just as it is about to be pronounced, creating a slight half-syllable effect.

Practice the following:
Nahuatl is pronounced "Nah-wahtl"
Quetzalqoatl is pronounced "keht-sahl-kowah-tl"
Mexica is pronounced "Me-shee-kah"
Huehuetlahtolli is pronounced "weh-weh-tlah-toh-lee"
Tenochtitlán is pronounced "te-no-sh-teet-lan"
Cuatlicue is proncounced "quat-lee-kway"

All English translations of *Nahuatl* and Spanish languages are from *Nahua* historian and philosopher Miguel León-Portilla.

Nahuatl is often mistaken as a language imposed by Aztec dominance, just as the Aztecs are often mistaken as those who established the commonwealth of Mesoamerican cultures. In the chronology below, note the late dates of the Aztec Empire in comparison to significantly earlier cultural developments in the Americas. There is no scholarly consensus regarding chronology, historical sources, dating methods, subject matter, and contrasting disciplinary methodologies. Readers should allow for margins of error in dates and subject matter.

Chronology (Gregorian Calendar)

50,000 BCE	Earliest known pictographs in Piaui, Brazil
50,000 BCE	Topper Site stone artifacts near Allendale, South Carolina
20,000 BCE	Projectile points and fragments of modified bone, central Mexico
12,500 BCE	Plank walls with animal hide covers in Monte Verde, Chile
11,500 BCE	Flint tools and weapons in Clovis, New Mexico
11,000 BCE	Foraging tools in Tamaulipas, Mexico
10,000 BCE	Speculated Mende African and Pacific Islander settlements
9000 BCE	Small nomadic bands in northern Belize

8500 BCE	Corn domestication in Oaxaca, Mexico
8000 BCE	Mound building settlements in Great Lakes region, North America
8500 BCE	Various settlements, pottery, and loom weaving throughout Mesoamerica
7400 BCE	Zea pollen, bottle gourds in Oaxaca Valley, Mexico
6300 BCE	Settlements across Cuba, the Dominican Republic, and Puerto Rico
3113 BCE	Starting date of the Epi-Olmec 5000-year time cycle
2500 BCE	Tlapacoya settlement and manufacturing center, southeast of Mexico City
2500 BCE	Zapotec urban culture and the construction of Monte Alto City
2400 BCE	Matanchén settlement along Mexican Pacific Coast
2000 BCE	Dzibilchaltún settlement in Yucatán
2000 BCE	Olmec urban culture and ceremonial architecture
1800 BCE	Capacha and El Opeño settlements in west Mexico, Maya settlements in Chiapas
1500 BCE	Flint tools on Catalina-California land bridge
1300 BCE	Toltec metropolis and kingdom controls Central Mexico
1200 BCE	Zapotec and Epi-Olmec urban cultures continue growth
1000 BCE	Teotihuacan metropolis and kingdom controls Mesoamerica
1000 BCE	Maya urban cultures
900 BCE	Cascajal Tablet, earliest known Olmec script
900 BCE	Teotihuacano, Ñuiñe, Xochicalco, and Mixteca-Puebla urban cultures
600 BCE	Earliest known Zapotec codex glyphs in Monte Albán
400 BCE	Maya control throughout Central America
300 BCE	Epi-Olmec writing to become a foundation for Maya script
200 BCE	Teotihuacan settlements, northeast of Mexico City
0	Year zero exists in Olmec, Hindu, and Buddhist calendars, not Gregorian
1111 CE	Aztec nomadic era, North America
1325 CE	Aztec establish imperial city of *Tenochtitlán* and rule over Mesoamerica
1491CE	Estimated population: 40 million
1650 CE	Estimated population: 10 million
1900 CE	Estimated population decline since 1492: 90–98 percent
2012 CE	End of the Epi-Olmec/Maya 5000-year time cycle

Further Reading

Boldurian, Anthony T., and John L. Cotter. *Clovis Revisited: New Perspectives on Paleoindian Adaptations from Blackwater Draw, New Mexico*. Philadelphia: University of Pennsylvania Museum Publication, 1999.

Bonnichsen, Robson, and Karen L. Turnmire, eds. *Ice Age Peoples of North America: Environments, Origins, and Adaptations of the First Americans*. Corvallis: Oregon State University Press, 1999.

Carmack, Robert, Janine Gasco, and Gary Gossen. *Legacy of Mesoamerica: The History and Culture of a Native American Civilization*. New Jersey: Prentice Hall, 1996.

Coe, Michael. *Mexico: From the Olmecs to the Aztecs*. 4th ed. Revised and Enlarged. New York: Thames & Hudson, 1994.

Fagan, Brian. *Ancient North America*. London: Thames and Hudson, 2005.

Haynes, Gary. *The Early Settlement of North America: The Clovis Era*. New York: Cambridge University Press, 2002.

León-Portilla, Miguel, and Earl Shorris, eds. *In the Language of Kings: An Anthology of Mesoamerican Literature—Pre-Columbian to the Present*. New York: W.W. Norton, 2001.

Mann, Charles. *1491: New Revelations of the Americas Before Columbus*. New York: Knopf Publishing Group, 2005.

Meltzer, David J. *Search for the First Americans*. Washington, DC: Smithsonian Institution Press, 1996.

Ramenofsky, Ann. *Vectors of Death: The Archeology of European Contact*. Albuquerque, NM: University of New Mexico Press, 1987.

Stannard, David. *American Holocaust: The Conquest of the New World*. New York: Oxford University Press, 1992.

Steelman, Karen, Richard Rickman, Marvin Rowe, and Thomas Boutton. "AMS Radiocarbon Ages of on Oxalate Accretion and Rock Paintings at Toca do Serrote da Bastiana, Brazil." Ed. Kevin Jakes. *Archeological Chemistry*. Washington, DC: American Chemical Society, 2002.

Weaver, Muriel Porter. *The Aztecs, Maya, and Their Predecessors: Archaeology of Mesoamerica*, 3rd ed. San Diego: Academic Press, 1993.

Williams, Stephen. *Fantastic Archaeology: The Wild Side of North American Prehistory*. University of Pennsylvania Press, 1991.

1

Mestiz@ Scripts and the Rhetoric of Subversion

We no longer belong to recognizable tribes or pueblos. Collectively, we do not know who our Spanish fathers and Indian mothers were, but we carry our indigenous ancestors in the stories we tell and the stories we deny.

—E.A. Mares

This book argues that Mestiz@ scripts subvert and revise hierarchical narratives of assimilation through symbolic mediation and border crossing. Using Gloria Anzaldúa's "new mestiza" consciousness as a powerful aesthetic, I analyze how Mesoamerican and Western cultural materials intersect and interact to produce new possibilities, through a dynamic strategy of Mestiz@ invention. By interpreting inscription practice in the realm of the material, of the corporeally generated, I analyze across conventional semiotic and disciplinary borders, between nonalphabetic and lettered graphic signs. That is, Mestiz@ sacred mural scripts in part rely upon bodily gestures—extension of the arm and upper back deltoid for support, as in mimicry sequences of layering, and ceremonial choreography. Meanwhile, Mestiz@ codex scripts depend upon graphic specific marks for support, such as painting, drawing, inscribing letters, pictography, and typesetting. My contribution involves crossing disciplinary territories to examine how Mestiz@ gestural and graphic symbols are enacted within colonial structures of power. Ritual mural and codex scripts are powerful rhetorical processes that metaphorically express, encode, and enact commentary about cultural relations in the borderlands, as well as about major forces that shape local Mestiz@ history.

Mestiz@ cultures emerged across the Western Hemisphere in the late fifteenth century as a consequence of "mestizaje," the fusion of bloodlines between American Indians and Spanish Iberian conquerors under colonial situations.[1] Today, the U.S. Census Bureau records the descendents of these groups, "Hispanics,"[2] as not only the fastest growing segment of the entire population of the United States, but also the nation's largest "minority" group with a mainland population of over forty-one million.[3] The expression "Mestiz@" as referred to here consists of a dynamic spectrum of shifting and contested subjectivity. At one extreme of this continuum are people who understand their individual and communal identity as primarily indigenous. At the other extreme are those who deny indigenous affiliation as part of their lineage and instead see themselves within a largely isolated Spanish Iberian inheritance of the past 400–500 years in America.[4] Throughout this analysis, semantic markers Mexican, Chicano, *Xicano*, and Latino are understood as part of this inclusive spectrum, though they certainly are not always interchangeable. While the intellectual province of Mesoamerica is crucial to the Mestiz@ continuum, I avoid placing cultures with tribal affiliation and/or community recognition, such as Pueblo Indians of the Rio Grande valley, within it.

Mestiz@ is an expression that also alludes to the larger milieu of *Latinidad* across the Americas and Caribbean at large, though the scope of this book attends to the scripts and cultures of Mexican-origin peoples who live north of the militarized border, who have been familiar with the dominant culture for quite some time. The reinvention of the typographic logogram "@" is primarily for purposes of gender inclusivity.[5] "@" in this study is also a marker of communal subjectivity among Mestiz@ cultures, a subjectivity that should never be exclusive.

Temporally, this study focuses on Mestiz@ scripts that are in use today—namely, the practice of painting in books and inscribing on architecture—although both must be comprehended historically: they are texts that speak to the Mesoamerican past while simultaneously addressing the colonial present. My aim is to illuminate the ways Mestiz@ inscriptions significantly revise dominant narratives of assimilation in order to critique enduring power structures and ensure culture. I apply the term "culture" in a way that is comparable to anthropologist Clifford Geertz's observation, that individuals are suspended within webs of experience that they themselves spin: "I take culture to be those webs, and the analysis of it to be therefore not an experimental science in search of law but an interpretive one in search of meaning."[6] Geertz's interpretive description supports culture as a meaning-making experience whereby people use shared symbols to mediate and legitimate lived experience. The study of Mestiz@ culture, therefore, can refer to the analysis of the variable ways this group interacts through material and symbolic means.

This interpretive explanation promotes an understanding of culture at the level of identifiable, individual systems. Raymond Williams argues that a culture is

> ...a particular way of life which expresses certain meanings and values not only in art and learning, but also in institutions and ordinary behavior. The analysis of culture, from such a definition, is the clarification of the meanings and the values implicit and explicit in a particular way of life, a particular culture.[7]

Studying a cultural system involves an examination of the fusions and fissures among the material and symbolic elements of particular lived experiences. I understand Mestiz@ ritual dance and painting/writing as symbolic practices that can be analyzed as part of a larger cultural system. Both are performances of meaning-making that provide arguments for and against certain things, namely, the dominant narratives of assimilation. Moreover, both Mestiz@ ritual dance and painting/writing embody a process of interactions whereby certain meanings and social realities specific to the Americas are shaped, destroyed, and sustained through official, resistant, and ritualistic uses of rhetoric. Analyzing Mestiz@ culture, then, involves studying how it is enacted as an everyday practice in the construction, articulation, and interpretation of those meanings. At a time when writing specialists are increasingly interested in the encounter of social difference and political struggle in a globalized world, this volume points to ways in which Mestiz@ rhetorics have continually worked to create "new" literacies: new ways of speaking, writing, and reading that promote anticolonial translations and revisions of colonial narratives. My hope is not only to influence emerging rhetoric and composition scholarship on borderland cultures, but also to point to literacy practices that might actually be prioritized in increasingly diverse classrooms of twenty-first century America. I believe we need to learn how to read in "new" ways.

It would be misleading, however, to suppose that explanations of culture could only emerge from British and Western intellectual traditions. Anthropologist Joann Keali'Inohomoku offers a helpful definition of culture with an understanding of the colonial experiences of denigration and permanent change that result from European conquest, particularly in Hawaii and the American southwest. That is, culture is a dynamic constellation of practices composed of tangible and intangible components with four fundamentals: material objects, perceptions and ideas, phenomenal behavior and events, and regulations that organize and maintain society.[8] In this study, culture refers to the extraordinary expressions, meanings, and values that both reflect and shape Mestiz@ social groups through selective focusing and embellishment. It is impossible to detach Mestiz@ culture from the colonial legacies of the Spanish Empire, U.S. imperial expansion into Mexico, and Mexican migration toward the United States. Culture, then, refers specifically to the affective, lived traditions and practices of the colonial borderlands, with an emphasis on ritual dance and writing.

Mestiz@ cultures have continually adapted to new social realities while at the same time retaining roots in older Mesoamerican civilizations. Mestiz@ rhetorics, then, are discursive manifestations of continuity and adaptation that comprise this survival. Rather than attempting to preserve or re-create a Mesoamerican "authenticity," Mestiz@ rhetorics generate new visions of history and subjectivity. The modern term "rhetoric" refers to the ancient Greek articulation, *rhêtorikê* (*tekhnê*), which appears in Plato's *Gorgias* and is usually translated as "the rhetorical art," or "the art of rhetoric."[9] *Rhêtorikê* derives from the verb *eirô*, meaning, "say" or "speak." The phrase pertains to the role of persuasion in oratory and public speaking as it was observed in Greek society beginning in the late fifth through the early fourth centuries BCE. What ancient Greeks recognized as rhetoric is comparable to what ancient Mesoamericans called *Huehuetlahtolli* (pronounced "weh-weh-tlah-toh-lee"). *Huehuetlahtolli* is a *Nahuatl* word formed by the compound *Huehue*, "ancient," and Tlahtolli, "word," "oration," or "discourse." Thus *Huehuetlahtolli* is translated as "proper discourse" or "discourse of the ancients."[10] I examine this expression at length in chapter 4, but I will note here that *Huehuetlahtolli* is stylistically characterized by cyclical movements, recurrent phrases, and the blending of two concrete terms to convey an abstraction. The present-day morpheme Mestiz@, for example, demonstrates a reflective syncretism in this tradition, one that straddles disparate cultural worlds.

Contemporary Mestiz@ rhetorics, this book argues, enact a strategy of invention between different ways of knowing. Crossing between comparative and conflicting elements creates a symbolic space beyond the mere coming together of two halves. The strategy implied here involves what I describe as "inventing between" the hierarchical tensions of Western and Mesoamerican practices. This notion of rhetorical border crossing is powerfully exemplified in Gloria Anzaldúa's landmark *Borderlands/La Frontera: The New Mestiza* (1987). Specifically, I advance Anzaldúa's new mestiza consciousness as an analytic for understanding Mestiz@ rhetorics. I argue that Anzaldúa's mestiza consciousness promotes the resistant movement between diverging cultural practices. By perpetually transitioning between worldviews (cultural, economic, spiritual, gendered, and erotic), mestiza consciousness offers the possibility of "thinking and writing from" the intersection of Mesoamerican and Western perspectives, where their collective expressions merge.

The study of Mestiz@ rhetorics not only calls for new ways to think about communicative practice; it also helps reveal the memories, politicization, colonization, and socioeconomic conditions of subjugated peoples across the United States and highlights the significance of studies of cultural subjectivities today. With the heightened globalization of trade, transnational employment, and economic transactions across nations, the place of Mestiz@s in the New World economy becomes even more crucial. And given that in many regions the number of college-age Mestiz@s is proportionately greater than the college-age segment in the rest of the population as a whole,[11] rhetoric and composition studies will benefit from learning about and learning from these cultures.

My analysis shows how such Mestiz@ rhetorical practices create symbolic spaces in which it becomes possible to understand multiple local histories, memories, and rhetorics coexisting, beyond dichotomous assumptions. Mestiz@ rhetorics defy hierarchical binaries by creating permeable ways of crossing and "inventing between" colonial oppositions, as illustrated by Gloria Anzaldúa's mestiza consciousness in *Borderlands*. Furthermore, these rhetorics offer powerful critiques of the dominant stories of assimilation, colony, and the border in an age where such things are hotly contested.

I argue that Mestiz@ rhetorics subvert, adapt, and revise historical narratives of assimilation, that they continue to do so today, and that rhetoric and composition studies can learn from these "border insurrections." By assimilation, I refer to the dichotomous process of conversion imposed by the framework of Western expansion across the north Atlantic beginning in the late fifteenth century. Lettered, monotheistic Europe was self-proclaimed as "civilized" in contrast to the "barbarity" of its binary other, Mesoamerica. Prior to conducting military assaults, officers would often recite, without an interpreter, an extensive *Requerimiento*, urging Mesoamericans to convert:

> If you do not, or if you maliciously delay in so doing, I certify that with God's help I will advance powerfully against you and make war on you wherever and however I am able, and will subject you to the yoke of obedience of the Church and of their majesties and take your women and children to be slaves, and as such I will sell and dispose of them as their majesties may order, and I will take your possessions and do you all the harm and damage that I can.[12]

Conversion here can refer to an abrupt alteration characterized by ritual acts symbolizing a shift in one's religious and political affiliation. Whether willing or coerced, the logic of conversion worked to alter Mesoamerican minds by subjecting them to the laws, obligations, and penalties imposed by the Church. Arguably, conversion is often not a public, well-reasoned, exemplary change but a gradual, often subtle process of shifting one's beliefs and practices from one cosmology to another. A common pattern was the Catholicizing of Mesoamerican beliefs in an environment dominated by Judeo-Christian ceremony, symbols, and rhetoric, where even daily and calendrical time was ordered by the Church. This type of progressive conversion often took place over generations. Another name for this sort of conversion, accumulated from thousands of consequential and inconsequential decisions, is assimilation.

The logic of assimilation is reproduced today by the escalation of Western dominance and economic capitalism on a global scale. Mestiz@s have continually faced dichotomous narratives that call the legitimacy of their existence into question. For example, a predicament of this narrative may be to either convert to the culture at large, or risk despising our collective difference, or to utterly reject the dominant culture and enact an extraordinary struggle against those forces that mark us as questionable. I assert that Mestiz@ rhetorics strategically undermine and reshape this binary configuration through "the stories we tell and the stories we deny," as E.A. Mares puts it, thereby inviting possibilities beyond it.

In the study that follows, I read codex writing, buon fresco painting, and ceremonial dance as rhetorical "texts" in order to draw conclusions about Mestiz@ resistance to dominant narratives of assimilation. I interpret these sites as cultural platforms that dialectically address ideas and experiences that are usually received as contrary. These sites invite the reader to think through apparently contrastive images and tools in a distinct visual and conceptual space. By pairing metaphors, crossing genres, shifting back and forth from one medium to another and borrowing from both Western and Mesoamerican symbolic material, Mestiz@ rhetorical strategies elude dichotomous categories. Such syntheses work to reveal the mythology and danger of rigid, binary thinking.

My examination of Mestiz@ scripts exposes the rigid evolutionary proposition that all writing systems progress toward the letter, that alphabetic literacy is the pinnacle of all other systems of recorded knowledge. Writing systems do not "evolve" so much as they shift and migrate across territories, technologies, and digital cultures. By digital here, most writing specialists may imagine N. Katherine Hayles' sense of the word as systems of complexity built upon simple binary codes, choices at the level between ones and zeros. While we all know that our computers are built on binary logics, scholars of written communication have yet to ground a study of writing on *human digits*, the appendages that produce a kinetic energy, a gestural force that in turn produces permanent or temporary marks of meaning. By digital, I am thus more influenced by the work of Cherokee writer Angela Haas, who applies a rhetorical analysis to the physical, corporeal production of American Indian material culture.

I will now review prior Mestiz@ research in rhetoric and composition studies in order to situate my contribution within this relatively new community of scholars. In the following chapter I present a preliminary account of how Anzaldúa's mestiza consciousness works, its major characteristics and basic lyrical properties. Then, I consider the critical reception of mestiza consciousness, including rhetoric and composition's recent publications that apply Anzaldúa's scholarship. These helpful considerations provide a framework for my extended argument that Anzaldúa's mestiza consciousness forwards a powerful aesthetic for understanding Mestiz@ ritual dance and writing. Moreover, I argue that mestiza consciousness is a "new" rhetorical strategy that radically revises the study and teaching of written language. In this spirit, I conclude this chapter by offering an outline of the larger project.

Mestiz@ Scholarship in Composition and Rhetoric

Jaime Armin Mejía's "Tejano Arts of the U.S.-Mexico Contact Zone" (1998) marks the first appearance of a Mexican-origin composition scholar in a major journal of the field. Mejía examines the shared writing practices of Chicano first-year college students in Texas. Using ethnographic and archival research, Mejía helps composition specialists understand how Mexican cultures are formed through matrifocal, clustered extended families. By applying what is known about these social networks to the cultural practice of classroom writing, Mejía offers what is likely one of the first modern freshman composition pedagogies that seriously accounts for Mexican literacies. Using collaboration as a cultural norm in the classroom, Mejía furthermore helps writing specialists consider the limitations of standard process-centered composition pedagogies.

Renee Moreno's "The Politics of Location: Text as Opposition" (2002) and Nancy Barron's "Dear Saints, Dear Stella: Letters Examining the Messy Lines of Expectations, Stereotypes, and Identity" (2003) furthermore assist the field in better understanding Mestiz@ composition practices. Both texts foreground the links between ethnicity, racialized identities, and formal education. In particular, Moreno and Barron demonstrate how social and pedagogical issues in higher education can work both for and against the possibilities of Mestiz@ student writing. The authors not only provide useful case studies of Latino youth, but point to ways these students can employ academic literacy and assigned class readings by exploring identities that straddle two or more cultures. Taken together with Ralph Cintron's ethnography *Angels' Town* (1997), Juan Guerra's *Close to Home* (1998), and *Latino/a Discourses* (2004), this research grants rhetoric and composition specialists helpful insights into the present-day linguistic practices of Latino first-year undergraduate students and/or youth. These authors moreover collectively confirm rhetoric as a mediating, identity-forming activity. As teachers of historically disfranchised student populations, these scholars emphasize that merely "reading about" them is not enough; a more progressive professoriate must pedagogically enact an understanding of the Mestiz@ rhetorics that students weave together, unravel, and connect.

While most rhetoric and composition scholarship examines Mestiz@ juvenile, postadolescent, and young adult linguistic issues in the classroom, remarkably few studies focus on the lived experiences of Mestiz@ professionals. Victor Villanueva's acclaimed *Bootstraps: From an American Academic of Color* (1993) provides the field with its first extended look at the teaching profession from the perspective of a Latino practitioner. Villanueva asserts that a primary aim of *Bootstraps* is to make explicit the material reality "that there is more to racism, ethnocentricity, and language than is apparent, that there are long-established systemic forces at play that maintain bigotry, systemic forces that can even make bigots of those who are appalled by bigotry" (12). Through a critical weaving of theory, autobiography, and exposition, Villanueva illustrates how even as Mestiz@s slowly shift and rise in class status in the academy, systemic racism impinges that experience.

By refusing to sever Mestiz@ lived experience and intellectual inquiry, Villanueva invites academics to read across these discourses as entwined, mutually informing literacies. *Bootstraps* suggests "new" possibilities for the practice of scholarly writing, innovative notions of rhetoric that might constitute new perspectives on invention strategies and the production of knowledge. By examining Mestiz@ experience beyond the first-year composition classroom, Villanueva promotes a more comprehensive understanding of Mestiz@ intellectual life. Moreover, *Bootstraps* aims to reconceive rhetoric and composition, to make it more inclusive and responsive to Mestiz@ intellectuals and all scholars of color.

While attention to Mestiz@ scholars in English composition is scarce, research on Mexican and Mesoamerican history is virtually absent.[13] Don Paul Abbot and Susan Romano present two exceptions. Abbott's *Rhetoric in the New World: Rhetorical Theory and Practice in Colonial Spanish America* (1996) treats *Huehuetlahtolli* as it was recorded by Franciscan Bernadino de Sahagún in the early sixteenth century. Sahagún was a key player in Spain's project of Christianization, which involved chronicling Aztec oratory and written practice with the primary aim of converting it to alphabetic, monotheistic literacy. Like Sahagún, Abbott's research misconceives *Huehuetlahtolli* and Mesoamerican pictography as "preliterate."[14] Constructive investigations of Aztec oratory and written practices become undermined when they are strictly imposed within provincial Eurocentric conceptions of alphabetic superiority. Abbott's work does, however, provide a helpful account of how Western rhetoric can be central to conquest and subjugation. Meanwhile, Susan Romano's "*Tlaltelolco*: The Grammatical-Rhetorical *Indios* of Colonial Mexico" (2004) examines North America's first Western writing program, the Colegio de

Santa Cruz de *Tlaltelolco*. Romano illustrates how rhetoric and writing pedagogies employed at *Tlaltelolco* are sadly familiar to present-day methods. Most recognizable is Spain's attempt to educate Mexican "cultural Others" through classroom debate about race and class identity against a backdrop of subjugated local rhetorical practice. While the term "Indio" is highly derogatory among Chicanas and Chicanos today, Romano's article contributes to a better understanding of the colonialist beginnings of composition and rhetoric in the New World. Notably, both Abbott and Romano highlight the fact that Spanish clergy failed to develop a "competent" pedagogy for colonized Mexicans. In the past four centuries, writing pedagogies have by and large instructed Mexican-origin peoples to "stop thinking Indian" and assimilate to European configurations. In this spirit I now offer the following episodes that organize this study.

Contemporary Mestiz@ rhetorics, chapter 2 argues, enact a strategy of invention between different ways of knowing and writing. Transgressing across comparative and conflicting elements creates a symbolic space beyond the mere coming together of two territories. The strategy of "inventing between" the hierarchical tensions of Western and Mesoamerican practices is unique to colonial situations among Mestiz@ peoples, and is not synonymous with Greco-Latin categories of communication. To further examine this notion of rhetorical border crossing, I turn to Gloria Anzaldúa's *Borderlands/ La Frontera: The New Mestiza*. Specifically, I advance Anzaldúa's new mestiza consciousness as an analytic for understanding Mestiz@ rhetorics. I argue that Anzaldúa's mestiza consciousness promotes the resistant movement between diverging cultural practices. By perpetually transitioning between worldviews, mestiza consciousness offers the possibility of "thinking and writing from" the intersection of Mesoamerican and Western perspectives, where their collective expressions merge.

Chapter 3 broadly accounts for the historical conditions of how Mestiz@ people came into existence, their consequent struggles during the aftermath of Spanish colonization, U.S. occupation, and the issues they face today. I begin with the *Popul Vuh* and the importance of Mesoamerican ancestries with particular emphasis on Aztec civilization leading up to the fall of *Tenochtitlán* in 1521. Then, I explain how early Spanish campaigns of genocide, enslavement, and Christianization lead to the historic Pueblo Revolt of 1680. My focus then shifts to the economic and social alliances forged between Mestiz@ villagers and Pueblo Indians along the upper Rio Grande river basin. While the Mexican revolution and the overthrow of Spanish imperialism were sources of political turmoil and unrest, Pueblo Indian-Mestiz@ relations cautiously continued. These details are helpful for understanding the allied resistance to U.S. occupation of the northern half of Mexico's territory. I offer a detailed account of the New Mexican Insurrection of 1847, including its casualties and legal ramifications. Then, I outline how poor relations between Mexicans and their Anglo aggressors were heightened with the Treaty of Guadalupe Hidalgo and its aftermath.

As rural villages were faced with the modernization of incorporating into urban American metropolitan centers over the next several decades, I account for the cultural shift that occurred at the local level, as well as some resistant strategies employed by villagers in response. Increasing cultural change in the early twentieth century often stemmed from continued linguistic and racial intolerance and acts of discrimination such as the Zootsuit Riots of 1943 and anti-Mexican repatriation acts that occurred well into the 1950s. These events help explain the rise of Mexican protection and mutual aid organizations as well as the Chicano Movement and its aftermath in the later half of the twentieth century. I account for the events leading up to Proposition 187 and conclude with a helpful example of how Mestiz@ memory symbolically opposes the triumph of conquest and assimilation.

Building on this foundation, I then argue in chapter 4 that Mestiz@ codex rhetorics revise and displace the narrative of assimilation through continuous symbolic play with pairs, doubles, corresponding expressions and twins. By fusing and embellishing Mesoamerican pictography into European inscription practices, Mestiz@ codex rhetorics promote a new dialectic, a new strategy of inventing and writing between worlds. My site of analysis is the *Codex Espangiensis: From Columbus to the Border Patrol* (2000), by Guillermo Gómez-Peña, Enrique Chagoya, and Felicia Rice. This revisionist codex fuses multiple writing systems and languages including Aztec pictography, alphabetic *Nahuatl,* twentieth-century Castilian, Chicano iconography, Spanglish, and English. My examination builds on prior landmark studies of earlier Mesoamerican manuscripts from Mexican historian and *Nahuatl* translator Miguel León-Portilla as well as art historian Elizabeth Boone Hill. My analysis is bolstered, moreover, by a careful account of *Huehuetlahtolli*, the Mesoamerican stylistic device for recording and transmitting wisdom. The codex is especially helpful to writing teachers, as it illustrates syncretic processes that express and enact commentary about rhetorical conventions and the hierarchical tensions between notation/illustration, writing/art, and temporal distinctions between sixteenth-century Christianization and twentieth-century global capitalism.

Chapter 5 analyzes internationally renowned muralist Frederico Vigil's buon fresco, *The Genesis of the Rio Grande*, a Mestiz@ ritual inscription practice that dates back to Mediterranean as well as Mesoamerican traditions. I argue that the buon fresco's rhetorical exchanges of intermediacy and border crossing work to resist and revise the hierarchical logic of monotheistic and alphabetic assimilation. I first describe the buon fresco itself, its major characteristics and primary figures of *Malintzin Tenepal* and *Moctezuma Xocoyotzin*. Using this description as a springboard, I synthesize key aspects of contrastive perspectives, images, and movements that are enacted within colonial structures of power. Specifically I examine how the Vigil's "Matachines" ceremonial participants strategically employ both Pueblo and Catholic iconography. Using the Matachines figures in Vigil's mural, I also address competing interpretations of Rio Grande cultures' origin: while many previous scholars promote the Spanish tale of Christian absolute conquest and Mexico's conversion, enduring local histories suggest that the river, as well as the Matachines dance, metaphorically derive from Aztec combat dances as a deliberate yet veiled strategy of subversion. This retelling symbolizes survival, not defeat, of Mesoamerican cultures.

Then, in chapter 6, I present a detailed consideration of how Mestiz@ rhetorics might revise the frameworks used to study and teach writing. I do not formally propose new curricula or course strategies, but instead flesh out promising responses to the inquiry: what curricular and pedagogical possibilities are enabled by Anzaldúa's mestiza consciousness? I first take up the inclusion of Anzaldúa's "How to Tame a Wild Tongue" in Patricia Bizzell and Bruce Herzberg's *The Rhetorical Tradition: Readings from Classical Times to the Present* (2001).

Finally, chapter 7 examines how Anzaldúa's expressions work simultaneously within and against Western configurations. By inventing from the colonial tensions produced between Mesoamerican and Western worlds, I argue that Anzaldúa invites an examination of parallel and coevolutionary histories of rhetoric and writing. Investigating rhetoric across national borders and cultural boundaries promotes a wider hemispheric view, beyond the path of Western expansion.

Accordingly, I propose three broad frameworks enabled by mestiza consciousness: Spacialization, Periodization, and Region versus Nation. Embracing an expanded geographic reach when studying rhetoric involves questioning the hierarchical progression from Greece to Rome to Western Europe to North America. New Spacializations would encourage teachers and students to question this linearity by confronting the very invention of the New World. Here I turn specifically to Walter Mignolo's illuminating *The Darker Side of the Renaissance*. By carefully investigating the coexisting territorialities of Mesoamerica and imperial Spain, Mignolo promotes a coevaluative understanding of alphabetic and pictographic cultures.

Rethinking Periodization includes a deeper historical outline that is no longer restricted by the pseudoscientific categories of Classical, Medieval, Renaissance, Enlightenment, and Modern. Argentine liberation philosopher Enrique Dussel's *The Invention of the Americas: Eclipse of the Other and the Myth of Modernity* effectively articulates a new paradigm of temporal sequences that break from Eurocentric designs. Dussel forwards the argument that while the dominant periodizations are undoubtedly European occurrences, they originate in dialectical relationship with Europe's colonial peripheries. Moreover, Dussel persuasively disengages from Europe's reductionist horizon by embracing a more planetary perspective. Affirming new periodizations that take into account the Aztec and Maya as well as Arab Muslim and Indo-Chinese circuits, for example, would advance massively revised accounts of how writing and rhetoric practices shift across time.

Finally, Alfred Arteaga's *An Other Tongue: Nation and Ethnicity in the Linguistic Borderlands* interrogates the tensions of identification between Region versus Nation. By questioning the processes of subjection that transpire under the nation-state, *An Other Tongue* helps teachers and students to understand the key role rhetoric plays in the push and pull struggle for self-definition. And as *Borderlands/ La Frontera* poetically illustrates, Mestiz@ rhetorics mediate and cross hierarchical distinctions between nationality, ethnicity, region, and colonial status. The frameworks I consider in chapter 5 are merely three of the many other "big picture" variations that could be derived from Gloria Anzaldúa's new mestiza consciousness. These modifications to the study of Western rhetoric and writing would equally emphasize connections, comparisons, and interpretive frameworks across and beyond national boundaries, thereby embracing a more hemispheric, perhaps even global plurality.

Collectively, these chapters make the case that Mestiz@ rhetorics significantly revise dominant narratives of assimilation. Gloria Anzaldúa's mestiza consciousness, if realized as a rhetorical strategy and new point of origin, subverts and revises Western colonial designs. Accepting Anzaldúa's contribution as a new framework promotes an understanding of parallel and coevolutionary developments of rhetoric, in which it becomes possible to perceive multiple histories and memories coexisting, without assumptions that all civilizations follow a linear, dichotomous trajectory. This intellectual tactic promotes new modes of invention, new ways to think, read, and write that provide not only much-needed historiographical correctives, but also advance political expressions better suited to current material realities of Western global expansion. Mestiz@ rhetorics resist the hierarchical logic of conquest and assimilation through, as E.A. Mares puts it, "the stories we tell and the stories we deny." This dynamic rhetorical strategy not only reinscribes our own history; it also asserts that the dominant narratives of Western rhetoric and writing must also be retold and revised.

II

New Consciousness/Ancient Myths

Let's all stop importing Greek myths and the Western Cartesian split point of view and root ourselves in the mythological soil and soul of this continent.

—Gloria Anzaldúa, *Borderlands/La Frontera*

The late Gloria Anzaldúa remains arguably one of the most widely read Chicanas today. Now in its twentieth anniversary third edition, *Borderlands/La Frontera: The New Mestiza* demonstrates its historical significance as it continues to be included on numerous course syllabi in Chicano and Latino Literature, Postcolonial Studies, Cultural and Ethnic Studies, Autobiography, Women's Studies, and some mandatory first-year English composition seminars. Anzaldúa is commonly recognized for her innovative ability to mediate the competing cultural forces that shape Mestiz@ experience, and her capacity to activate that mediation toward creative, revisionary strategies for social change. Born in a ranch settlement of Jesus Maria in South Texas, Anzaldúa writes from the lived experience of a native border dweller. *Borderlands/La Frontera* tells of a radical Chicana history across the México/U.S. boundaries using a form of visual writing Anzaldúa calls autohistoria. In *La Frontera/The Border: Art About the Mexico/United States Border Experience*, Anzaldúa explains that her visual form "...supersedes the pictorial. It depicts both the soul of an artist and the soul of the *pueblo*. It deals with who tells the stories and what stories and histories are told....[t]his form goes beyond the traditional self-portrait or autobiography; in telling the writer/artists' personal story, it also includes the artist's cultural history" (113). Thus, both the individual and the ancestral are consciously woven together to form a new retelling of history. Mestiz@ ways of life are informed through living, contextualized, cultural networks. Through this visual rhetorical form, Anzaldúa conveys this interconnectivity at the crossroads between cultural histories of the México/U.S. borderlands. This interconnectivity is further emphasized as Anzaldúa weaves autobiography, exposition, poetry, and history in a manner that defies conventional classification.

In "*La conciencia de la mestiza*: Towards a New Consciousness," Chapter 7 of *Borderlands*, Anzaldúa further explains this convergence of voices and cultures.[1]

> At the confluence of two ore more genetic streams, with chromosomes constantly 'crossing over,' this mixture of races, rather than resulting in an inferior being, provides hybrid progeny, a mutable, more malleable species with a rich gene pool. From this racial, ideological, cultural and biological cross-pollinization, an 'alien' consciousness is presently in the making—a new *mestiza* consciousness, *una conciencia de mujer.* It is a consciousness of the Borderlands. (99)

Anzaldúa's thoughts on the biological mixing between races come primarily from Mexican nationalist Jose Vasconcelos and his *La Raza Cósmica* (1945). Vasconcelos inverts the Arian myth of racial purity by claiming an elitist assumption of "mixed-blood," mestizo peoples. Many Mestiz@s avoid Vasconcelos' discriminatory cultural construct, as his proposal furthermore places a Spanish cosmology as the "civilizing," paternal influence upon Mesoamerican cultures. By claiming "a new mestiza" consciousness, Anzaldúa simultaneously begins with and departs from Vasconcelos' hierarchical expression. By employing lower case letters and feminizing the expression a new mestiza, Anzaldúa effectively revises the nationalism of Vasconcelos' racial mixing. As Anzaldúa's larger corpus illustrates, mestizaje is not merely a matter of genetics, but one of memory, culture, and epistemic potential. Concurrent with Anzaldúa's project, questions of biology and blood quantum identity politics are largely outside the scope and concern of this analysis. What is helpful in the passage above is the articulation of a powerful Mestiz@ rhetorical strategy: thinking from the intersection of Iberian, *Nahuatl*, and Anglo-European traditions to "invent between" different ways of knowing, where individual and communal expressions across the borderlands intersect.

Forming what Chicana theorist Norma Alarcón calls a "panmexican collective,"[2] Anzaldúa's border crossings in effect link together dual expressions and symbolic oppositions, from pre-Columbian deities to Mexican icons. Snake Woman, *Coatlicue*, Señora de Guadalupe/ *Coatlaxopeuh*, and *La Chingada* are only a few of the varied icons that symbolize Anzaldúa's cyclical enunciation of Mesoamerican and Mexican historical knowledge. *Coatlicue*, the mother figure of all Aztec gods[3] is woven together and fused with Guadalupe, the post-Columbian recreation of the Christian Mary. This admixture is further embroidered with *La Chingada*, a pseudonym for La Malinche, the mistress to conquistador Hernán Cortéz, the military strategist behind Mesoamerica's brutal invasion. Like the constantly shifting subjectivities of the Mestiz@ spectrum, the deities Anzaldúa names become a pantheon of cultural possibilities. Through disparate Aztec, Olmec, Maya and contemporary Mexican icons, the dominant narratives of assimilation can be unlearned. By placing herself at the intersection and crossing between these historic figures and traditions, Anzaldúa reinvents and reconstitutes divergent cultural memories through snake-like rhetorics of the border, both material and symbolic:

> 1,950 mile-long open wound
> dividing a *pueblo*, a culture,
> running down the length of my body,
> staking fence rods in my flesh,
> splits me splits me
> *me raja* *me raja*
> This is her home
> this thin edge of barbwire. (24–25)

Anzaldúa's narrative interweaves and unfolds across "dangerous terrain," linking the individual rhetor to collective myth, this time reimagined from the border struggles of the present. The split geography of México and the United States is a continual referent in *Borderlands*. Moreover, Anzaldúa builds upon and expands the material experiences of *La Frontera* by questioning and defying psychological, erotic, and sacred borders under colonial situations.[4] It is precisely the fracture between boundaries, "this thin edge of barbwire," that Anzaldúa activates as a space of rhetorical potential.

Anzaldúa advances mestiza consciousness as a dynamic methodology that gives voice to progressive political agendas of the new mestiza, a subjectivity that claims much more than the narrow biological definition that Vasconcelos' Mestizaje allows. Anzaldúa clearly opposes all forms of hierarchical dichotomies, yet her political ideology is grounded in the colonial legacy of the México/U.S. borderlands in its relation to larger hemispheric and global events. Mestiza consciousness mobilizes pre-Columbian intellectual history as a process of coming to awareness as a political agent of resistance and transformation. This awareness reactivates pre-Conquest historical sites such as Aztec ceremonial centers to affirm Mesoamerica's place in a history that has been subjugated. This "new" knowledge reasserts the importance of Mesoamerican gestural and graphic expressions rendered "barbarian" and passive by Christianization and alphabetic literacy. Moreover, by fusing Olmec and Quiche Maya legacies into the Aztec, Anzaldúa resists the military dominance of the Triple Alliance, the most powerful imperial force in Mesoamerica prior to European invasion. Anzaldúa's declaration of Mesoamerican deities and traditions enacts a transformation of rhetorical performance from a Greco-Roman Western practice to a site of Mestiz@ resistance.

Critical Reception of Mestiza Consciousness

Anzaldúa's mestiza consciousness is considered a significant contributor to gender studies, antiracist scholarship on the construction of identity within multiple contexts of domination, the pursuit of resistance to oppression, and the struggle for "minority" recognition.[5] Because mestiza consciousness enacts a subjectivity that subverts and defies gendered, political, erotic and sacred binaries, many academics have adopted the trope of border crossing in their research. Numerous critics, especially in the late 1980s and early 1990s, began using mestiza consciousness as a way to bring these Western dichotomies into question and offer possibilities for rethinking a world organized otherwise.[6] Generally regarded as Anzaldúa's chief political manifesto, mestiza consciousness assists researchers aiming to understand the complex and competing political and cultural forces that shape Mestiz@ experiences in the U.S. borderlands. Mestiza consciousness has been largely welcomed as a useful method for understanding and mobilizing these experiences toward creative and revisionary efforts for social change.

Because mestiza consciousness is undoubtedly worth further inquiry, Anzaldúa has commented on the troubling lack of critical attention that it sometimes receives within various academic circles. Such silence may indicate volumes about the expectations some critics place on "minority" writers. As Gloria Anzaldúa comments, "...whatever position we may occupy, we are getting only one point of view: white middle class. Theory serves those that create it...[w]e focus on the cultural abuse of colored by white and thus fall into the trap of the colonized reader and writer forever reacting against the dominant."[7] This trap or double bind that Anzaldúa refers to is one that critics often duplicate when analyzing the work of nonwhite, "non-Western" intellectuals. For writers of color, Anzaldúa suggests, the double bind is framed by a recurring reaction against dominant narratives, which, by its very repetition, might be interpreted as a reinstatement and affirmation of the dominant as center.

In an interview at the end of *Borderlands/La Frontera*, Anzaldúa suggests that white middle-class educators fetishize this double bind and often overlook how mestiza consciousness can strategically revise and move beyond white/nonwhite hierarchical dichotomies of subjectivity. When asked directly about the use of her work in classrooms, Anzaldúa responds,

> They teach it as a way of introducing students to cultural diversity. However, some of the writing is glossed over as, particularly, white critics and teachers often pick just some parts of *Borderlands*. For example, they take the passages in which I talk about mestizaje and borderlands because they can more easily apply them to their own experiences. The angrier parts of *Borderlands*, however, are often ignored as they seem to be too threatening and too confrontational. In some way, I think you could call this selective critical interpretation a kind of racism. (232)

Indeed, it is understandable that many educators might find Anzaldúa's work inaccessible. Without serious, sustained training in the historical legacies of the Spanish Empire and imperial expansion of the United States into Mexico, educators would likely find the operations of colonial power difficult to navigate in their scholarship and teaching. Moreover, conventional curricula that focus strictly on European, Anglo-Saxon, and Anglo-American traditions will not help teachers adequately work through Anzaldúa's prevalent use of Mesoamerican and Mexican inscription practices, icons, and intellectual histories.

Anzaldúa's use of Mesoamerican legacies in particular has met with some controversy from Mestiz@ scholars. Poet Benjamin Alire Saenz, for example, takes issue with the application of indigenous elements throughout *Borderlands/La Frontera*. Saenz is concerned that Anzaldúa's use of Aztec mythology is ultimately not helpful for present-day Chicanos, many of whom live in modern metropolitan settings that are undeniably contrastive to the lived experience of pre-Columbian Mesoamericans as well as present-day tribalized native peoples:

> I, like Anzaldúa, have a mixed ancestry. My great-grandmother was a Tahurumaran Indian from Mexico. But for me to claim her material culture as mine rings hollow. I was raised in a far different environment, and I was formed by that environment. It is too late for me to forge a return to my great-grandmother's culture. This does not mean that I am unconcerned about the deforestation that is destroying the Tahurumaran people of northern Mexico, but I cannot mistake myself for them...I sympathize with Anzaldúa's strategy....By calling herself a mestiza, she takes herself out of a European mind-set. She refuses to refer to herself as "Hispanic"—to do so would be to embrace an identity that admits no competing discourses, that admits only a European history and erases any indigenous consciousness. Her impulse is to defy that her "Indianness" has been destroyed. But her "Indianness" has been destroyed—just as mine has. (85)

Saenz puts pressure on an enduring struggle and debate within Mestiz@ communities that share indigenous memories and practices in an assortment of diverse and complicated ways. Certainly, the material realities of most Mestiz@s including Anzaldúa cannot be directly equated with those of tribalized indigenous cultures. Furthermore, it is not historically plausible that most Mestiz@s are biological descendants of the Aztec. An affinity with pre-Columbian Aztec symbolism, Saenz asserts, may result in a utopian escapism that is not grounded in the lived experiences of either Mestiz@s or tribalized American Indians. Some Mestiz@s, like Saenz, share a Tahurumaran heritage, while others might descend in part from Yaqui, Navajo-Dine, or a variety of northern Rio Grande Pueblos of the México/U.S. borderlands. These cultural groups bear distinct and fluid subjectivities, and furthermore face contemporary struggles that may not necessarily link directly to the Aztec.

Despite Saenz' disagreement with the use of Aztec mythology, he clearly aligns himself with Anzaldúa's political strategy of resisting dominant narratives of cultural assimilation. While the tensions produced by Mesoamerican cultural symbols in mestiza consciousness are deserving of these and other critiques, in "How to Tell a Mestizo from an Enchirito®: Colonialism and National Culture in the

Borderlands," Michael Hames-Garcia argues that Anzaldúa's use of Aztec spirituality does not imply a romantic escape, but conversely creates a syncretic force that binds the corporeal act of writing with the concrete realities of colonialism, past and present.[8]

While Anzaldúa's *Borderlands* no doubt incorporates the material realities of lived experience along the U.S./Mexico border, Debra Castillo and María Socorro Tabuenca Córdoba's *Border Women: Writing from La Frontera* (2002) challenges the U.S.-centered nature of her scholarship:

> ...critics have made Anzaldúa "the representative" of "the border." In Anzaldúa's work the border also functions primarily as a metaphor, in that the border space as a geopolitical region converges with discourses of ethnicity, class, gender, and sexual preference. Nevertheless, Anzaldúa's book, despite its multiple crossings of cultural and gender borders—from ethnicity to feminisms, from the academic realm to the work of blue-collar labor—tends to essentialize relations between Mexico and the United States. Her third country between the two nations, the borderlands, is still a metaphorical country defined and narrated from a First World perspective ... Anzaldúa's famous analysis does not take into cognizance the many other othernesses related to a border existence; her "us" is limited to U.S. minorities; her "them" is U.S. dominant culture. Mexican border dwellers are also "us" and "them" with respect to their Chicana/o counterparts; they can in some sense be considered the "other" of both dominant and U.S. resistance discourses. (15)

Castillo and Córdoba would agree with Saenz, I presume, that the lived experiences of Mestiz@s north of the border cannot be equated with those to the south. Yet the authors are quick to point out that it is the *critical reception culture* of Anzaldúa that has positioned her work as "representative" of the border. Rethinking Anzaldúa's U.S. borderlands calls into question the relationships between geohistorical locations across the U.S./Mexico matrix, the disparate consequences of unregulated capitalist expansion, and the relationships between border writing and local epistemologies. The political tensions between Mestiz@s to the north and south as well as those between Aztec and Mestiz@ cultures substantiate further inquiry and debate, especially in classrooms that investigate the links between rhetoric, writing, and subjectivities specific to the Americas.

Critical Reception in Composition and Rhetoric Studies

Recent publications in composition and rhetoric indicate that the field is beginning to recognize the intellectual contribution of mestiza consciousness. Patricia Bizzell and Bruce Herzberg's *The Rhetorical Tradition: Readings from Classical Times to the Present* (2001) includes "How to Tame a Wild Tongue," a selection from *Borderlands/La Frontera* that poetically recounts how linguistic discrimination can be deeply embedded within formal sites of English literacy instruction. This painful narrative illustrates Anzaldúa's experience with physical retribution for speaking a Spanish variety in a composition classroom. Later, Anzaldúa again receives pressures to assimilate to English literacy from her mother. Using these moments of conflict and dissonance, Anzaldúa explores and affirms her many languages and voices, refusing to submit her tongue and mind to pedagogical designs of assimilation. In its place, Anzaldúa interweaves an assortment of Spanish varieties with English and *Nahuatl*. Anzaldúa's appearance in *The Rhetorical Tradition* represents the first contemporary incorporation of an indigenous Mexican into the Western rhetorical canon, thereby inviting a fruitful cross-cultural dialogue that moves with, against, and beyond Western practices. In chapter 5, I address Bizzell and Herzberg's treatment in detail.

"How to Tame a Wild Tongue" also appears in David Bartholomae and Anthony Petrosky's *Ways of Reading: An Anthology for Writers* (2002) along with "Entering the Serpent," also from *Borderlands*. *Ways of Reading* is a collection of essays and writing assignments designed primarily for first-year college composition seminars. The editors provide the field with one of the first pedagogical applications of Anzaldúa for lower-division writing classrooms. A brief consideration of Bartholomae and Petrosky's text helps clarify how Anzaldúa fits into their composition pedagogy. Here's an excerpt from the preface to instructors:

> We know that a reader is a person who puts together fragments. Those coherent readings we construct begin with confusion and puzzlement, and we construct those readings by writing and rewriting—by working on a text. These are the lessons our students need to learn, and this is why a course in reading is also a course in writing. (vi–vii)

Recognizing the dynamic processes and interconnections of reading and writing, they continue, now directly addressing composition students:

> Strong readers, we've said, remake what they have read to serve their own ends, putting things together, figuring out how ideas and examples relate, explaining as best they can material that is difficult or problematic... At these moments, it is hard to distinguish the act of reading from the act of writing. In fact, the connection between reading and writing can be seen as almost a literal one, since the best way you can show your reading of a rich and dense essay... is by writing down your thoughts, placing one idea against another, commenting on what you've done, taking examples into account, looking back at where you began, perhaps changing your mind, and moving on. (12)

The editors propose that "working" on texts requires not merely the interrelated activities of reading and writing, but the deliberate acts of rereading and rewriting. The textbook contains selections that are meant to be challenging for students, with the expectation that the essays will necessitate multiple readings. It follows that reading through a challenging essay is a counterpart to the demands of piecing together its fragments through continuous writing exercises.

Bartholomae and Petrosky expect students to engage the selections on more than a surface level. Prompts follow each essay, usually emphasizing strategies for rereading or something the editors note as necessary to the writing process. Writing assignments ask students to engage with the major themes of the essays and sometimes to read them with and against other essays in the collection. It is in this context that the editors ask students to respond to Gloria Anzaldúa's "How to Tame a Wild Tongue":

> Write an essay in which you present a reading of *Borderlands/La Frontera* as an example of an autoethnographic and/or transcultural text. You should imagine that you are writing to someone who is not familiar with either Pratt's argument or Anzaldúa's thinking... your work, then, is to present Anzaldúa's text to readers who don't have it in front of them. (812)

The primary aim of the exercise requires students to reflect upon and articulate the content and style of Anzaldúa's essay. Student responses would be primarily descriptive in nature, yet students would also consider the significance of weaving between languages and voices, the clashing images of Mexico and the West, dual expressions, symbolic oppositions, and other rhetorical effects. Anzaldúa textually inscribes and collides cultural worlds that undoubtedly contrast with the conventions of academic prose. One can easily imagine classroom discussions that raise awareness of the wider range of expressive potential emerging from the borderlands. I see this kind of application of Anzaldúa as a productive first step for composition specialists. The assignment prompt directs students to compare "How to Tame a Wild Tongue" to a previously assigned selection, Mary Louise Pratt's "Arts of the Contact Zone," which elaborates on Afro-Cuban Fernando Ortiz' rhetorical concept, transculturation. I address the parallels and differences between Anzaldúa's writing, Ortiz' transculturation, and Pratt's "contact zone" in chapter 6. The distinctions I draw there further clarify the intervention my argument advances through positioning mestiza consciousness as a powerful rhetorical strategy.

Composition specialist Andrea Lunsford's 1998 interview with Gloria Anzaldúa points in this direction. In a field where most attention to Mestiz@s has thus far focused on linguistic practices of lower-division undergraduate students, Lunsford welcomes rhetoric and composition scholars to consider Anzaldúa's mestiza consciousness, which has direct implications for scholarship in the discipline. Throughout the interview Anzaldúa discusses her relationship to language and writing, remarking that

> In the process of writing, you're reflecting on all of the things that make you different, that make you the same... [p]ostcoloniality looks at this power system discipline—whether it's a government, whether it's anthropology, or composition—and it asks, Who has the voice? Who says these are the rules? Who makes the law? (14)

The perpetual grappling and analysis of conflict implied in mestiza consciousness promotes new possibilities, a composition that makes visible the lived contradictions and transformations of diverse writing practices between Mesoamerican and Western worlds. Lunsford's interview with Anzaldúa helps define and clarify the dynamic interrelations between colonial power, resistance, and multiculturalism as it is contested within U.S. institutions of higher education. These linkages furthermore share many pressure points with debates in composition and rhetoric studies such as the relationship between diverse inscription practices and the material realities of lived experience. This interview offers the field much for further discussion and debate. Using prior rhetoric and composition scholarship on Anzaldúa, I will now examine how mestiza consciousness advances a powerful new aesthetic for understanding Mestiz@ rhetorics of resistance.

Mestiza Consciousness as Rhetorical Strategy

This book adds significantly to composition scholarship by arguing that mestiza consciousness is a unique Mestiz@ strategy of invention. This rhetorical tactic is not to be confused with the mere encounter of disparate cultures. Consider Anzaldúa's explanation of borderland subjectivity:

> In a constant state of mental *nepantlism*, an Aztec word meaning torn between ways, la mestiza is a product of the transfer of the cultural and spiritual values of one group to another. Being tricultural, monolingual, bilingual or multilingual, speaking a patois, and in a state of perpetual transition, the mestiza faces the dilemma of the mixed breed: which collectivity does the daughter of a dark-skinned mother listen to? (25)

Nepantla, which also translates as "the space between two oceans," is a *Nahuatl* expression coined in the early sixteenth century. The first generation of offspring between Mesoamericans and Spaniards recognized that "authentic" pre-Columbian ways of life were impossible to reconstruct. In addition, the Spanish colonial world of Christianization was not a suitable alternative. *Nepantlism* is a strategy of thinking from a border space through dual expressions and symbolic oppositions. Inventing from *nepantlism*, suspended between paradoxical frames of reference, was first a possibility in the mind of the Aztec, not the Spaniard. Both worlds experienced and negotiated cultural difference. Mestiza consciousness is a borderland articulation that emerges specifically from the underside of colonial relations of power.

Mestiza consciousness, I argue, can revise Western rhetoric and composition traditions by articulating "new" memories, subaltern recollections in which Aztec writing practices and Mesoamerican ritual acts are strategically reconfigured and embroidered within the post-Columbian world of colonial and global power. Chapter 6 of *Borderlands*, for example, is titled "Tlilli, Tlapalli: The Path of the Red and Black Ink," which directly appeals to both Mesoamerican and colonial histories of writing and rhetoric in the borderlands. One of the earliest known expressions for writing in America, Tlilli Tlapalli literally means "the black [ink], the red [ink]" and directly references the formal transmission of knowledge at the *Calmecac*, a highly structured Mesoamerican conservatory and ceremonial center. Chapter 6, like much of *Borderlands*, juxtaposes opposing cultural memories and writing practices. Anzaldúa borrows multiple Spanish verses from the *Colloquios y Doctrina Christiana*, a recorded dialogue between the first 12 Franciscan friars and representatives of the early Mexican nobility, who gathered in Mexico in 1524 after the military conquest of *Tenochtitlán*, the Aztec administrative and spiritual center.[9] The dialogue largely recounts answers of the Mexican intelligentsia to the Franciscan "proposal" that they convert to Judeo-Christian doctrine. The passages in *Colloquios* were first inscribed in an alphabetized *Nahuatl*, collected, and later translated into Spanish by the missionary Bernardino de Sahagún around 1565. Anzaldúa's "Tlilli, Tlapalli: The Path of the Red and Black Ink" narrates the moment in which the Aztec nobility refer to Tlamatinime, the philosophers and composers of Mesoamerican writing, and the teachers of *Huehuetlahtolli*.

At this critical moment of early Western expansion, which recalls the near destruction of Mesoamerican rhetorical practices, Anzaldúa reactivates the power of the pictograph and the value of the codex, four centuries later. References to the códices correspond to *amoxtli*, the pictographic "codex books" that were systematically destroyed by Spanish combatants as a strategy for taming and subjugating indigenous minds. Spain's campaign of Christianization and the alphabetic literacy aimed to rewrite and redefine the Mesoamerican world under European-imposed categories. Thus, Anzaldúa invites readers to simultaneously dwell in the tragic Christianizing mission of the sixteenth century and the present stage of global border crossing. As passages throughout *Borderlands* illustrate, the present era of globalization continually questions, through the expansion of capital, mass migrations and permeable borders, the integrity and hierarchy of assimilation. Moreover, Anzaldúa's script in "Tlilli, Tlapalli" asserts an active entangling of Spanish, English, *Nahuatl*, Quechua and pictographic memories in the present, thereby inviting comparative and contrastive practices that continually shift between Greco-Roman and Mesoamerican rhetorics.

One of the most significant contributors to understanding Mesoamerican rhetoric today is Mexican historian and philosopher Miguel León-Portilla. His landmark translation of the *Huehuetlahtolli* documents the discursive properties that were systematically taught at the *Calmecac*. León-Portilla illustrates that although Mesoamericans did not have rhetoric from the regionally provincial Greco-Roman understanding of persuasion, their Tlamatinime and Tlacuiloque understood and mediated their world through *Huehuetlahtolli*, an equally functional and valuable discursive practice. León-Portilla supports the case that *Huehuetlahtolli* is far from extinct as a communicative art, and such practice cannot be reduced to a static or "authentic" pre-Columbian property of Mesoamerica.

In collaboration with Native American studies scholar Inés Hernández-Avila, León-Portilla recognizes present-day writing practices in and beyond Mexico to compose in *Nahuatl*/Spanish/English hybrids as well as other idioms. To properly account for these present-day rhetorical manifestations of dual expressions and symbolic oppositions, the authors advance the phrase "Yancuic Tlahtolli." With the *Nahuatl* root Hue ("ancient") replaced, the modified expression becomes translated as "The New Word."[10] Thus, an ancient rhetorical vehicle for inscribing wisdom and history revitalizes a new consciousness that fuses Mesoamerican culture and knowledge into contemporary variations. Mestiza consciousness follows in this dynamic tradition through figurative contradictions, parallel expressions, and dual symbolism. I interpret this strategy as a resistant rhetoric that addresses the larger backdrop of colonial subjugation and resistance in the Americas. Through continuous symbolic play with doubles and corresponding expressions, mestiza consciousness revises the dominant narrative of assimilation.

Throughout *Borderlands/La Frontera*, Anzaldúa's rhetoric denaturalizes English literacy as the normative tool of writing by entwining a myriad of languages, including at least two forms of English and six varieties of Spanish. The Castilian variations confront readers with both the standardized dialect of an ex-colonial power as well as some of its hybridized, countercultural admixtures. In his *Local Histories/Global Designs: Coloniality, Subaltern Knowledges, and Border Thinking* (2000), Walter Mignolo explains the complex layering of power among the various Spanish languages embroidered throughout Anzaldúa's tapestry:

> Spanish is both a hegemonic language allowing for the subalternization of Amerindian languages and a subaltern language of North Atlantic modernity. And I would add, it is three times subaltern.

> Spanish was first displaced toward a subaltern position within the European community itself during the seventeenth century...when French, German, and English became the languages of reason and science...Second, after World War II and the division of the world into three ranked areas, Spanish became the language of a significant portion of the Third World, Hispanic America. Spanish was devalued a third time when it became the language of Latino communities in the United States. (268)

In "How to Tame a Wild Tongue," Anzaldúa elaborates on pachuco and Chicano Spanish, two of the many language varieties that have emerged in the U.S. borderlands as a partial consequence of both Castilian and English colonization.[11] Linguist Rosaura Sánchez' *Chicano Discourse: Socio-Historic Perspectives* confirms that these varieties, while they share some similarities to the standard Spanish Peninsula dialect, are rural and working-class variants unique to the México/U.S. borderlands.[12] Through these linguistic and rhetorical variations, Anzaldúa opens up an imaginary that is no longer tied to hierarchical orders of imperial history. In the preface to *Borderlands*, Anzaldúa states,

> The switching of "codes" in this book from English to Castilian Spanish to the North Mexican dialect to Tex-Mex to a sprinkling of *Nahuatl* to a mixture of all of these, reflects my language, a new language...we Chicanos no longer feel that we need to beg entrance, that we need always to make the first overture—to translate to Anglos, Mexicans and Latinos, apology blurting out of our mouths with every step. Today we ask to be met halfway. This book is our invitation... (20)

Accepting this invitation, I argue, points toward rethinking Western historical foundations of rhetoric and writing from a "new" understanding that invents across and beyond nations, from a new mestiza consciousness.

Thus, mestiza consciousness as a rhetorical strategy invites readers not only to think with, against, and beyond the first language to impose rhetoric instruction-proper in America. It furthermore confronts readers with so-called Third World transformations of Spanish and the memories that are kept alive through matrifocal Mestiz@ ritual acts such as *brujaria* and *curanderismo*, healing arts of Mexican folk Catholicism and Aztec sacred practice.[13] Alongside this heterogeneous backdrop, Anzaldúa furthermore introduces the potential to displace the dominance of alphabetic literacy by continually evoking pictographic record-keeping practices, which reinscribe the Aztec concept of *Tlaquilolitztli*, another of the earliest expressions for writing in America. Readers are confronted with an Aztec cosmology, influenced by the preceding 5,000 years of development in the Valley of Oaxaca, which cultivated their own complex rhetorical traditions and equally suitable, "civilized" societies. Rhetoric and composition historians, if they take up mestiza consciousness as a rhetorical strategy, must confront the pictographic writing of pre-Columbian Mexican civilizations in meaningful ways.

By merging Western and Mesoamerican practices of writing, Anzaldúa is no longer obliged to accept the Western philosophy of a grammar, of linguistic control and "taming the wild tongue" and mind, as universal components of writing instruction. Mestiza consciousness potentially reveals a new politics of teaching that no longer privileges speaking, writing, and thinking within a single language controlled by conventions of scholarly prose. The matter raised here is not whether Standardized Academic English should still be taught or employed in U.S. colleges and universities. College English is merely the dominant institutional language of our day, and attaining fluency enables possibilities to intervene from the periphery to the center of contemporary theoretical dialogue and debate, as the widely read *Borderlands* illustrates. Not exercising the hegemonic imperial language of English at all in her scholarship would guarantee Anzaldúa's marginalization before ever having an opportunity to participate in academic conversations among U.S. rhetoric and composition specialists.

By rejecting the colonial legacy of taming the tongue and mind, mestiza consciousness does not refuse the teaching of English. Rather, mestiza consciousness as a rhetorical strategy effectively challenges the first wide-scale colonialist pedagogy of writing, a pedagogical campaign articulated just prior to and during the earliest moments of Western global expansion. At the end of the fifteenth century, Andalusian writer Antonio de Nebrija published the first grammar for Spanish in *Gramática Castellana*. This pedagogy forwards a political philosophy that privileges alphabetic literacy by linking it directly to colonization and nation-state formation. In the minds and hands of Franciscan missionaries, this ideology was to be used for teaching European customs to Mesoamericans, including conversion to Christianity. One of the most noteworthy features of Nebrija's pedagogy is his claim for a linkage between alphabetic literacy, military occupation, and the Christian nation-state:

> Now that the Church has been purified, and we are thus reconciled to God, now that the enemies of the Faith have been subdued by our arms, now that just laws are being enforced, enabling us all to live as equals, what else remains but the flowering of the peaceful arts. And among the arts, foremost are those of language, which sets us apart from the wild animals: language, which is the unique distinction of man, the means for the kind of understanding which can be surpassed only by contemplation. (5)

Here Nebrija refers primarily to written alphabetic speech, in its narrow Western conception. Alphabetic literacy thus hierarchically distinguishes "civilized" humanity from "barbarian" living systems in Mesoamerica and other colonial peripheries. Nebrija understood that the power of a regulated language, through grammar, lay in teaching it to "cultural Others," as well as in controlling "barbarian" languages by writing their grammars.[14] As history demonstrates, this European theory of written language was to become a foundation for the massive campaign to colonize the Western Hemisphere, and later Africa and Asia. It is this hierarchical narrative, this pedagogical legacy that mestiza consciousness rhetorically subverts and revises.

If writing specialists today accept Anzaldúa's mestiza consciousness as a starting point, then possibilities for accessing rhetorical and pedagogical potentials, no longer constrained by dichotomous frameworks of Western expansion, become available. If, in place of theorizing rhetoric and writing based on a Western narrative and mestiza consciousness is advanced as a point of origin, scholars might be encouraged to think about, practice, and teach rhetoric in ways that are directly responsive to comparative developments of writing, both past and present, from Olmec hieroglyphs to Aztec pictography to present-day Mestiz@ codices. No longer limited by parochial assumptions about writing as the representation of speech through alphabetic or syllabic systems, new studies could examine the construction of knowledge through various practices of information storage and transmission, whether one writes with letters or with pictographs. New translations of rhetoric that emerge from colonial peripheries also contribute to a materialist, historically grounded theory of writing as it has changed across time.

Mestiza consciousness is a distinct enunciation, grounded in the lived experiences of the peripheral colonial world that expresses new potentials that surpass the hierarchical logic of assimilation. The intellectual province of the borderlands contributes a thorough knowledge of critical moments of colonization and capitalist global expansion. Mestiz@ rhetorics, beginning with the brutal encounter between disparate worlds, invoke the idea of temporal simultaneity in which it becomes possible to envision multiple histories and memories coexisting, without assertions that all cultures across the Americas and the globe follow along the same hierarchical axis of development.

While mestiza consciousness might be described as "comparative" between Mesoamerica and the West, there is a crucial distinction between this articulation and comparative approaches from a colonial point of view. Comparative rhetorics should not erase the complex differences between contrastive civilizations by using European descriptions of Western rhetorical practice as a universal frame for understanding diverse cultural traditions in Mesoamerica. A comparative methodology along these lines is a product similar to what was articulated during colonial expansion to the Western Hemisphere beginning with Franciscan ethnographers such as Bernardino de Sahagún. In contrast, mestiza consciousness challenges a colonialist foundation by inventing alternatives from the vantage point of its conceptual borders and limits. A passage from Walter Mignolo's *The Darker Side of the Renaissance: Literacy, Territoriality, and Colonization*, is helpful:

> I prefer to think that if comparative processes need an origin, it—like many others—should not be looked for among the Greeks but among some of the features common to living organisms. Discerning differences by identities, and vice versa, also seems to be a feature of human intelligence, and, consequently, so are comparative attitudes. Why should comparatism be interpreted as a Greek invention instead of as a human need for adaptation and survival? Comparative categories formulated in disciplinary terms are what we might attribute to the colonial expansion of the fifteenth through seventeenth centuries, which implies that only the Western foundation of knowledge was an authorized way of knowing, comparing, and formulating comparative categories. (19)

Accordingly, a mestiza consciousness comparative approach to rhetoric and writing need not be limited to only those expressions and explanations provided by the Western world.

Effectively rethinking rhetoric and writing in a more comparative or coevolutionary context, therefore, includes at least two simultaneous long-term objectives. First, scholars would need to reconstruct a history of rhetoric and writing practices specific to the Americas. By reconstruction, I am not suggesting an essential mining or reclamation of "authentic" Mesoamerican history. Furthermore, nostalgia is not the motivation of this project. A careful reconstruction would instead involve an investigation of material and historical plausibilities in order to develop "new" ways of thinking about writing and rhetoric, both yesterday and today. Second, writing specialists could reinscribe Mesoamerican and Mestiz@ writing practices and knowledges into the dominant frameworks of the contemporary study of written language.

Mestiza consciousness is a powerful conceptual and analytic tool that significantly revises how writing and rhetoric can be studied and taught. In a small but hopefully significant way, this study contributes to both long-term objectives. Mestiza consciousness, as a Mestiz@ rhetorical practice, creates a locus of enunciation not where Spanish Iberian, African, and Mesoamerican legacies are mere alternatives to Western rhetoric. Mestiz@ rhetorics suggest, conversely, that Western practices are not necessarily superior alternatives to the immense hemispheric and global plurality that remain obscured.

III

Mestiz@: A Brief History, from Mexicatl to Chican@

And then the earth arose because of them, it was simply their word that brought it forth. For the forming of the earth they said "Earth." It arose suddenly, just like a cloud, like a mist, now forming, unfolding. Then the mountains were separated from the water, all at once the great mountains came forth. By their genius alone, by their cutting edge alone they carried out the conception of the mountain-plain, whose face grew instant groves of cypress and pine.

—*Popul Vuh*, Chapter 1[1]

In 1524, Chief Lieutenant Pedro Alvarado and Spanish armed forces occupied the Quiche Maya civilization of Guatemala and proceeded to burn their ancient libraries and schools. Secretly, some Maya intelligentsia managed to translate copies of centuries-old hieroglyphic manuscripts into a Latin alphabetic script. Because most transcriptions were kept hidden as a deliberate tactic of survival, over time many were inadvertently lost. One manuscript, discovered not until 1701 by an indigenous priest, Francisco Ximénez, was the *Popul Vuh*, or "Book of Council," which offers an extensive account of Maya creation myths and rituals.[2] Mexican historian and philosopher Miguel León-Portilla argues that an indigenous Quiche, Diego Reynoso, was likely responsible for the first translation of the *Popul Vuh* into Spanish.[3]

Plausibly the oldest "book" in the Western Hemisphere, the manuscript is now read by Mestiz@ and countless others as a powerful tribute to ancestral creation myths and lineages of identity across the Americas. Chapter 1 of the *Popul Vuh* references the earth and its formation, which today recuperates an indigenous understanding of the cyclical nature of time, change, and growth while simultaneously speaking to the importance of the land that was stolen and appropriated first by Spain and later by the U.S. government in its imperial expansion. Arturo Aldama's *Disrupting Savagism: Intersecting Chicana/o, Immigrant, and Native American Struggles for Self-Representation*, confirms the material and symbolic importance of geographical space in America:

> Land is a source of revitalization, renewal, and sustenance that was in the stewardship of campesinos and indigenous communities before the creation of the slave-like Spanish and Mexican croillo hacienda systems, the bloody acquisition as U.S. territory, and the control by U.S. multi-national agribusiness. (99)

This chapter on history begins with the *Popul Vuh* creation story because Mestiz@ peoples identify their collective historical legacy with pre-Columbian cultures that flourished throughout the hemisphere from 30,000 to 100,000 years ago, and see themselves as related to a number of the over 500 North American nations and the 250 linguistic groups in Mexico and Central America as well as some in the Caribbean and South American Amazon.[4]

Over 3,500 years ago, the ancestors of Mestiz@s laid the foundations for three major Mesoamerican civilizations: the Inka, the Maya, and Aztec. The phrase "Mesoamerica" literally means "Middle America" and applies widely to the cultural legacies of indigenous cultures across the central Mexican plateau as well as the Maya lowlands. As an umbrella term, Mesoamerica is employed not to suggest a sweeping generalization, but in recognition of long processes of interrelated yet diverse cultures in a constant state of transformation. Cultural transformation took after Spanish customs, and later Western European and Anglo-American traditions were imposed upon Mesoamerica. Moreover, the expression is not necessarily fixed along a chronological scale and has been used as an enduring cultural identifier in a perpetual state of flux.[5] Mesoamerica did not disappear, in a matter of speaking, but adapted.

The Olmec developed as one of the first highly complex Mesoamerican civilizations around 1,500–2,000 years prior to the birth of Jesus of Nazareth. The Olmec people knew themselves as *Xi* (pronounced "shee"), and emerged along the tropical lowlands of Mexico. As early as 1300 BCE, *Xi* villages gave way to a complex society governed by kingdoms, with impressive ceremonial centers, calendrics, and glyphic inscription practices. A greenstone slab known as the "Cascajal block," dated 900 BCE, contains the earliest glyphic etchings in the Western Hemisphere. The script features horizontal symbols, complete with their own syntax and language-specific word order. While some scholars suggest that the *Xi* document has a ritual purpose, the meaning of the text has yet to be fully deciphered at the time of this publication.

The Inka civilization emerged much later than the *Xi*, around 1200 CE, and thrived until Spanish occupation in 1535. The impressive population extended from the equator to the Pacific coast of Chile, although most cities emerged on the Peruvian slopes of the Andes Mountains. Remarkably, the vastly organized and complex Inka civilization recorded information not through glyphs but the *khipu*, a collection of knotted cotton cords. Color-coded strands operated as a kind of textile abacus, and are today compared to the binary-coded systems of computer programming languages.[6] In *Signs of the Inka Khipu: Binary Coding in the Andean Knotted-String Records* (2003), Gary Urton notes:

> "I believe that a consideration of computer information technology, and in particular a careful thinking through of the nature of the 'interface' between a code and the script(s) that it encodes, may provide a useful model for conceptualizing what I hypothesize to have been the relationship between the storing of information and the reading of messages in the khipu. I suggest that this relationship may be likened to that between the signs of a binary code, on the one hand, and the message—usually in the form of some recognizable, 'readable' script—transmitted by means of that binary code, on the other hand . . . In the technology of communicating by means of, for instance, e-mail, we work on a keyboard that allows us to produce on the computer monitor in front of us a typewritten version of a message. The message that we perceive on the screen before us in a familiar script (e.g., Spanish, Japanese, English) exists inside the computer in the form of binary-coded sequences in which each mark (e.g., alphabetical letter, comma, hyphen, etc.) that is produced by touching a key on the keyboard coincides with, or is carried by, a particular eight-binary-digit (abbreviated as 'bit') sequence of 1s and 0s." (38–39)

If we understand the khipu codes as related to those of computer technologies, we open doors to new ways of thinking about how information is recorded as well as how our computers work and what they do. The khipu system not only calls scholars to rethink computer languages, but invites writing specialists to reconsider what counts as so-called visual and multimedia modes of communication. The Quiche Maya typically receive the most attention among the vast diversity of Mesoamerican civilizations. Originating in the Yucatan around 2600 BCE, the Maya rose to prominence around AD 250 in what is today southern Mexico, Guatemala, northern Belize, and western Honduras. Building on the inherited inventions and ideas of the Olmec, the Maya developed complex astronomy, calendrical systems, and hieroglyphic writing. The Maya were noted as well for elaborate and highly decorated ceremonial architecture, including temple pyramids, palaces, and observatories, which were built without metal tools. They were also skilled farmers, clearing large sections of tropical rain forest and, where groundwater was scarce, building sizeable underground reservoirs for the storage of rainwater. The Maya were equally skilled as weavers and potters, and cleared routes through swamplands to foster extensive trade networks across the region. Of all Mesoamerican groups, however, those of central Mesoamerica and the Aztec empire often hold the most resonance with Mestiz@ collective memory.

The Aztec Before Spanish Conquest

The word Aztec simply means "people of Aztlán," and was used heavily by nineteenth-century German scientific explorer Alex von Humboldt. Humboldt proposed the expression as a universal reference to all *Nahuatl* speakers in central Mesoamerica at the time of Spanish conquest[7] The Valley of Oaxaca and surrounding regions were linguistically diverse, yet most cultures were able to communicate with others through *Nahuatl*. The Aztecs knew themselves as the *Mexica* ("Me-shee-kah") or *Culhua-Mexica*, when wanting to emphasize their affiliation with the lineages established at *Culhuacan*, a community in the center of the Mexican plateau.

Prior to Spanish invasion, the *Mexica* held the largest political concentration of power, with *Tenochtitlán* ("Te-nosh-teet-lahn") as its administrative center. Inhabited by some 300,000 people in the early sixteenth century, *Tenochtitlán* was built upon an island and reclaimed wetlands around Lake Texcoco ("Tesh-ko-ko"). This shallow body of water occupied a large portion of the Central Valley of Mexico. Today, the lake is drained and the ruins of the Aztec capitol lie beneath the modern metropolis of downtown Mexico City. *Tenochtitlán* was approached by long passageways that stretched from the mainland across the marshes. Four wide pedestrian walkways led in from the points of entry, quartering the residential zones and converging on the impressive civic and religious core of the city.[8] Royal palace compounds stood by an open market plaza, while a large quadrangular enclosure defined the ceremonial center area. In the middle of this sacred precinct, a tall pyramid rose above smaller pyramids and connected buildings. Upon the pyramid were paired temples of the ancient rain and fertility deity Tlaloc, and the hero god *Huitzilopochtli/ Mexitli* (literally, "Hummingbird of the South"). Reportedly, among surrounding temples and other buildings stood a tall scaffolding with poles strung with hundreds of skulls of *Mexica* adversaries. The skulls were to serve as reminders of the *Mexica's* powerful military strength.[9]

Ancient pictographic manuscripts indicate that the *Mexica* were nomadic hunter gatherers who, in the thirteenth century, migrated into the Central Highlands from the deserts to the north.[10] This movement followed a very old pattern of migration seen throughout Mesoamerican history. In response to drought or other harsh ecological conditions, famine, the pressures of other desert peoples or war among city-states in the center, tribes from northern arid regions migrated into the fertile, well-watered highlands where agricultural, urban populations had long flourished. *Mexica* myth explains that their place of origin was, Aztlán, "place of white cranes."[11] Aztlán is described as an island-hill rising from a lake. It was there that the *Mexica* emerged from caves and the earth itself. After a while they decided to leave and embarked by canoes to the mainland, where they began their long migration south.

When the *Mexica* arrived in the northern end of the Valley of Oaxaca sometime in the late thirteenth century, they encountered an impressive people with prestigious lineages. The *Toltec* were primarily responsible for cultivating the region, establishing trade routes, agricultural production, and erecting most of the great pyramids. While some intermarriage took place, notably between a *Mexica* chieftain and a woman from the *Toltec* royalty, the newcomers were regarded as somewhat primitive. Over time trouble broke out between the settlers and their hosts when the *Mexica* reportedly sacrificed the daughter of a *Culhuacan* chief as an offering to the earth and fertility god.[12] An ensuing battle drove the *Mexica* into the marshlands by the western shore. Taking shelter in an unclaimed area of the lake, the *Mexica* occupied a permanent settlement that became *Tenochtitlán*. The industrious *Mexica* established a marketplace and traded natural resources from the lake, built their economic base, constructed ceremonial centers, and so on.

Approximately a hundred years after the founding, the establishment had become a formidable city under the leadership of *Itzcóatl*. The *Mexica* quickly formed alliances causing a decisive shift in Mesoamerica's balance of power. The allied city-states of *Tenochtitlán*, *Tetzcoco*, and *Tlacopan* formed what is today remembered as the Triple Alliance, a federation of the most economically and politically powerful nations in the Valley of Oaxaca.[13] Noteworthy was the *Tlaltelolco* market, one of the cultural hubs of the *Mexica* metropolis. In this highly structured commercial space, traders from numerous townships brought produce from lakeside plantations and other goods from the plains and mountains of the highland region. Long-distance traders imported goods through long trains of human carriers from sources on the tropical lowland coasts and the forests and mountains to the far south.

As the alliance flourished under *Itzcóatl's* control, the *Mexica* saw the need to reconsider its past and define a new national historical identity. Itzcóatl assembled a council in *Tenochtitlán* to review old migration accounts. The council concluded that the obscure origins of the migrating *Mexica* were unacceptable for their new imperial status. Older records were then burned and a new official history began to be written. At this time *Huitzilopochtli/Mexitli* was recognized as the official god of the *Mexica*.[14] With this information, modern scholars have analyzed the existing migration texts and the legend of *Huitzilopochtli/Mexitli*, noting especially its mythological episodes. Findings show that the *Mexica* migration story shares episodes closely reflecting the older migration stories of the *Tolteca-Chichimeca*.[15]

Indeed, the whole sequence of events beginning in Aztlán conforms to a widespread pattern of origin and migration stories found among the Quiche Maya, the *Toltec*, the *Tarascans*, as well as the *Tewa*/San Juan Pueblo on the Rio Grande valley in northern New Mexico. The sequence begins in a faraway land or a lake to the north at the onset of a new era. According to the biblical concept of creation, humans were created from elements. Migration from the homeland is typically directed by a deity in response to dissention, famine, or war. The departing group is frequently joined by others, and a supernatural leader or messenger guides the route of migration. Undoubtedly, the "official" account of the *Mexica* migration reflects earlier well-established models. Through *Huitzilopochtli/Mexitli*, the *Mexica* created a new point of reference for the development of a rising religious and governmental social dynamic. The migration legend and *Huitzilopochtli*/Mexitli's symbolism inspired their culture with pride.[16]

In 1440, *Moctezuma Ilhuicamina* came to power over the Triple Alliance. *Moctezuma* I dispatched a royal delegation of priests to find Aztlán, the *Mexica* ancestral homeland. Legends explain that when the group reached the birthplace of *Huitzilopochtli/Mexitli*, they were transformed into birds and other winged beasts. The delegation took flight and arrived in Aztlán where they resumed human form. Soon, the priests were guided to a relative of *Huitzilopochtli/Mexitli* who scolded them for the material and political excesses of *Tenochtitlán* and the Triple Alliance. The royal delegation then came to the presence of Coatlicue, *Huitzilopochtli/Mexitli's* ancient mother, who prophesied that *Tenochtitlán* would eventually fall under conquest[17] With this news, the delegation returned to inform *Moctezuma* I.

Moctezuma Xocoyotzin, a high priest and educator, was to become *Tenochtitlán's* next leader in 1502. Following the appointment, messengers reportedly found him cleaning a temple. After taking charge, Moctezuma II dismissed most council authorities including those who appointed him, replacing them with philosophers and priests.[18] A mutual dislike between the new ruler and many in the Alliance led Moctezuma to create elaborate rituals that physically separated him from others. Well-studied in philosophy and divination, Moctezuma sent emissaries to find a legendary prophet, Huemac, who was to predict the arrival of Quetzalcoatl (literally, "feathered serpent"), a powerful Mesoamerican deity. Huemac refused to assist Moctezuma, and instead urged *Tenochtitlán* to abandon all luxuries and seek atonement.[19]

Later, in 1519, Moctezuma II received reports of bearded strangers landing on the east coast of the Triple Alliance. Here's an account recorded after the conquest:

> All of us who were there saw gods arriving on the coast in great houses of water.... Moctezuma remained alone, pensive, and quite suspicious of this great novelty in his kingdom...and he called to mind his prophet's predictions.... He began to believe that it was Quetzalcoatl whom they once adored as a god...and who long ago had left for the far east.[20]

Moctezuma then sent ambassadors carrying elaborate costumes as offerings, one after the rain deity *Tlaloc*, and the other of *Quetzalcoatl*.

Whereas Tlaloc's mask had two large circular eyes, *Quetzalcoatl's* featured a long beard. Upon meeting the Spaniard Hernán Cortéz, the ambassadors decided that the conquistador had the attributes of *Quetzalcoatl*, and dressed him like the god.[21]

Hearing that Cortéz and his men continued to advance toward *Tenochtitlán*, Moctezuma sent philosopher priests with more offerings hoping to prevent his approach. Of the assorted gifts, Moctezuma included gold:

> They gave the Spanish gold flags, flags of quetzal feathers, and gold necklaces. And when they had given them this, their faces were smiling, they were very glad (the Spaniards), they were delighted. As if they were monkeys they picked up gold, because they seated in such gesture, as if their hearts were renewed and illuminated. *Because true it is that that is what they yearn for with great thirst. Their chests widen, they are furiously hungry for it. Like hungry pigs they crave gold.*[22] (Italics in original)

Moctezuma was unaware of the consequences of his offerings. Even though it was rare for people to get close to Moctezuma, even though no one was permitted to look into Moctezuma's face, the leader realized a meeting with Cortéz was inevitable. On November 8, 1519, Moctezuma Xocoyotzin met Hernán Cortéz, whom he believed to be the god *Quetzalcoatl*. When Cortéz arrived at *Tenochtitlán*'s great entrance, Moctezuma honored him with flowers from his personal garden. One of Cortéz' soldiers, Bernal Díaz del Castillo, writes of the historic meeting:

> What men have there ever been with such daring?...The great Moctezuma descended from his platform...Cortéz was told that the great Moctezuma was coming...so he approached Moctezuma and they did each other homage.[23]

After Moctezuma received Cortéz and his men, the Spaniards departed for Yucatan to covertly recruit native allies and prepare to extinguish the Triple Alliance.

Conquest of Tenochtitlán

At Spain's first arrival, the Mesoamerican region was one of the most populous areas in the world, with an estimated 25 million people residing in the Valley of Mexico alone.[24] On August 13, 1521, Spanish combatants proceeded to ransack *Tenochtitlán*. Of Cortéz' first victims were his native allies from the coastal Zempoala. European smallpox annihilated that entire population. Conquistadors furthermore destroyed all 6,000 inhabitants of *Cholula*.[25] Notable is conquistador Pedro Alvarado's massacre of the *Mexica* at *Tenochtitlán*. Alvarado invited the warriors to lay down their arms and partake of a ceremonial feast in a great courtyard new the temples:

> The Spaniards took up positions at the exits and entrances... so that none of the Aztecs could leave. The Spaniards then entered the sacred patio and commenced murdering people. They marched forward carrying wooden and metal shields and swords. They surrounded those dancing and pushed them toward the kettledrums. They hacked into the drum player, cutting off both his arms. They then decapitated him, and his head fell to the ground at a distance. Swiftly the Spaniards thrust their lances among the people and hacked them with their swords. In some cases they attacked from behind, carving out entrails, which spread all over the earth, leaving bodies lifeless. They wounded those partying in the thighs, the calves, and the full abdomen. Entrails covered the earth. Some Aztecs ran, but in vain, since their own intestines wrapped their feet like a net and tripped them up. These victims could find no way to escape since the Spaniards slaughtered them at entrances and exits. Some victims attempted to scale the walls, but they could not save themselves.[26]

Estimates of the temple death toll range around 1,000. The *Mexica* revolted in response, and the Spanish seized Moctezuma as a captive. On July 1, 1520, in an effort to diminish the raging mob, Moctezuma appeared on the balcony of his palace, appealing for a retreat. Reportedly, arrows and darts delivered fatal wounds to Moctezuma.[27]

It took Spanish forces two years to completely destroy the immense city—its gardens, temples, libraries, schools, and houses. In 50 years after this bloody encounter, all but 10 percent of the population was destroyed due to smallpox, slaughter, and starvation.[28] Spain quickly imposed encomiendas, a feudal system whereby the Spanish Crown assigned "grants" of natives within specific Mesoamerican regions to the authority of encomenderos, Spanish lords in the New World. The encomiendas functioned to control, reeducate and indoctrinate surviving Mesoamericans in Catholicism. In fact, encomenderos with 50 or more natives were to educate one person in reading and writing and religious doctrine, who was then forced to teach the other natives.[29] Moreover, natives were required to pay encomenderos tributes in return for "protection" and religious instruction.[30] The encomienda system did not directly require land occupation by the encomendero. Officially, land was to remain in native possession and was supervised by the Spanish Crown.[31] Encomenderos often owned land nearby, however, and forced natives into slave labor in mines and on plantations.[32]

While the Valley of Oaxaca endured some of the greatest casualties, regions to the north along the Rio Grande river basin were also brutally colonized. The feudal system encouraged Spanish and Mesoamerican intermarriage as a deliberate strategy of subjugation through constant and direct contact. Spain also hoped this would help their efforts to convert native minds to a Christian worldview. However, what the encomienda system actually accomplished was a guaranteed labor supply because they could easily force the Indians to produce food and supplies.[33] Quickly, the rights of Mesoamericans, meager as they were, were ignored on every occasion involving commerce, because they provided a source of "immediate revenue" for the encomenderos.[34] Because of this, Mesoamericans were forced into positions of starvation and then into death.[35]

From this historical narrative, we come to understand that European arrival did not "civilize" or advance Mesoamerican culture. Conversely, it enslaved the majority of its inhabitants while forcing them to become Christians and subordinates to an arbitrary Spanish administration. Immense deposits from gold and silver mines were transferred to Europe. At the same time, Western Africans were taken captive and shipped across the Atlantic as replacements for the quickly dying population of Mesoamerican slaves.[36] Together, these acts created one of the vast sources of accumulation that allowed Europe to expand its economic system into a global phenomena and an unparalleled age of transatlantic imperialism. Such strategies played a decisive role in diverse Mestiz@ historical experiences, experiences complicated by an expanding capitalist system and its attendant cultural forces, including pervasive racism.[37] From its eruptions in early modern Europe to its imperial projects thereafter, the feudalist and eventually capitalist system became fused with the logic of Western expansion.

In only a few hundred years' time, Spain, Portugal, England, France, Belgium, the Dutch, and Germany gained control of most of the Americas and Caribbean, the African continent, the Middle East, India, South Asia, Pacific Asia, and some parts of China. While North

America fell to the armed forces of England and France, the majority of the continent remained under Spanish and Portuguese control. Under the campaign of Christianization, a fully globalized slave system encompassing millions of kidnapped Africans lasted for 450 years until slavery was abolished in the 1800s.[38]

England, and later the Anglo-American leaders of the United States, managed to massacre or separate natives while also settling their lands with large numbers of English, Irish, Scottish, and other Western European peoples. Chicano historian Tomás Almaguer characterizes the later European conflict as genocide:

> Undoubtedly, the most brutal aspect of Anglo-Indian relation was the state policy of genocide. This policy was initially advocated by the first Anglo governor of California, Peter H. Burnett, who informed the state legislature in 1851 that "a war of extermination will continue to be waged between the two races until the Indian race becomes extinct." (22)

As for Mexico, the remaining native populations were kept as slaves to the comparatively smaller Spanish populace. While many Spanish and natives did intermarry, thereby creating the biological emergence of Mestiz@s, it is important to remember that there were few Spanish settlers around. In *The Discovery and Conquest of Mexico 1517–1521*, foot soldier Bernal Díaz del Castillo records that Spanish numbers only reached a height of 150,000 during the early years of conquest in the early sixteenth century, whereas African slaves reached a height of 300,000, twice the Spanish numbers (22). Of those Spaniards that did settle in the "New World," the number of Sephardic Crypto-Jews was high.[39]

Anthropologist Martha Menchaca's *Recovering History, Constructing Race: The Indian, Black, and White Roots of Mexican Americans* adds to this cultural complexity. By placing *Afro-Mestizos* of Spanish, Mexica, and African ancestries at the foundation of Mexican racial subjectivity, Menchaca further emphasizes the expansive range of the Mestiz@ spectrum. One of the most notable Mexicans of African decent is Gaspar Nyanga, who violently rebelled against Spanish colonial rule and established what is often regarded as the first self-governed African community in the Western Hemisphere: San Lorenzo de los Negros, later renamed Yanga for its forefather.

As the sixteenth century reached its end, the mixed-blood, Mestiz@ population had already grown beyond 25,000 in greater Mexico. In the first half of the seventeenth century, Mestiz@s grew to 400,000, and two centuries after that their numbers reached 1.5 million.[40] After the colonial rule was overthrown in the early 1800s, the Spanish came to Mexico only in small numbers if at all. By then, 60 percent of the Mexican population was estimated to be indigenous. Today, 10 percent of the Mexican people are "officially" recognized as indigenous, another 10 percent is reported as European, and the rest of the population is 80 percent Mestiz@ of mixed indigenous, Spanish, and/or African ancestry.[41]

Indeed, as the Spanish Iberian settlers were relatively small in number, it is understandable why today such a large percentage of Mexican peoples would share cultural memories and cultural practices that are largely indigenous. Despite the 500-year project of Hispanicization, Chicano intellectual work maintains that Mexican-origin people today are generally of indigenous Mesoamerican cultures. Mexico reportedly has more traditional indigenous tribal people, 10–20 million, speaking close to 80 languages, more than any other country in the hemisphere.[42] It is for these reasons that Guillermo Gómez-Peña and Yareli Arismendi refer to greater Mexico as "the largest Indian Reservation of the United States" (1).

The Pueblo Revolt

Syncretic mixing between Spanish and indigenous cultures was by no means utopic. The brutality and savagery of Hernán Cortéz' destruction of *Tenochtitlán* was mirrored in numerous other bloody campaigns across the Western Hemisphere. Noteworthy are the events surrounding colonizer Don Juan de Oñate and his heavily armed 1598 expedition along the Rio Grande valley. Oñate's soldiers, accompanied by Franciscan friars, regularly murdered natives, forcefully confiscated their lands and imposed the Judeo-Christian faith system. The Spanish naturally encountered native resistance to forced occupation, especially from the Acoma, a small nation 40 miles west of Albuquerque. Strategically built atop a 357-foot sandstone mesa, the Acoma Pueblo maintained a natural and effective defense against its opponents. In December of 1598, Acoma soldiers resisted Spanish terrorism in a minor battle that ended with the significant death of Oñate's nephew and 10 other Spanish soldiers. In retribution of his nephew's killing, Oñate attacked the mesa in 1599.[43] The epic battle lasted three days resulting in the systematic slaughter of hundreds of Acoma men, women, and children. After executing surviving Acoma leaders, Oñate cut off the right foot of every male over 25 years of age. Acoma women over 25 were sentenced to 25 years of slavery.[44]

Decades of Spanish intolerance and brutality ensued throughout the Rio Grande river basin. In 1675, 47 various Pueblo religious leaders were hauled into the administrative center of Santa Fe and publicly flogged and jailed. Four of them were martyred. Among those who survived was the San Juan *Tewa* religious leader Popé, who began covertly organizing a revolt against Spanish regimes.[45] When the day of the revolt approached, lengths of knotted cord were sent to over two dozen Pueblos, each knot signifying one day until the revolt. In August of 1680, surrounding Pueblo nations and the neighboring Navajo and Apache collectively rebelled against the Catholic Church and Spanish oppression, killing up to 400 colonizers.[46] Pueblo warriors drove the surviving 1,000 Spaniards back down the Rio Grande valley all the way to El Paso. For the next 12 years the Pueblos occupied government buildings in Santa Fe and began restoring the landscape for its original inhabitants.[47] Pueblo organizing was so complete that most Spanish remnants were destroyed, including their institutions, churches, libraries, administrative buildings, and particularly the encomienda mines that exploited native slave labor. Popé's Pueblo Revolt is widely regarded as the most successful indigenous uprising in North American history.

In 1693, Spanish forces under Don Diego de Vargas returned, engaging in a somewhat more diplomatic, gradual reclaiming of colonial governance. Some fighting continued in and around Santa Fe, which lead to the execution of 54 "rebels" for treason against God and the Royal Crown. Of those who surrendered at Santa Fe, 400 were seized and distributed to Spanish soldiers in servitude for 10 years.[48] Some Pueblo natives committed suicide rather than live under the harsh rule of the Spaniards yet again.[49] Continued deaths so angered Pueblo leaders along the Rio Grande river basin that they took to the mountains to prepare for a long skirmish with the colonizers. It took de Vargas practically the rest of the century and the loss of many more lives to end the military operations along the Rio Grande.

Pueblo-Hispano Alliances

In the aftermath of the Pueblo Revolt, the two cultures slowly fostered a more integrated economic, political, and social network. Beginning in the very early seventeenth century, for example, Hispano villages shared the same water resources with the Pueblos and planted and harvested their crops in the eternal calendrical cycle of spring, summer, fall, and winter. A large and far-flung trade network between Pueblo and Hispano also evolved during this time. The necessary kind of red ochre used for ceremonial use and pottery was only to be found in the Mesa de las Viejas area northwest of the contemporary village of Canjilón in Rio Arriba County.[50] Hispanos of the Canjilón-Cebolla area learned to gather and deliver the ochre to *Tewa* Pueblos for trade. Also traded was an important medicinal and folk herb, osa, used by both groups to combat ailments.[51]

Cultural exchanges between Pueblos and Hispano villagers slowly increased as Spanish officials had their eyes on France. Spain diverted much of its administrative attention spent on Christianizing natives to instead monitor rapidly expanding French colonial forces from Louisiana to the Texas coast. In the northern New Mexican territory, Pueblo and Hispano alike turned their attention to growing common concern with power struggles against Apaches to the east and south, Comanches to the north and east, and Navajos to the north and west.

During the eighteenth century Pueblos and Hispanos increasingly found themselves defending their communities and crops against nomadic raids. Pueblo soldiers served as auxiliaries to Hispano expeditions, and in time the necessity to combine forces against common pressures fostered layers of mutual respect and collaboration. For the Pueblos, the fact that the Spaniards no longer imposed the brutal encomienda system led them to relax their defenses.[52] In the religious realm, the Pueblo people learned that they would be left alone to perform their ceremonial dances if they scheduled at least some of them on major Catholic holidays and saints' birthdays.[53] Meanwhile, the friars were content to know that the Pueblos were dancing for the practices of the Church even if for their own reasons as well. In chapter 5, I attend to some detailed examples of this cultural merger as they are illustrated through the contemporary resurgence of ritual folk dances along the upper Rio Grande valley.

In addition to the friars and their Christianizing, Pueblo cultures were also altered by the introduction to metal tools and weapons, horses, new fruits, crops, and so on. Returning to life before Spanish foot soldiers marched up the Rio Grande basin was an impossibility. Slowly, cultural admixtures evolved during the early eighteenth century where Pueblo and Hispano communities came to embody indispensable aspects of each culture. For example, many "mixed-blood" villagers with no tribal affiliation nevertheless became familiar with the spirituality of the landscape that was an intrinsic part of the Pueblo world.[54] This population largely discarded the notion of Spanish purity, as is indicated by their chosen ethnic identifier, Españoles Mexicanos ("Spanish Mexicans"), widely recorded on birth certificates, marriage records, and other official documents.[55]

Mexican Independence and Political Unrest

Far from the gradual and cautious syncretism between the "Españoles Mexicanos" and Rio Grande Pueblos, French forces initiated the Peninsular War by invading Spain and Portugal. In 1808, Napoleon appointed his brother José Bonaparte as king of Spain, thereby sending the colonial administration into chaos. Criollos, cultural elites born in Mexico of Spanish parents, took this opportunity to organize a wide-scale revolution for Mexican independence. One of the most notable figures of the Independence War was Miguel Hidalgo y Costilla, a criollo priest stationed in the Mexican city of Dolores who helped organize a Mesoamerican alliance against Spanish authorities. Former Spanish military commander Agustín Iturbide, a Mestiz@ supported by the criollo elite, worked with Hidalgo and other Mexican revolutionaries to implement a new government in 1821.[56]

Plans for a constitutional monarchy called for an independent Mexican nation with a limited monarchy, granting Spanish royalty with first right to the throne. Unable to persuade a royal family member to accept, Agustín Iturbide was elected emperor of Mexico in 1822.[57] In a year's time, a military revolt overturned the monarchy and Mexico's Congress drafted a new constitution for a federal republic. In 1824, Mexico became a republic with a president, a two-house Congress heading the national government, and governors and legislatures heading the states. Guadalupe Victoria, a follower of revolutionary priest Miguel Hidalgo y Costilla, became the first Mexican president. Mexican life remained difficult due partially to declining economic conditions. One of the republic's burdens was the assumption of substantial debt contracted during the late colonial period and the empire. Mexico's ability to service the debt was severely constrained by the costs of maintaining a 50,000-strong army and the insufficiency of revenues generated by tariffs, taxes, and government monopolies. To cover the deficit, President Victoria accepted loans on stiff terms from British merchant houses.[58] The British supported independence movements in Spanish colonies and saw the loans as an opportunity to further displace Spain as the New World's dominant mercantile power.

In 1829, as a new president was elected, 3,000 Spanish soldiers attacked the city of Tampico with the aim of retaking Mexico. President Vicente Guerrero sent general Antonio López de Santa Anna to dislodge Spanish forces, but the Mexican general could not launch an effective assault and instead dug in for a siege. Cut off from supplies and weakened by disease, the Spanish surrendered to the Mexicans in October. In the aftermath of the Spanish withdrawal, Santa Anna was widely hailed as the savior of the republic.[59] With the Spanish threat gone, President Guerrero enacted several liberal reforms, including the abolition of slavery in September 1829. But his forceful style of governing, made possible by Guerrero's retention of emergency presidential powers obtained during the Spanish invasion, gave renewed cause for another rebellion.[60]

In early 1830, the conservative vice president, Anastasio Bustamante, led a successful military-backed revolt against Guerrero and installed himself as Mexico's third president. While attempting to flee the country, Guerrero was captured and executed under Bustamante's orders.[61] In early 1832, Santa Anna denounced Bustamante in Veracruz, occupied the city, and appropriated its custom revenues. Santa Anna's defiance spurred additional revolts throughout the states, leading to the eventual collapse of the conservative government. In the aftermath of the rebellion, the highly popular Santa Anna was elected president. In 1836, Santa Anna led Mexican forces to repress an uprising of advancing Anglo settlers in Mexico's northern province of San Antonio. Santa Anna ruled Mexico in an imperious fashion, disbanding Congress when it tried to pass a constitution guaranteeing human rights and an end to special monopolies. Northern and Yucatan rebellions in 1844 led to the overthrow of Santa Anna and the election of Jose Joaquin de Herrera as president.[62]

Constant regime change, bureaucratic turmoil, and Mexico's ailing economy impinged on Mestiz@ life. Despite political corruption at the highest levels of government, communities worked to maintain equitable life at the local level, especially regarding the distribution of political and legal rights. Unlike the European settler colonies in the expanding United States, Mexico protected the legal rights of women and men alike. For generations, in fact, it was customary and socially acceptable for women to vote, own property, access the courts, and engage in estate management.[63] Due in part to deep-rooted matrifocal, extended clustered family structures, it was normative, not disruptive, for Mexican women to exercise considerable political power.[64] While women in political roles such as holding public office may have been nonexistent, Mestiz@ villages nevertheless did not adhere to rigid sexual divisions of labor. Socially, economically, and politically, the Mexican republic was largely unprepared for the approaching American invasion.

U.S. Occupation

U.S. aggression in 1846 initiated a process of adaptive change across Mexican communities. It was a relatively slow process, however, until the Great Depression and the eventual introduction of welfare led to a diaspora of Mestiz@ farm workers following the harvests around the nation. The massive introduction of science and technology hastened the process of village and Pueblo change. Mexicans living in the northernmost regions became part of the United States after the Mexican-American War of 1845–1848. That war was hastened in part by the removal of Texas from Mexican lands through bloodshed led by Southern slaveholders to expand their slave territories.[65] After Texas briefly declared itself a republic, it eventually joined the United States and became part of the slave-holding states and then the Confederacy. As Mexico had abolished slavery, the republic refused to turn over escaped slaves from the South. An estimated 10,000 slaves escaped this way, in another important underground railroad to the south of the border.[66]

To expand territory and to rebuke Mexico for refusing to turn over U.S. "property" in the form of human slaves, the United States invaded. By 1847, General Winfield Scott led armed forces across Veracruz and marched into Mexico City/*Tenochtitlán*, which soon fell in battle. Rodolfo Acuña's landmark *Occupied America: A History of Chicanos* effectively recounts how congressional and media pressures to take over the whole country stopped when a civil war between Mexican peasants and other indigenous people turned on the U.S. invaders. As U.S. forces took Mexico's capitol city, troops under General Stephen Watts Kearny invaded the northern territory along the Rio Grande valley. In 1846, Kearny and his troops entered Santa Fe and informed residents that he had taken possession of the northernmost region of the Republic of Mexico.[67] Local officials were forced to take oaths of allegiance to the U.S. regime. A civil government was effectively put into place as Kearny appointed Charles Bent as the territory's first American governor. In addition to the governorship, Kearny appointed an American secretary and several judicial and civil officers. Despite Kearny's rapid attempts to absolve them of their loyalty to the republic, Mexicans legally maintained their citizenship at this time.[68]

Mestiz@ Insurrection

In January of 1847, a contingent of Mexicans organized an uprising against Governor Bent's residence in Don Fernando de Taos, 70 miles north of Santa Fe along the Rio Grande valley. In defiance of U.S. occupation, Mexicans killed Bent and six other officials stationed at his home. In response, 400 troops with several pieces of artillery were deployed to counter this and other numerous uprisings that erupted along the Rio Grande river basin.[69] In an act of retreat and reorganization, Mestiz@ "rebels" regrouped at the Pueblo village of Taos. Under the direction of Colonel Sterling Price, U.S. forces commenced an artillery barrage against the Pueblo of Taos. American troops fought past the outer defenses but were unable to dislodge Mexican and Pueblo forces from the church of San Geronimo, whose massive adobe walls provided protection. Colonel Price's troops reportedly used the largest gun they had, a "six-pounder," to breach the wall. With the wall opened, troops wheeled the cannon to point blank range and poured several rounds into the hole, killing up to 200 defenders. Casualties in the surrounding battlefield bring the estimate of Mestiz@s who died to at least 300.

Several captured survivors were indicted and convicted of high treason against the U.S. government, and were condemned to public execution by hanging. The first sentence was to Antonio Maria Trujillo, believed to be one of four principal organizers of the insurrection. Trujillo's case was plausibly the earliest death sentence in New Mexico's territorial judiciary. This is Judge Joab Houghton's verdict:

> Your age and grey hairs have excited the sympathy of both the Court and the jury.... It would appear that your old age has not brought you wisdom nor purity or honesty of your heart.... You have nourished bitterness and hatred in your soul. You have been found seconding the acts of a band of the most traitorous murderers that ever blackened with the recital of their deeds the annals of history.... For such foul crimes, an enlightened and liberal jury have been compelled from the

> evidence...and by a sense of their stern but unmistakable duty, to find you guilty of treason against the government under which you are a citizen.... And their only remains to the court the painful duty of passing upon you the sentence of the law, which is, that you be taken to prison, there to remain until Friday the 16th of April next and that at 2 o'clock in the afternoon of that day you be taken thence to the place of execution and there be hanged by the neck till you are dead! dead! dead! And may the Almighty God have mercy on your soul.[70]

Admittedly, Houghton's address is one of the most impassioned death sentences in New Mexico's judiciary history. Within days of Trujillo's sentence, a number of individuals, reportedly including the U.S. district attorney, questioned the authority of American courts to condemn Mexican citizens for treason.

Meanwhile, a separate civil court assembled to convict 40 or more other Mestiz@s who had been captured earlier that year. The presiding judge was the father of one of the men killed in Don Fernando de Taos at the onset of the revolt. On the first day of court, a grand jury convened with George Bent, brother of the recently assassinated governor, serving as foreman.[71] For killing governor Bent and his officials, five Mestiz@s were hanged in the Don Fernando plaza: Jose Manuel Garcia, Pedro Lucero, Juan Ramon Trujillo, Manuel Romero, and Isidro Romero. In retaliation for the executions, three U.S. soldiers were killed in Los Valles, a small settlement south of Santa Fe. A detachment of American troops quickly descended on Los Valles, killed six villagers, and within hours burned down the entire township. Forty villagers were imprisoned, out of which seven were convicted for murder. Between February and August of 1847, well over 20 Mexican citizens were publicly executed for treason and slaughter.[72] For Mestiz@s, these events constituted a harsh introduction to U.S. jurisprudence.

The Treaty of Guadalupe Hidalgo

The United States officially ended its war against Mexico with the 1848 ratification of the Treaty of Peace, Friendship, Limits and Settlement. The document is typically referred to as the Treaty of Guadalupe Hidalgo, after the name of the Mexican city where the treaty was signed. Among the treaty resolutions was Mexico's cession of what are today the states of California, Colorado, Nevada, Utah, Arizona, and New Mexico. These regions collectively amount to just over half of Mexico's territory.[73] Under Articles VIII and IX of the treaty, Mestiz@s in these regions were guaranteed property rights according to preexisting Spanish and Mexican laws.[74] To implement the treaty's property protection provisions, the U.S. Congress created a commission in 1851 to review and confirm community land grants where a city or village existed.

Conflict continued between Mestiz@s and their new land rulers. The former Mexican territories were sparsely populated agricultural communities unfamiliar with the English language, the U.S. legal system, and American culture. The earlier Mexican system relied on Spanish and Mexican laws that were often interpreted according to local custom rather than through a formal court system. Furthermore, Mexican and Spanish systems were rooted in a rural, community-based system of land-holding based on the region's relationship with the sustenance of surrounding populations. Land boundaries were articulated with reference to regional landmarks, and therefore often lacked cartographic precision. The results of this commission are hotly debated today. Many land grants were rejected and became part of the U.S. public domain, while the grants that were awarded often provided less acreage than was claimed.[75] As Mexicans lost much of their territory, the continued influx of immigration radically altered their cultural landscape.

Anglo immigrants soon outnumbered the Mexican and native Californian populations, although the increase in population included Chinese laborers, immigrants from Australia, Chilean miners, and former African slaves. Mexican resistance and adjustment to their new neighbors lasted for several decades. Mestiz@s were lynched and in some cases slaughtered by vigilante groups and official law enforcers such as the Texas Rangers[76] In 1913, an estimated 3,000 Mexican lives were lost in the crushing of the so-called Plan de San Diego revolt in the Rio Grande Valley of Texas, led by the Texas Rangers and involving lynching and outright murder as reprisals.[77] These episodes lasted throughout the first half of the twentieth century.

On January 5, 1931, in San Diego California, the all-white school board of Lemon Grove Grammar School voted to prohibit 75 Mestiz@ students from entering the 5-room building. Instead, Principle Jerome Green ordered the students to go to a hastily built structure across some railroad tracks in a largely Mexican section of town. The board decided not to notify the parents of the children about the relocation. With help from the Mexican consulate, parents sued the school board over racially segregating their children, most of whom were born in the United States. On March 11, 1931, San Diego Superior Court Judge Claude Chambers ruled that the school board lacked the authority to segregate the children.[78] Later that year, California Assemblyman George Bliss of Carpinteria tried to legalize the segregation of Mexican children by classifying them as Indians. His bill failed. The Lemon Grove case did not gain national attention, though the United States would confront institutionalized racism 23 years later with *Brown v. the Board of Education.*

Decades of racial tensions continued across the country. For example, Arturo Rosales' *Chicano! The History of Mexican American Civil Rights* effectively documents how, in the 1940s, Anglo servicemen, policemen, and citizens attacked these pachucos during the so-called Zootsuit Riots of 1943 and in the infamous Sleepy Lagoon Murder Trial, where 22 Mexican youth were convicted and imprisoned for murder in a case that was later thrown out (103). Mexicans were labeled by the press and many politicians as the most violent criminal element in the city. During the Great Depression of the late 1920s and early 1930s, the United States rounded up tens of thousands of Mexicans, including many U.S.-born citizens, to deport them to Mexico in one of the first anti-Mexican repatriation acts; similar round-ups occurred during World War II and in the 1950s.[79]

Despite this, Mexicans entered the armed forces in large numbers during World War II. Yet they returned to their barrios in places like Texas where Mexicans could not be buried alongside whites and there were still separate nights for movies and timings for swimming for Mexicans in public theaters and swimming pools.[80] In many areas across the country, strict neighborhood zoning laws forbade Mexicans, Indians, and African-Americans from living in areas where Anglos predominated. Anglos, of course, could live anywhere they wanted to. Mestiz@s, although started organizing since 1848, began to create with renouned a number of Mexican protection and mutual aid organizations such as the League of Latin American Citizens, the Government Issue Forum (GI), and others.[81] By the mid-1950s, they participated in struggles to integrate segregated schools, parks, and other public places. While Anglo America might have paid greater attention to African Americans due to massive boycotts and marches during the same time, Mestiz@s also contested Anglo discriminatory practices throughout the U.S. southwest.[82]

The Chicano Movement

In the 1960s, civil rights battles escalated. In California, Mestiz@s in the migrant camps and agricultural fields organized with the leadership of people such as Dolores Huerta and Cesar Chavez, and the burgeoning United Farm Workers Union, one of the first successful workers union in the United States.[83] Other organizational efforts such as Tijerina Alianza occurred, particularly in urban areas where Mestiz@s lived in segregated housing with inadequate schooling and job prospects. In *From Indians to Chicanos: The Dynamics of Mexican-American Culture*, James Diego Vigil notes, "The farm union fought to correct injustices against workers, and the Alianza sought the return of treaty-guaranteed land; both issues, land and labor, are at the center of this historical account" (241). After years of organizing, East Los Angeles, then the largest community of Mexicans in the United States, made headline news in 1968 when thousands of students walked out of their schools that at the time had the lowest reading and writing scores and the highest dropout rates in the country.[84] Collectively, these events propelled what was to become El Movimiento and the communal naming ceremony that embraced the highly politicized term "Chicano" in order to signify pride in the Mesoamerican past and a commitment to indigenous struggles of the present.[85]

The word "Chicano" is a Spanish derivative of an older *Nahuatl* root, Mexitli (pronounced "Meh-shee-tlee").[86] Mexitli is part of the dual expression *Huitzilopochtli*/Mexitli, which points to the *Mexica* and their historic migration from Aztlán to the Valley of Oaxaca. Mexitli is the linguistic progenitor of "Mexica" and its singular "Mexicatl." Notably, the word "Mexico" derives from "Méjicano," an early sixteenth century Spanish mispronunciation of Mexicatl ("Me-hee-cah-no"), with the "x" pronounced like the English "h," and the glottal stop at the end disappearing altogether. Given this etymology, some Chicanos began reverting back to the *Nahuatl* use of the letter X, forming Xicano. While the first two syllables are *Nahuatl*, the last syllable is Castilian. The morpheme Xicano enacts a reflective syncretism that is akin to Gloria Anzaldúa's new mestiza consciousness.

Use of either Chicano or Xicano is important for Mestiz@s who understand their individual and communal identity as primarily indigenous to the Western Hemisphere. Employing the term Chicano symbolically counters centuries of attempts to colonize indigenous minds. For example, Spanish forces called Mesoamerica "Las Indias" (The Indies) to the very end of their colonial days. The inhabitants of Las Indias were called "Indios," the origin of the anglicized word still in use today, "Indian." While "Indian" has been subversively adopted by many native communities, its Spanish relative "Indio" continues to carry negative connotations. As a consequence of Christianization, millions of Indians within the boundaries of New Spain were intentionally detribalized. Then, Indians were fused together and "Mexicanized" into a new but colonized and separate group from the Hispano elite. The war between the United States and Mexico from 1846 to 1848 separated the inhabitants of the northern region from the rest of Mexico. Under the Treaty of Guadalupe Hidalgo, villagers were again colonized and "de-Mexicanized." Chicano is thus a semantic marker of insurrection, rebellion, liberation, and an affirmation of indigenous identity, both past and present. It is noteworthy that the term was communally self-selected, indicating Chicano agency in knowing their own name. Especially in the latter half of the twentieth century, this strategic subjectivity was deeply embedded in a hotbed social activism.

In the late 1960s and 1970s, East Los Angeles had nine major civil disturbances, the most significant being the Chicano Moratorium against the Vietnam War. In August 1970, some 30,000 people converged onto Laguna Park after marching for several miles before being attacked by Los Angeles County Sheriff's deputies. Several people were killed, hundreds arrested, and property was burned.[87] Community efforts later led to the creations of groups such as the Brown Berets, a paramilitary Chicano activist group; Catolicos Por La Raza; La Raza Unida Party; as well as the United Mexican-American Students that laid the foundation for the Movimiento Estudiantil Chicano de Aztlán (MeCha), which in 30 years would become the leading Chicano student activist organization on many U.S. high school, college, and university campuses.[88] In the years following, Mexican murals exploded on the walls, along with literature and music, various media projects including independent newspapers, radio, film, and so on. And just as the United States resisted the Black Panthers, the American Indian Movement, Students for a Democratic Society, and Puerto Rican Young Lords, and other Independence for Puerto Rico groups, Mestiz@ organizations were being infiltrated, spied on, and disorganized.[89]

The 1970s saw the Nixon cuts, which eliminated government funds and support for community-based justice and antipoverty efforts. In

California, the Proposition 13 Tax Revolt also pulled needed property taxes from social services, forcing the elimination of teen posts and housing and educational reform projects.[90] At the same time, major industries in steel, auto, tires, meatpacking, and textiles were closing down across America, adversely affecting the Mexican communities that were largely created to deed into those industries in places like Los Angeles and Chicago, the two largest industrial centers of the country.

By the mid-1980s, whole communities were devastated with millions of jobs lost, which also impacted African Americans, Puerto Rican, Native American, and other working-class peoples.[91] Despite this, or perhaps because of it, a new stirring of Mestiz@s came about during California Governor Pete Wilson's support of initiative efforts like Proposition 187 that denied vital social, educational, and health services to undocumented immigrants in the state. Other laws like "three strikes and you're out" and Proposition 21, which gave prosecutors the power to try youth as adults, also garnered more Chicano participation in politics and demonstrations.[92] Today, Mestiz@s have spread throughout the country, with large numbers in low-paying jobs throughout the northeast, midwest, and southern parts of the country.

Mesoamerican, Matrifocal Family Structures

Mestiz@ historical narratives are far from the America that commences with the Mayflower reaching Plymouth Rock, with the New England settlers and the Massachusetts Bay Colony. For Mestiz@ cultures, Anglo-Protestants are not necessarily synonymous with the foundation of human progress and development, and the idea of European arrival in general is associated with the violent upheaval of the sixteenth century. As Tzvetan Todorov notes in *The Conquest of America*, the invasion of Mesoamerica was "the most astonishing encounter of our history, which heralds our present identity as citizens of the world and interpreters of culture" (4).

Long before the arrival of Europeans, cultures across the hemisphere had developed their own civilized ways of life, many with matrifocal social organizations and networks that, perhaps surprisingly, persist today in Mestiz@, Mexican and other indigenous communities including those across Latin America and the Caribbean. Carlos Vélez-Ibáñez' ethnographic and archival project, *Border Visions: Mexican Cultures of the Southwest United States*, examines the structured clusters of Mexican extended families. In "Living in *Confianza* and Patriarchy: The Cultural Systems of U.S. Mexican Households," Vélez-Ibáñez asserts that Women's cultural transmission define them as the interpreters, carriers, and creators of Mexican culture in the United States and the borderlands (177).

In his study of Mexican-origin clustered families, Vélez-Ibáñez' furthermore illustrates just how much a role women have historically played and continue to play in the household , thereby countering the harmfully narrow stereotype that all Mexican cultures operate under a dominating patriarchy:

> If anything, Mexican households are mostly in the control of women; expenditures are made jointly; funds of knowledge are divided by gender but distributed in an even-handed manner; most Mexican children are made responsible very early on for each other regardless of gender; and in fact, it is women, especially in the late stage of development, upon whom the entire structure of the household cluster rests or falls in economic and political terms. (147)

More importantly, Vélez-Ibáñez finds that women in these household clusters are "the primary agents of change and stability;" mothers, and especially grandmothers, are the center of the extended family structure. This research is consistent with historical analysis that suggests that matrifocal and female-headed households are an older pattern of family organization across Latin America and the Caribbean.[93] Mexican familial hubs, primarily matrifocal in nature, have never been without power struggle, as is demonstrated in Cherríe Moraga's "Queer Aztlán: The Re-Formation of Chicano Tribe," Alma García's *Chicana Feminist Thought*, and other helpful sources that are too numerous to name here. Vélez-Ibáñez' research underscores the fact that Mexican and Mestiz@ ways of life cannot be properly understood without examining the material contributions and struggles of women in those cultures. Furthermore, it is clear that the home consists of relationships closely linked to each other, forming a small matrifocal cluster. Most, if not all, of these clusters were closely linked together by kinship, by intimate friends and neighbors, and by both formal and informal institutions. Altogether, Mesoamerican and Mexican villages remained giant clusters of closely connected families and neighbors despite the disruption and turmoil that came with the eventual assault of European invasion.

Uses of Mestiz@ History

Throughout their past Mestiz@s have continually interacted with and mediated the larger world around them. Often, they are raised without knowing the intellectual and cultural isolation across the borderlands. Mestiz@s had been almost severed from their indigenous and Mexican roots. Some community elders who were raised during the racially heated decades of the early twentieth century even insisted, perhaps desperately, that Mestiz@s were actually "Spanish," not Mexican or indigenous at all.[94] With hindsight, this can be interpreted and explained as an adaptive communal, collective attempt to buy time, to buy breathing space from the aggressive campaign of Westernization. Sadly, U.S. educators too often presented little that is historically candid or accurate about Mesoamerican intellectual histories, nor even the aesthetic and scientific heritage of the Latin world extending to Iberia. In some schools, Spanish was often tolerated, though certainly never encouraged. In many communities across the United States, however, children were routinely physically beaten for speaking Spanish.[95]

As a result, Mestiz@ peoples from the United States have lived as much of their culture as they could under politically negative situations. Village communities were overwhelmed by forces in the region such as the railroad, the university, the health industry, military bases, national weapons producers, tourist industries, and so on. Far from being a model for an isolated village, small communities might serve as a model for how a local culture subjected to such pressure by change, shifts much of its prior cultural subjectivity. Of course, the "prior subjectivity" referred to here was not and is not static. As Miguel Montiel, Tomás Atencio, and E.A. Mares argue in *Resolana for a Dark New Age* (forthcoming), from the founding of the original Old Town Albuquerque in the early decades of the eighteenth century until 1846 and the entry of military forces as conquerors and occupiers, for over two centuries this community had evolved with the influx of new families, expanded agricultural activities, a variety of contacts with indigenous cultures, and the impact of Mexican Catholicism with its missions, schools, and annual religious celebrations and rites of passage. The U.S. occupation had the strongest impact on the later and current sequence of developments. It is not so much that Mestiz@s assimilated to the United States, but rather they had no choice but to slowly blend, to intermix their own values and lifestyles with Western worldviews.

Over time, Mestiz@ villages had diminishing feedback mechanisms, intellectually and culturally speaking, from the provinces of Spain, Mexico, and Latin America. Mestiz@s largely rejected the historical mythologizing of Spain as a medieval wonderland from whence came kings and queens, nobles, and a false Spanish Iberian pride. Also rejected was the Spanish and Anglo historical narrative of Mesoamerica as a backward land filled with savage people. Instead, Mestiz@s identify their history through dynamic and ever-changing indigenous worldviews. Consider the following lines from E.A. Mares, who dedicates his poem to *Popé* and the Pueblo Revolt of 1680:

My name was the promise of summer,
A cornucopia overflowing
With food for the pueblos...

My name was the harvest of gold,
The gathering of life-giving maize,
Fields of ripe squash, beans, and chile
To feed the people of *O'ke Owinge*
And all the pueblos of our land...

I visited the sacred hills and mountains.
I knew the Summer People.
I knew the Winter People.
I knew my own name.
My authority returned to me...

Then the Spaniards took me.
They flogged me.
They could not take away my name.
My authority returned to me...

When the war leaders came,
I spoke with authority.
I sent forth the runners
Bearing the knotted cords
To the twenty four pueblos,
To the six different languages,
To all the directions and their colors
From Taos to the Hopi villages...

We unraveled the last knot
In the searing light of day.
We struck everywhere at once.
We raked a fire across the sun.

We let those Spaniards go
Who had lived with us in peace.
We let them go. We drove the rest
South from Santa Fe,
Down the valleys of sweet rivers
To the mountains of Mexico...

We broke their arrogance
Like bits of dry straw.
We drove them away.
We let them go.

When the Spaniards came back,
We fought them from our pueblos
Until tendrils of peace pushed up
Through the hateful crust of war.

My authority flows
Within and around the earth,
Within and around the mountains,
Like the waters flow
Through the pueblo lands.

I know my own name.
I know my own name.
I know my own name.[96]

Mares is a nontribalized Mestiz@ with bloodlines that trace back to both Spanish and indigenous populations along the Rio Grande river basin. The fact that Mares may not legally identify biological ties directly to Popé, the San Juan Pueblo, or even neighboring Pueblos to the north is entirely beside the point. By writing from the perspective of the great *Tewa* religious leader, Mares symbolically opposes the triumph of Spanish conquest and assimilation.

Repeated references to the sacred hills and mountains call upon the Pueblo ritual assertion that the material earth is connected to a larger cosmology. Evoking *O'ke Owinge*, the *Tewa* self-expression for the San Juan village, links directly to the *Tewa* creation narrative. Blue Corn Woman and White Corn Maiden sent messengers to the upper world to see how they might emerge from the lake. Once they were accepted by the natural world above, the Summer and Winter chiefs were called forth, from whom the *O'ke Owinge* descended.[97] Their landscape was ripe and fertile, which fostered self-sufficient rural *Tewa* communities. The *Tewa* did not first appear in world history merely to provide living labor for the Spanish encomiendas that subjected them to starvation. Mares privileges *Tewa* ritual creation myth and recognizes native authority to name one's own place in history.

By writing from the perspective of Popé, Mares metaphorically rereads his own history through the eyes of the oppressed. The Pueblo Revolt has become engrained in Mestiz@ memory and embodies the resistant past as well as the tragedy of Western conquest. The continuity of the Pueblo Revolt as a locus of indigenous insurrection contributes strongly to its symbolic elevation. Mares' poetic reconstruction operates as a corrective to the vanguard narrative of European history. While Mares respects the bravery and vision of *Popé* in the Pueblo Revolt, he avoids romanticizing. Muted resentment is counterbalanced with implicit optimism: the wounded and persecuted find strategic possibilities of survival.

This is a dynamic notion of the interaction of memory with the ongoing rush of history. Mestiz@s, transformed after 1848 from being the center of a Spanish colonial outpost into an ethnic curiosity on the borderland peripheries of the United States, had to invent from a space of memory where they could recreate the past in response to U.S. imperatives. Events like *Tenochtitlán* in 1521, the Pueblo Revolt of 1640, and the New Mexico Insurrection of 1847 smolder in the memories of Mestiz@s who refuse European interpretations of conquest and assimilation. The history recounted in this chapter asserts that Mestiz@ culture is alive, developing, expanding, and interacting with all cultures of the United States and beyond. There is no singular Mestiz@ or Mexican culture, but rather there are "many Mexicos."[98] Mestiz@s and their communities are interacting and connecting with each other and with the larger world around them, forming intricate cultural networks of persons and communities. Mestiz@ historical legacies, this chapter illustrates, have attempted and do attempt to mediate the devastatingly negative consequences for their cultures. Mestiz@s are a mixed group in terms of their values, customs, and communities. Mestiz@ history, I hope to have shown, refers to a complex and dynamic legacy that today remains contested, fluid, and adaptive.

IV

Codex Scripts of Resistance: From Columbus to the Border Patrol

The Chicano Codex is a map back to the original face, una peregrinación to an America unwritten. América: the brown swell of tierra indígena debajo de la Calavera.

—Cherríe Moraga

In 1992, over 20 Mestiz@ artists showcased their work in a traveling exhibit, *Chicano Codex: Encountering Art of the Americas*. Each piece creatively resembled Mesoamerican *amoxtli*, the pictographic "codex books" that were destroyed by Spanish combatants as a strategy for subjugating indigenous minds. Spain's campaign of Christianization and the art of letters aimed to redefine and remap the Mesoamerican world under European-imposed categories. The consequences of this massive colonial operation were so brutal that it could be assumed that European writing practices completely destroyed and replaced Mesoamerican pictography. The *Chicano Codex* exhibition intervenes in this reigning narrative and suggests instead that pictographic rhetorics are strategically in use today. Chicana essayist Cherríe Moraga argues that the codices point to "a map back to the original face" (21) thereby recharting and revising the dominant historical narrative of assimilation. While contemporary codex productions differ from pre-Columbian *amoxtli* manuscripts, the link to Mesoamerican pictography and the enduring struggle against colonization is crucial to understanding this distinct rhetorical emergence.

This chapter analyzes the dialectic of oppositions and reversals in modern-day codex manuscripts, namely the *Codex Espangliensis: From Columbus to the Border Patrol* (2000), a mass-produced publication from Moving Parts Press. I first describe the *Codex* itself, its textual structure, major characteristics, featured characters and storyline. I then consider prior studies of Mesoamerican *amoxtli* from historians Miguel León-Portilla and Elizabeth Boone Hill. Using the perspectives of Miguel León-Portilla and Cherríe Moraga as a springboard, I offer a rhetorical study of the manuscript's contrastive symbols and characters as they are inscribed against past and present colonial powers. As I explained in chapter 1, this analysis aims to decipher strategies of resistance encoded in Mestiz@ cultural symbols. I interpret such symbolization as a resistant rhetoric that addresses the larger backdrop of colonial subjugation and resistance in the Americas. Specifically, I argue that Mestiz@ codex rhetorics revise and displace the dominant historical narrative of cultural assimilation through continuous symbolic play with pairs, doubles, corresponding expressions and twins. By fusing and embellishing Mesoamerican pictography into European inscription practices, Mestiz@ codex rhetorics promote a new dialectic, a new strategy of inventing and writing between worlds.

Codex Espangiensis

In 2000, three artists collaborated on a commercial publication, *Codex Espangliensis* from City Lights Books and Moving Parts Press. Lithographer Enrique Chagoya provides colorful illustrations and montages of American popular culture, mass media icons, transnational corporate entities, Aztec pictography, and sixteenth-century images of colonial exploitation. Graphic designer Felicia Rice weaves alphabetic script over and against Chagoya's visual imagery. The alphabetic text is stretched and distorted across each page, often slanted and squeezed around images and consequently bleeding across the manuscript's margins. Performance artist and cultural critic Guillermo Gómez-Peña provides the alphabetic text, which derives primarily from his previous performance scripts. Written in English, Spanish, Spanglish, and Mexican-Spanish varieties, the poetic scripts critique Spanish colonization of the Americas, the North American Free Trade Agreement, and the consequences of globalization in the territories of immigration, language, and popular culture.

The rectangular manuscript opens from the right and invites a reading from right to left. Without pagination, 15 "pages" or screens fold into an accordion file that can expand over 21 feet in length. In addition to being read as one continuous extended mural, the manuscript may also unravel from left to right. Screen 2 therefore doubles as screen 14 depending on the selected reading order. The entire left panel of screen 14/2 supports a pictographic representation of *Quetzalcoatl Ehecatl/Mictlantecuhtli*, a twin Mesoamerican deity. The divine skeletal couple is graphically adjoined, facing opposite sides. *Ehecatl's* black figure carries a royal staff and is accompanied with graphic manifestations of an eagle and stone temple. Costumed in white, *Mictlantecuhtli* embraces an elongated steel-tipped lance. Imposed over the bottom right of the bulky pictograph is a miniature Disney icon, Minnie Mouse. Minnie's polka-dot skirt and flower-tipped hat underscore her jovial gaze toward the ambivalent *Quetzalcoatl*.

Emerging from the right panel of screen 14/2 is a generously sized ideograph of an injured Aztec warrior and philosopher king, Nezahaulcoyotl. A blue-feathered suit scales the soldier's trunk and connects to a short tunic. The bloodstained warrior extends a decorated shield before him with a sword drawn from behind. Two lively DC comic icons engage him from the sky. Superman and Wonder Woman mutually struggle to subdue the combative pictographic soldier. Uneven lines of alphabetic script intertwine between the besieged warrior and *Quetzalcoatl*:

In 1492, an
Aztec Sailor
Named Noctli
Europzin Tezpoca
Departed From The
Port Of Minatitlan
with a small flotilla of
wooden rafts, 3 months later
He Discovered A New
Continent And Named It
Europzin After Himself.
In November 1512, the
Omni-Potent Aztecs Began
The Conquest Of Europzin
In The Name Of Thy Father
Tezcatlipoca, Lord Of Cross-
Cultural Misunderstandings

y entonces el desmadre so comenzo a multiplicar
logo-rhythmically and logo-aritmicamente. (Screen 14/2)

The multilingual passage alternates between capitalized bold type and an erudite cursive font. An amalgam of typography, typeface, and lettering weave between pictographs, bloodstains, and American cultural icons. This assorted visual composition extends across each fold of the *Codex*.

Symbolic representations of Christianization likewise appear throughout the panels. On screen 13/3, an archaic image of Christ's face is imprinted over a blood-spattered surface. A crown of thorns decorates the suffering image. Pictographic representations of various Mesoamerican ceremonial costumes and combat gear fill the screen fold. Covering a small quarter of the pictographic inventory is a catalogue of miscellaneous travel items written in alphabetic Spanish. A daunting headline in English reads: AMNESIA IS AT THE CORE OF THE PROBLEM. Straddled between the itemized list and sacrificial Christ, a wounded Superman exchanges dialogue with a Mexican child in an apple orchard. The hero guides the boy away from a long line of watchful migrant workers: "LISTEN MANUEL—I WON'T FIND OUT WHAT'S BEEN GOING ON FROM THESE HOTHEADS! TELL ME *YOUR* STORY... YOUR *PROBLEM*." Manuel responds: "SEÑOR SUPERMAN—I COME FROM *MEXICO!* AS MY FATHER LAY DYING, HE TOLD ME TO COME TO THE *U.S.A.* FOR A BETTER LIFE" (italics in original).

Admixtures of popular culture and religious iconography continue on screen 12/4, where a solemn image of Guadalupe stands atop a writhing serpent. The snake twists across the panel, spraying venom without direction. Guadalupe prayerfully nods to Wonder Woman, who emerges from the opened carcass of an unidentified woman. The woman appears to remain alive in spite of the massive wound opening her torso. Bordering the figures of Guadalupe and the dissected woman are fragments of contrasting alphabetic scripts. For example,

IN A COUNTRY AT WAR
IN A CITY AT WAR
IN A NEIGHBORHOOD AT WAR
MY AUDIENCE IS ALL COMPOSED OF VICTIMS OF POLITICAL
 TORTURE
BUT THEY DON'T KNOW IT
THEY DON'T REMEMBER
THEY DON'T WANT TO BE REMEMBERED... (Screen 12/4)

Wonder Woman firmly grasps an oversized high-tech firearm that appears modeled after American science fiction films made in the 1950s. Half-concealed by grotesquely displayed internal organs, Wonder Woman aims her weapon squarely at the reader with the declaration: "GO TO HELL!" Guadalupe counsels the comic superhero: "OH, *DEAR*. IS THAT A *NEURAL IMPACTER?* DO THEY STIL MAKE THOSE?...I'D ADVISE YOU TO TRY THE *PLASM DISRUPTER*. IT'S SMALLER." Guadalupe's final caption, "I LOVE YOU" (italics in original).

An unnamed conservatory spans across screen 10/6. This sixteenth-century illustration features two rectangular worktables. At one table an ethnically ambiguous scribe dutifully paints an image of a Spanish bureaucrat onto a codex manuscript. Hovering above the neighboring table, a severed hand paints undecipherable pictographs. A bloodred warning extends the length of the conservatory wall: NEW DEFINITIONS. Adjacent to this scene of writing, Disney icon Mickey Mouse stands in a state of distress, his oversized white gloves are stained with blood. Against the mouse's backside, graphically slanted multiple-choice descriptions are set alongside the right-hand margin of the folded screen, as if someone is literally pushing them off the manuscript. The First World is described as the small geographic region that controls the majority of the world's resources, whereas the Third World references "ex-underdeveloped countries," the Fourth World is a conceptual convergence of indigenous and deterritorialized cultures. Finally, the Fifth World is associated with virtual space, mass media, art education, the White House and Disneyland. The script is superimposed over footprints of blood that align with the steps of Disney's mouse. To the immediate left are a series of isolated, unanswered questions: "Where exactly is the United States located? In which world are you located? For which world does your art speak? Are you experiencing once again an identity crisis? Has your community been left out of the above categories?" At the bottom margin of the screen fold is a proclamation: "EL DIALOGO DEBE SER PUBLICO," which in English translates as "the dialogue should be made public."

The dual reading order of the *Codex Espangliensis* presents viewers with at least two possibilities for a conclusion and introduction. On the right panel of screen 15/1, pictographic depictions of ethnically diverse Mesoamericans consume severed body parts and remains of Mickey Mouse. A Mexican ritual priest adds salt to the constrained mouse. Juxtaposed over this scene of cannibalism and barbarity are itemized cultural categories attributed to the SAN DIEGO NATURAL HISTORY MUSEUM:

AZTEC........................[ ]
APACHE.......................[ ]
SEMINOLE.....................[ ]
TAINO.................... [ ]
LACONDON.....................[ ]
CHICANO..................[ ]
ANGLO SAXON...............[ ]
MARXIST...........................[ ]

The ritual priest sits atop a stone temple, its steps splattered with blood. Beneath the temple in small script is the accompanying questionnaire to the taxonomy above: "Please place the following species in the appropriate category: (A) a threatened species is likely to become endangered within the foreseeable future; (B) an endangered species is in danger of extinction; (C) an extinct species no longer exists." Against the left panel of the same screen, a multicolored Superman battles his black and white, inverted twin. Against Superman's overturned double are unanswered, fragmented queries: THREATENED? ENDANGERED? OR EXTINCT?

Screen 1/15 provides the alternative introduction/conclusion to the codex manuscript. Pictographic depictions of Aztec warriors decorated in conventional headdresses and weaponry advance from the left fold. Multiple zoomorphic graphs of eagles, jaguars, and serpents accompany the soldiers. Opposing these Mesoamerican symbols is an airborne Superman. His suit and skin are bloodred, and a human skull replaces the angular S traditionally embroidered across the hero's chest. Stretched along the top margin of the screen a bold, cursive script reminiscent of nineteenth-century political cartoons reads: "¿donde radica la diferencia entre el arte de libre comersio y un tratado de libre cultura?" A varied English translation of the unanswered query is repeated across the bottom margin: "QUESTION: WHAT IS THE DIFFERENCE BETWEEN FREE-TRADE ART AND A FREE ART AGREEMENT?"

Pictograph and Codex History

Mesoamerican codex writing belongs to a pictorial system consisting of images structured to create visual messages. The graphic elements of these messages appear as figural representations, icons, and symbols. Mesoamerican writing is considered to be "semasiographic," a configuration of permanently recorded marks that signify thought, ideas, and imagery rather than visible speech. Notably, this writing practice fuses into a single symbolic account what for Western minds are separate and hierarchical concepts of annotation and illustration. While early Mexicans did designate some symbols to voice specific words, their larger graphic system did not correspond directly with spoken language. Because the symbols did not replicate any single linguistic system, speakers of *Nahuatl*, *Yucatecan*, *Mixtec*, *Zapotec*, and *Quiche Maya* had the advantage of translating the pictographs into their own respective tongue. Readers mediated a combination of naturalistic images, pictorial conventions, and abstract symbols that were recorded within an organized structure. By knowing the basic conventions and the meanings of the symbols and recognizing their arrangement, readers interpreted the pictographic messages.[1] A precise reading order is not set, however, so that different readings and interpretations remain possible.

The *amoxtli* and pictographic writing system are inheritors of multiple and ancient traditions, though it is believed that they draw primarily from three Mesoamerican societies.[2] The *Teotihuacános* (100 BCE–900 ADE), the culture that built the pyramids near modern-day Mexico City, provided the template for civilization that was taken on by later *Nahuatl*-speaking groups including the Aztec and to some degree the Maya. The *Zapotec* (500 BCE–900 ADE) developed a calendrical literacy and a logographic writing system that used separate glyphs to represent syllables. Finally, the traditions of the *Olmec* (1000–400 BCE), whose hieroglyphic inscription practices predate the Greek alphabet, are the progenitors of Mesoamerican culture. Some speculate that the *Olmec* are actually ancient *Náhua*, which would designate Mexicans as a progeny of the first culture to advance an inscription system in the Western Hemisphere.[3] Scholars generally agree that the *amoxtli* are rooted in a cultural web of commonalities shared by these as well as other diverse Mesoamerican groups.[4]

Given this extensive history, it is not surprising that pictography was one of the only major Mesoamerican rhetorical practices to survive the imposition of European literacy. Early Mexicans provide the earliest known North American expressions for writing. *In tlilli, in tlapalli* is a metaphor for books that translates literally as "the black [ink], the red [ink]" and also implies knowledge or wisdom. The

Nahuatl verb for writing, *Tlaquilolitztli*, means both "to write" and "to paint."[5] While the *tlacuiloque* composed the images, it was the *Tlamatinime* who assumed ownership as well as the task of textual interpretation. *Tlamatinime* are described as philosophers, women and men who studied and transmitted *Huehuetlahtolli*, translated as "proper discourse" or discourse of the ancients.[6] *Nahuatl*, the Aztec lingua franca, is gender-neutral and thus *Tlamatinime* cannot be affixed as an exclusively male occupation. An English translation of *Tlamatinime* as "female and male philosophers" is consistent with surviving Mesoamerican manuscripts that represent women as well as men in the profession of *amoxtli* production.[7] Sometimes as early as eight years of age, students would begin their study of *Huehuetlahtolli* at one of several conservatories collectively known as the *Calmecac*. In addition to training male and female apprentices, Mexican conservatories systematically transmitted *Huehuetlahtolli* for students from "common" as well as noble lineage.[8]

The *Calmecac*, influenced by the preceding 10,000 years of cultural development in the Valley of Oaxaca, can be understood broadly as a fully subsidized higher education network with a remarkable influence in Mesoamerican society. The conservatories supported the realization of an organized and operative legislature, civic courts, and other public forums; an exact science of time, mathematics, and astronomy; a complex faith system; advanced knowledge of herbal medicine; elaborate architecture, sculptures, paintings, and so on. All of this was supported not with letters or books, but with systematic education in the arts of *Huehuetlahtolli* and *amoxtli* manuscripts.

Such instruction served an important social and cultural function. *Huehuetlahtolli* organized and transmitted wisdom for the purposes of intelligent and effective governance. When presented publicly, the discourse took the form of ritualistic and ceremonial orations, prayers, business and governmental speeches, and so on. The most commonly employed stylistic devices of *Huehuetlahtolli* include parallel expressions, repetitive and recurrent phrases, and a stylistic device known as *difrasismo*, the blending of two concrete terms to convey an abstraction.[9] For example, what the Western world understands as poetics or art is articulated by the Aztec through the idiomatic expression "in *xochitl*, in *cuicatl*," translated as "flower and song."[10] In *xochitl*, in *cuicatl* may hold a key to understanding how early Mesoamerican culture understood *Huehuetlahtolli*, as flower and song was one of the ways they thought about their system of writing. Because the *amoxtli* were typically memorized in the form of verse, it's not difficult to imagine how a poem like the following might have been represented in pictographic script and then reconstituted for ritual performance:

> With flowers you write,
> Oh Giver of Life!
> With songs you give color,
> with songs you shade
> those who must live on the earth.
>
> Later you will destroy
> eagles and tigers;
> we live only in your painting
> here, on earth.[11]

Although recorded in alphabetic script during the sixteenth century, the prior generation of Mesoamerican artists would have represented this poem with pictographs of flowers—the symbols for writing—songs, and color. Earth, for example, could have been represented by its conventional symbol of a serpent. The destruction of eagles and tigers, shorthand for the warriors of those ranks, was easily depicted through pictographic techniques. The expression "Giver of Life" corresponds with the belief that *Quetzalcoatl*, patron god of writing, offers flower and song as a gift. The practice of inscription using pictography or any other sign system is a result of divine providence. Through the dual concept of flower and song, the experiences and histories of Mesoamerica are graphically preserved.

The duality of *Huehuetlahtolli* at the syntactic level corresponds with the larger configuration of Mesoamerican worldviews. It is noteworthy that at the roots of Mexican consciousness is a belief in divine pairs. The pictographs of early *amoxtli* and other manuscripts continually reference the dual god, *Tonantzin/Totahtzin*, meaning Our Mother/Our Father. This She/He creator, also known as *Ometeotl*, represents not a binary opposition, but a sense of balance in life. *Ometeotl's* two children, *Quetzalcoatl* and *Tezcatlipoca*, are credited with creating the heavens and earth. *Quetzalcoatl*, in addition to being identified with the gift of writing, is widely associated with water and fertility (see chapter 3). One manifestation of *Quetzalcoatl*, *Ehecatl*, is the god of wind who appears in the breath of living beings and the breezes that bring rain clouds. *Mictlantecuhtli*, *Quetzalcoatl's* second manifestation, represents the god of death and rules the underworld. At the rhetorical level, *Huehuetlahtolli* intertwines a twofold poetic structure, human character, and divine foundation together. The organization of Mesoamerican life around equilibrium, duality, and symmetry is a recurring theme in Mexican discourse and plays an important role in pictographic rhetoric.[12]

The *amoxtli* manuscripts were produced using bark paper or strips of animal hide and were colorfully marked or painted on one or both sides. While civilizations to the far north such as the Great Lakes and the Mississippi made use of rolled scrolls,[13] Mesoamerican cultures traditionally folded their manuscripts into accordion-like files or folded screens with protective wooden end pieces attached at both sides. Most scholars sort the *amoxtli* into two general categories according to their function. The first group, *xiuhtlapiualli* or "annals," contain government-sanctioned histories that record community migration patterns, tribute rights, genealogies of nobility, the mapping of territories, and other political affairs. Collectively, the surviving annals account for each year of *Mexica* life beginning with the twelfth-century departure from the island of *Aztlán* (see chapter 2). The other group, simply referred to as ritual *amoxtli*, provides a glimpse of the core beliefs and practices of Mesoamerican culture. Recorded in the surviving nine ritual texts are creation narratives, day-to-day customs of civic and religious life including annual feast cycles, the economies of agriculture, and cultural practices surrounding birth, marriage, burial, and so on. Some manuscripts record explicit behavior codes for useful and constructive citizenry.[14]

The ritual *amoxtli* were stretched flat against a wall or floor and delivered orally by the *Amoxoaque*, "those who understand the paintings that conserve memories."[15] The manuscripts were literally performed, often accompanied with music and dance.[16] A poem written by a sixteenth-century Aztec scribe reflects the performative nature of the *amoxtli*:

> I sing the pictures of the book
> as I unfold [its pages]
> I am like the flowery parrot
> as I make the codex pages speak
> inside the house of the picture-writings.[17]

Mesoamerican rhetoric required use of the entire body through choreography, recitation, chanting, and choral production. The flowery parrot is a metaphor for vitality and spirituality. References to flowers and singing reinforce the sacred association with the act of writing. The expression "house of the picture-writings" drives home the notion that Mesoamerican rhetoric was an institutionalized practice deeply embedded within the culture with its own recognizable buildings and locations. A mere "reading" of the *amoxtli* constituted a communal ritualistic and ceremonial event. The syntactic form of *Huehuetlahtolli* varied in rhythm, and it is reasonable that each delivery would have mirrored such creative variability. The orations were designed to pass on ancient wisdom during special occasions: to children who had reached an age of discretion, to those about to marry, for birthrights, and funerals. Archaeological records, especially from the lowland Maya, assert that these ritual events flourished for at least 1000 years before Hernán Cortéz and his conquistadors arrived at *Tenochtitlán*.

With the defeat of the Aztec Empire and the Triple Alliance, Mesoamerica's highly developed education system and agricultural economy were brought to a virtual standstill. Spanish forces, attempting to reinforce their political authority, imposed a new social and economic system of Christianization. For Spain to justify its mission, Mesoamerican pictography was denigrated as inherently inferior to the Western art of letters. Spanish combatants regarded the *Calmecac* and the *amoxtli* manuscripts as "devil's work" and set out to systematically destroy them.[18] As a replacement for the *Calmecac*, missionaries established the first European and officially patriarchal education system in the Western Hemisphere. By 1536, the College of the Holy Cross in *Tlatelolco*, *Tenochtitlán* began working with writers from the Mexican intelligentsia. The function of subjugated Mexican writers was twofold. First, the scribes were to help Franciscan missionaries to translate Latin and Spanish religious texts to an alphabetized *Nahuatl* in order to further colonize Mexican minds. Their second responsibility was to reconstruct Mesoamerican memory by literally rewriting the codices that had been systematically destroyed.[19] The colonial codices employed the contrastive and conflicting writing practices of pictography, alphabetized *Nahuatl* and Spanish.

The first European writing specialists in the New World, in full compliance with the colonial administration, oversaw the commission of 54 new codex productions. Some manuscripts aimed to reorganize Mesoamerican memory according to European categories. Other codices negotiated legal and economic claims with institutions across the colony. The early colonial codices also served as a method of negotiating cultural identity under colonial circumstances.[20] Under Spanish rule, the early colonial codices were converted to something closer to "artifacts" instead of the living commemorative manuscripts they once were in the hands of the *Amoxoaque* and their fellow performers. The *Codex* Mendoza, for example, was composed in 1542 by the order of Virrey Mendoza, the first viceroy of New Spain. Recounting the history of the fall of *Tenochtitlán*, the manuscript also includes pictographic information about Aztec cycles of life at the time of the conquest. Such books of the early colonial era, although composed by Aztec and a growing number of Mestiz@s, presented the dominant historical narratives of Mesoamerica's defeat as seen and authorized by Spanish imperial perspectives. Mexican pictography was marginalized, at least according to Spanish eyes, as supplementary illustrations next to the Spanish-Iberian alphabet and an alphabetized *Nahuatl*, the new prevailing tools of literacy and civilization in the borderlands.

Despite the campaign of Christianization and alphabetic literacy, Mesoamerican pictographic traditions persisted. Codex production continued in central Mexico and the Valley of Oaxaca at least until the seventeenth century.[21] Mesoamerican rhetorics continued in various non-codex formats as well, including scrolls, *lienzos* (sheets), and *techialoyan* or "landbook," documents used to defend communities against changes in colonial law until as late as the nineteenth century.[22] Spanish courts and administration in colonial New Spain evidently preferred Mesoamerican pictographic histories for mediating land disputes. Presumably the pictography was seen as more ancient, and thus more "authentic" than the more recent alphabetic records. Some remnants of these practices survived into modern times and some villages continue to guard their pictographic documents carefully.[23]

The twentieth century was a powerful period of Mesoamerican rhetorical revival. Only 50 years earlier, the Treaty of Guadalupe Hidalgo created an international border across what was northern Mexico. On the northern side of these borderlands the strongest capitalist nation would develop. By waging war against Mexico in part to expand slave territories and secure key ports on the Pacific Coast, the United States ushered in a new imperialist era of Western economic and cultural dominance.

Pictographic murals, cultivated by the Chicano civil rights movement in the mid-1960s, work to revise this dominant narrative by reestablishing Mesoamerican aesthetic structures for critiquing recent colonizing events. Chicano murals were an important adjunct to *El Movimiento* in the 1960s as they articulated a desire for social and political change, instilled ethnic pride in Mesoamerican artistic roots, and raised cultural consciousness about prevailing economic injustice. Building upon the resonance of Mesoamerican pictography, these mural rhetorics advance a multilayered script of protest that was spiritual, social, economic, aesthetic, and political.[24] To the south of the México/U.S. borderlands, Western imperialism produced an industrialized Mexico that, rather than developing Mexico's internal economy, established and favored the markets of other nations, namely the United States. By the early twentieth century, the United States became the main foreign investor in Mexico, claiming the majority of its produced goods, mineral holdings.[25] Penetration into the Mexican economy left even more workers landless and jobless, thereby fostering a mass migration of Mexicans into the United States. Under this particular stage of globalization, Mexicans became the kind of labor required for the rise of capitalist production: propertyless wage labor.

Amidst this turmoil, the Mexican Revolution (1910–1917) fostered a cultural agenda that embraced Mesoamerican writing practices and their histories. Notable artists such as David Alfaro Siqueiros and Diego Rivera weaved Aztec pictography with muralist art and Marxist idealism. As movements on both sides of the border occurred almost four centuries after the imposition of the Spanish alphabet, much of what was produced was limited within the European conceptualization of art as graphically and ideologically distinct from "true" writing. The spread of Western literacy did not only assume the dominant form of reading and writing. It also advanced a massive colonial operation in which the materiality and ideology of Mesoamerican rhetorics were intermingled with, and in some cases, replaced by the materiality and ideology of Western writing practices.[26] Despite the limits of the categories used to comprehend them, the resurgence of Mesoamerican graphic practices informed what would eventually come. Indeed, from the revolutionary and Marxian images of Mexican muralists of the early twentieth century to the Chicano social movement images of the past 30 years, the practice of incorporating Mesoamerican pictography remains steady.

The Codex Literature

A fundamental concern for scholars of the *amoxtli* and pictographic manuscripts has been determining the accuracy of "native" interpretation. Further complicating this concern is the enduring Western intellectual tradition of denying the existence of literacy and history in pre-Columbian cultures. Thus, as the argument goes, the *amoxtli* do not record proper history nor do they employ a true written form. The first Europeans to write of the codices regarded them with some interest but quickly dismissed them. Pedro de Gante, one of the first Franciscan missionaries to arrive in Mexico, wrote to Phillip II that the Aztecs were a "people without writing, without letters, and without any kind of enlightenment."[27]

The sixteenth-century European bias that Mexicans lack true writing and history continues today. The dominant Western approach has long been to categorize and define codex writing according to its cultural and symbolic inadequacy in comparison with European monotheistic, alphabetic literacy. In some cases, Aztec pictographic rhetoric is omitted altogether from academic fields of inquiry. Not only are Mesoamerican codices absent from rhetoric and composition, for example, but hybrid and alphabetic texts in *Nahuatl* and Spanish are missing as well. Don Paul Abbott's "The Ancient World: Rhetorics in Aztec Culture" (1987) is the field's first notable exception. In his preliminary study of *Huehuetlahtolli*, Abbott draws comparisons between Aztec practices and epideictic oratory as it was articulated and recorded by elite males in ancient Greece. By asserting Greco-Roman terms as a global measuring stick, Abbott unmistakably translates "Discourse of the Ancients" as a mere appendage of Western rhetoric. As I explained in chapter 1, Abbott's analysis remains clouded by the assumption that early Mexicans were preliterate compared to the literacy attained by Ancient Greeks.[28] Thus, "Mesoamerican rhetoric" is reconfigured as an inferior practice in the periphery of a civilized center of tradition.

This alphabetic bias works against constructive readings of pictorial documents and reduces them to quaint artifacts of an apparently extinct culture. In the mid-nineteenth century, both sides of the Atlantic began to recognize the few remaining pre-Columbian codices and published their facsimiles. Lord Kingsborough's 1831–1848 *Antiquities of Mexico* includes nine color lithographs in its first three volumes. Although the massive collection contains no analysis, the publication directed international attention to *amoxtli* productions. French Mexicanist Joseph Aubin offers the first modern scholarly attempt to interpret the codices, further fueling Western interest.[29] By the early twentieth century, a half-dozen other facsimiles and commentaries were published by Alfredo Chavero, Franz Ehrle, Zelia Nuttall, and Antonio Peñafiel.[30]

Anthropologist Paul Radin's *Sources and Authenticity of the Ancient Mexicans* (1920) is the first modern Western work to argue that codex pictography is a legitimate system for inscribing Mesoamerican memory.[31] Radin furthermore offers the first classification of the codex documents, a model still in use today. He distinguishes first between primary sources of pre-Columbian pictography and secondary sources of chronicles written by Spaniards or Mestiz@s that relied on older pictographs. Among the primary sources Radin also distinguishes between earlier accounts of the Aztec migration period and subsequent accounts during the Triple Alliance.

Art historian Donald Robertson groups the codices according to organizational principles or "styles" in his *Mexican Manuscript Painting of the Early Colonial Period* (1959).[32] Robertson identifies three principal types: "time-oriented" histories like annals, where history is a sequence of events according to time; "place-oriented" histories organize around geography; and "event-oriented" histories in which the narrative moves from event to event. These styles represent a developmental sequence, Robertson claims, in which the time-oriented history establishes the latter two. Henry Nicholson's "Pre-Hispanic Central Mexican Historiography" (1971) expands Robertson's typology by comparative analysis of pictographic manuscripts, archaeological monuments and records of oral transmissions. Combining format and content, Nicholson recognizes five categories: continuous year-count annals, cartographic histories, genealogies and dynastic lists.[33]

Mexican archeologist Alfonso Caso examines codex historical content, language affiliation, and brief reading approaches in his *Reyes y Reinos de las Mixteca* (1979). Caso's approach of combining rather than separating pictorial manuscripts to fuse a larger history of early Mexican dynasties significantly influenced archeological works such as John Pohl's *Politics of Symbolism in the Mixtec Codices* (1994). In this spirit, anthropologist Joyce Marcus' *Mesoamerican Writing Systems* stands out as it looks equally at historical records in four early cultures: Aztec, *Mixtec*, *Zapotec*, and Maya. Marcus focuses on hieroglyphic writing rather than on codices themselves. Drawing examples from manuscripts, stone monuments and ceramics, Marcus compares how each culture presents, through its texts and images, its calendars, people and places, as well as its ideas about divine ancestry, royal marriages, territory, and warfare.

Latin American art historian Elizabeth Boone Hill provides, overall, one of the most complete accounts of codex writing. Her *Stories in Red and Black: Pictorial Histories of the Aztecs and Mixtecs* (2000) applies manuscript analysis to the insightful matters of colonization, native agency and resistance, and writing in cross-cultural situations. Boone provides an overview of the corpus of manuscripts produced during the first three generations after conquest, noting the way Indigenous and Mestiz@ artists structured and recorded their manuscripts. This work significantly privileges pictography over the alphabetic glosses that typically accompanied the early colonial codices. By examining the visual elements comprising the vocabulary of the pictographic system and the grammar that drives it, Boone suggests codex reading conventions based on historically plausible Mexican understandings. Giving priority to pictographs as an independent system is vital, Boone maintains, as the alphabetic script sometimes may not correspond with the adjacent pictorial content (11).

One of the most significant contributors to understanding codex rhetoric is Mexican historian and philosopher Miguel León-Portilla. Since his *Aztec Thought and Language* (1959), León-Portilla has been recognized worldwide as the leading authority on *Nahuatl* writing and cosmology. His landmark translation of the *Huehuetlahtolli*, published in a massive edition at the quincentenary of European invasion, illustrates the formalized discursive properties that were systematically taught at the *Calmecac*. León-Portilla helps writing specialists understand that while Mesoamericans had no "rhetoric" from the regionally provincial Greco-Roman view of persuasion, their *Tlamatinime* and *Tlacuiloque* understood and mediated their world through *Huehuetlahtolli*, an equally suitable discursive practice. As a distinguished translator of *Nahuatl*, León-Portilla presents evidence for an Aztec pictographic rhetorical tradition and compares several alphabetic and pictographic versions of indigenous texts to show how "an authentic thread of the Mesoamerican cultural weaving" can be reached.[34] León-Portilla asserts that ancient Mesoamerican concepts are in fact achieved through alphabetic translations. Some of the alphabetic hybrid texts, those that translated and mediated pictography in *Nahuatl* and Spanish do preserve pre-Columbian form.[35]

León-Portilla supports the case that *Huehuetlahtolli* is clearly far from extinct as a communicative practice, and such practice cannot be reduced to a static or pure pre-Columbian rhetoric of Mesoamerica. In collaboration with Native American Studies scholar Inés Hernández-Avila, León-Portilla recognizes contemporary writing practices in and beyond Mexico to compose in *Nahuatl*/Spanish hybrids as well as other indigenous idioms. To properly account for these present-day rhetorical manifestations of dual expressions and symbolic oppositions, the authors apply the phrase "*Yancuic Tlahtolli.*" With the *Nahuatl* root *Hue* ("ancient") replaced, the modified expression becomes translated as "The New Word."[36] Thus, a rhetorical vehicle for inscribing wisdom and history for over 2,000 years works to revitalize a new consciousness that fuses Mesoamerican culture and knowledge into its contemporary variations. My analysis follows a similar approach by deciphering, through the investigation of symbolic oppositions and parallel expressions, rhetorical strategies of resistance encoded in the codex manuscript. I interpret such symbolization as a resistant rhetoric that addresses the larger backdrop of colonial subjugation and resistance in the Americas. Through continuous symbolic play with doubles and corresponding expressions, Mestiz@ codex rhetorics revise the dominant narrative of assimilation.

Analysis

> *First, the works...conceptually replenish the void that has remained in indigenous American culture since the original picture books were burned by colonial administrations. Second, the gathering of codices...counters the dispersion of the surviving codices and colonial facsimiles to libraries and art collections throughout this continent and Europe. Third, the exhibition provides an important national cultural forum from the Chicano community on the merits, issues, and debates of the 1992 quincentenary.*
>
> —Marcos Sanchez-Tranquilino

Marcos Sanchez-Tranquilino, Mexican Museum of San Francisco curator, recognizes that the production of codices today intervenes in the dominant account of conquest and assimilation. This narrative corresponds to a religious and historiographic imaginary supported by Western writing conventions. *Chicano Codex: Encountering Art of the Americas* illustrates syncretic rhetorical processes that express and enact commentary about these conventions and the hierarchical tensions between notation/illustration, writing/art, and temporal distinctions between sixteenth-century Christianization and twentieth-century global capitalism. Sanchez-Tranquilino emphasizes that rather than seeking authentic *amoxtli* recreations, the codices amount to a reactivation and variation of the earlier forms in response to the colonial quincentenary (3). By intertwining Mesoamerican pictography with Mexican murals and Chicano iconography, codex rhetorics at once look back to the Mesoamerican past while critiquing the present and inventing possible shared futures.

The exhibit's revisioning notably involves the restoration of Mexican women's roles to *amoxtli* production. In *Codex Delilah: Journey from Mexicatl to Chicana*, for example, Delilah Montoya weaves pictographs with alphabetic script to tell of initiation into curanderismo, the practice of indigenous Mexican folk medicine. Intertwining healing arts with mixed script conventions corresponds with the dual Mesoamerican expression "in *xochitl*, in *cuicatl*/flower and song," which affirms the link between the act of writing and spirituality. By depicting her journey toward *Aztlán*, the mythic homeland of the *Mexica*, Montoya transposes the great Aztec migration narrative referenced in earlier *amoxtli*.[37] Thus, Montoya's representation of self-discovery and initiation does not seek an idealized pre-Columbian identity but instead sets in motion a distinct Mestiz@ subjectivity. The *Codex Delilah*, like the other works in the exhibit, takes its name from its composer, thereby symbolically opposing the earlier European appropriation of Mesoamerican *amoxtli*.[38]

In her postscript to the *Chicano Codex* published companion, Cherríe Moraga notes how the exhibit's interweavings propose a chart for cultural affirmation: "The Chicano Codex is a map back to the original face, *una peregrinación* to an America unwritten. América: the brown swell of tierra indígena debajo de la Calavera" (21). America, as a cultural and national marker of colonial power, must be remapped and revised. To inhabit Moraga's double inscription of America/América, readers must straddle both possibilities to invent a new, "unwritten" potential. Moraga's insertion of *Calavera* evokes the renowned Mexican revolutionary and artist José Guadalupe Posada Aguilar. Posada created lithographic images of skeletal figures to critique bourgeois culture and oppressive governance. The satiric *calaveras* heavily influenced Mexican and Chicano muralists, and are often seen as an aesthetic variation in the tradition of *Quetzalcoatl's* bare-boned twin manifestation *Ehecatl/Mictlantecuhtli*. Moraga's intersection of cultural voices and inscription conventions guide readers along an anticolonial map, backward and forward in time, from Mesoamerica to the present. Mestiz@ codices do not appropriate or "recover" early *amoxtli* expressions, Moraga implies, but instead advance a rhetorical process of reactivation and variation.

This framework cultivates an understanding of another present-day emergence, the *Codex Espangliensis: From Columbus to the Border Patrol* (2000), perhaps the most revisionist codex ever assembled and one that directly addresses colonial narratives of assimilation. As a collaborative effort between lithographer Enrique Chagoya, performance artist and cultural critic Guillermo Gómez Peña, and book artist Felicia Rice, the manuscript resists the Western ideology of writing as a solitary act. Performing the multiple stations of codex production mirrors the work of Mesoamerican *Tlacuiloque*. The manuscript conveys a tale of civilizing missions, colonial conquests, and rhetorical heterogeneity using Spanglish, Mesoamerican pictography, twentieth-century Mexican iconography, and transnational corporate imagery to weave yet another mythic retelling of history. This time, in *Noctli Europzin Tezpoca* (1492), the Aztec sailor departs from *Minatitlan* only to "discover" a new continent and name it *Europzin* after himself. Framing this encounter as a discovery foregrounds the larger problem of ethnocentrism and bias that plagues the ways in which *amoxtli* and pictography have been misunderstood by the colonial imaginary from the start. The sailor titling the continent after himself underscores not only the egotism of imperial conquest but also America's unique colonial predicament of being the only continent in the world to be christened with the name of an explorer.[39]

In November 1512, Aztec soldiers begin their wide-scale invasion of *Europzin* in the name of the "Lord of Cross-Cultural Misunderstanding." The early sixteenth-century Aztec conquest parallels the invasion of colonist Hernán Cortéz and the consequent fall of *Tenochtitlán*, Mesoamerica's metropolitan and political center. Such a satiric reversal necessarily undermines the project of Christianization and the myth of Mesoamerican barbarity. The cultural reorganization of the continent of *Europzin* parallels America's violent restructuring under European-imposed categories. *Anahuac*, the *Nahuatl* regional conceptualization of the *Aztec* federation, for example, was geopolitically remapped and renamed as a new European periphery, the frontier of New Spain. Readers are confronted with multiple cartographies that symbolically counter an American subjectivity with historically fixed national and cultural borders.

The reversal of Europe and Mesoamerica in the *Codex Espangliensis*' remapping of world history works to dislodge the integrity of Christianization and the dogma of European assimilation as they have operated in the past and continue today. Moreover, this retelling constructs a new perspective of global history that emerges from the lived experiences of the México/U.S. border. As described in chapter 2, the borderlands are both material and discursive territories of asymmetrical power that impinge on Mestiz@ communities.

Chicana theorist Norma Alarcón describes such power dynamics as follows:

> These borderlands are spaces where, as a result of expansionary wars, colonization, juridico-immigratory policing, coyote exploitation of émigrés and group vigilantes, formations of violence are continuously in the making.[40]

Alarcón's notion of the borderlands correlates with Gloria Anzaldúa's articulation of *Nepantlism*, the rhetorical strategy I explained in chapter 3. Inventing from Anzaldúa's borderland identity requires movement between cultural places, a perpetual transition amid contradictory and hierarchical worldviews. Between the borders of Latin America and Anglo America, between a so-called developing nation and monopolizing capitalism, between the Aztec and the European, the *Codex Espangliensis* critiques across both real and imagined boundaries of a brutal, globalized world.

On each panel of the manuscript, border violence forms a visual history of oppression that runs both forward and in reverse. Observing the tradition of pre-Columbian *amoxtli*, the *Codex* reads from right to left and proceeds without pagination. In place of pages, 15 folded screens disrupt the traditional Western physical practice of reading. While advancing through each unnumbered screen in the order of Mesoamerican tradition, possibilities of alternative readings are revealed: in addition to being read as one continuous, extended mural, the narrative may also unravel from left to right. Thus, screen 1 may also be reread concurrently as screen 15 in an alternate account. Because narrative and logical order are ultimately not fixed in the text, each folio or screen simultaneously functions as a potential beginning, middle, or end. Multiple reading orders represent an anticolonial collage, a set of variations around themes of colonialism and civilizing missions. Fundamental Aristotelian laws of aesthetic invention and organization that demand a linear beginning, middle, and end are therefore called into question. The material practice of reading the *Codex* requires a complex visual dance, forward and back, sometimes circular, other times broken.

It is through this strategy of reading and rereading history, forward and in reverse, that Mestiz@ codex rhetorics invite readers to envision the Spanish colonial sixteenth century and the present era of late global capitalism simultaneously. By fusing different temporalities, the *Codex Espangliensis* mirrors the same tactic employed by early pictographic artists during the time of the early conquest. The suggestion of Mesoamerican chronology recuperates the Aztec and Maya cyclical nature of time, change, and growth. But this time, readers are confronted with the Mestiz@ past and present in light of the capitalist development that permeates the United States, the highly militarized borderlands, and the world. The theft and appropriation of Mesoamerican land and culture by Spanish colonial regimes is juxtaposed with contemporary images of Mexico symbolized as cheap labor and raw materials—a source of profit for the new conquistadors and lords of *Aztlán*: landowners, foreign investors, and transnational corporate entities.

This strategy neither opposes material history nor the lived experiences of colonial exploitation. Instead, codex rhetorics propose a detour, a revision or creolization of dominant assimilation narratives, of taking them in a plurality of directions, toward new ways of reading. The *Codex* calls for new ways of reading and knowing that "invent between" syncretic visions and revisions of geographical colonialism and economic imperialism. In this context, Mestiz@ rhetorical practice refers to the available means of identification that are mediated at the intersection of knowledge constructed by the dominance of Western colonialism on the one hand, and on the other hand, knowledge emerging from anticolonial perspectives in the borderlands.

The full name of the *Codex* illustrates this kind of intermediation. *Espangliensis* is a satirical fusion of two language systems that, when intertwined, supports no intelligible meaning in either tongue. The first morpheme is cut and derives from the Spanish word for Spain, *España*. The Latin suffix *-sis* refers to a pattern or state of sickness. Merged between these is a severed and potentially hidden stem, anglo, a Mexican-Spanish expression for people of Western European and European-American descent. It is noteworthy that the Spanish tongue not only represents a standardized dialect of an ex-colonial power of Christianization and assimilation. In the present age of market fundamentalism, Spanish has also developed subalternized countercultural admixtures. We are invited not only to think with, against, and beyond the first language to impose rhetoric instruction proper in America. We are also confronted with so-called Third World transformations of Spanish, and the memories that are kept alive through Mestiz@ cultures.

To understand *Espangliensis*, the reader must think in and through each discourse to arrive at one of several possible explanations. This practice is further complex because, apart from the creators' aspirations, as a mass-marketed "book" from City Lights and Moving Parts Press, the manuscript is open to consumption and interpretation by Mestiz@s and non-Mestiz@s alike. Yet this only amplifies the import of *Codex Espangliensis* as a reactivation of Mesoamerican pictographic rhetoric. The pre-Columbian *Amoxoaque*, after all, had always applied multiple interpretations and multiple performances of the *amoxtli.* The syncretic mixing of such disparate elements thus creates a complex rhetorical space beyond the mere coming together of two halves. The rhetorical strategy implied here involves an invention beyond the hierarchical logic of assimilation. As a stylistic device, this syncretic process is akin to Inés Hernández-Avila and Miguel León-Portilla's articulation of contemporary Mesoamerican rhetoric, *Yancuic Tlahtolli.* This Mexican strategy sustains a long tradition of *difrasismo*, the combining of different terms to convey new ideas and abstractions. In the *Codex Espangliensis*, as with *The Chicano Codex: Encountering Art of the Americas* and the numerous Mexican murals before them, *Yancuic Tlahtolli* functions as a metaphorical and critical tool that expands earlier commemorative rhetorical nature to condemn present-day colonial injustice and human suffering. The Mestiz@ codex pairs celebration and struggle as a tactical refiguring.[41] Because the refiguring of Europe/Mesoamerica in world history is an intentional work of fiction, the *Codex* might not be seen as a parallel structure to the earlier historical work of the pre-Columbian *amoxtli.* However, the *Codex* symbolically references the long-established interplay of telling and retelling Mesoamerican history; the Aztec intelligentsia, after all, rewrote their *amoxtli* in order to be understood as biological descendents of the prestigious *Toltec.*

The continuous symbolic play with pairs, doubles, corresponding expressions, and twins is scattered throughout the *Codex Espangliensis.* Screen 14/2, where the mythical Aztec sailor *Tezpoca* engages in colonial invasion of *Europzin*, is such an example. In place of sacred Judeo-Christian symbols, readers are confronted with a massive pictograph of *Quetzalcoatl Ehecatl/Mictlantecuhtli*, the twin deity symbolizing the duality and balance of life and death.[42] *Quetzalcoatl* is the sacred hero recognized for creating human life from ancestral bones who also represents the patron of scribes and artists.[43] *Mictlantecuhtli*, *Quetzalcoatl's* manifestation of death, carries a steel-tipped lance that is remarkably comparable to the one Hernán Cortéz presented to Moctezuma during their fateful encounter at *Tenochtitlán.*[44] The immediate pictographic reference of twin spirituality emphasizes the Aztec philosophical belief that Mesoamericans were literally, corporally composed of the past.[45] History is not merely a factor of ancient knowledge, but a deep-rooted awareness that material life itself is made possible by the past. The assertion of the Mesoamerican living past counters Cortéz' attempt to erase it. At the moment of colonial contact and conflict between worlds, not only is the Mesoamerican spiritual world affirmed, but the boundaries between the colonial past and the colonial present become infused.

Placed in opposition to the *Quetzalcoatl Ehecatl/Mictlantecuhtli* deity and Mesoamerican pictography are cartoon action heroes of twentieth-century American popular culture. While the D.C. Marvel icons Superman and Wonder Woman convey their own kind of twin identity with their respective alter egos, what is most striking is the way in which these figures become a stand-in or double for the cultural imperialism perpetuated in commercial as well as political realms under a global age of market fundamentalism. In place of human inequity under a Spanish colonial administration, Chagoya, Rice, and Gómez-Peña shift readers' attention to injustice in an era of telecommunications.

Representing exaggerations of Anglo-European strength and presence in the Western Hemisphere, these cartoon superheroes permeate every bloodstained screen in the *Codex*, just as American popular culture now saturates the screens of television, cinemas, and computers across the globe.

Syncretic play with pairs and double expressions can also be seen in the manuscript's symbolic representation of Christianization. In the context of anticolonial critique, Catholic imagery may appear on the surface as an impulsive embrace of Christian conversion. Images of Christ and the saints make several appearances across most screens in the *Codex*. Mexican historian Davíd Carrasco suggests we reread these Christian symbols as they are appropriated or reappropriated by Mesoamerican and Mestiz@ cultures. Responding to Mexican crucifixions, Carrasco observes,

> Many appear, on first glance, to be symbols of a European Christian presence. But on closer view it is clear that many echo preconquest designs, emotions, conceptions of spatial arrangement, and style. Further reflections leads to the realization that these crosses are neither European nor Indian, but Mexican—a fluid syncretic image of new power, decoration, and combined meanings.[46]

On screen 13/3, a multicolored image of Christ's body serves as an ambivalent trope of sixteenth-century Catholic conversion on the one hand, and as an image of persisting Mesoamerican suffering and martyrdom on the other. A reading of subversion is possible as Christ literally bleeds along with afflicted Mesoamericans, thereby critiquing methods of Spanish brutality and European regulation over Mexican bodies.

This critical arrangement of intermixing religious figures is likewise illustrated on screen 12/4, where a solemn image of the Virgin of Guadalupe peers down on Wonder Woman emerging from the opened carcass of an unidentified woman. The DC comic icon, with a caption that reads "GO TO HELL!" grips an oversized high-tech firearm appearing as if modeled after 1950s' science fiction films. While Mary traditionally signifies an intermediary to the Christian God and as a fostering, loving guardian to the faithful, an alternate Mestiz@ narrative also endures. In 1531, only 10 years after Cortéz waged war against the Oaxacan confederacy, the Holy Mother appeared next to a shrine on a hilltop dedicated to the goddess *Tonantzin*, the Aztec sacred mother. Guadalupe spoke in *Nahuatl* to Juan Diego *Cuauhtlatoatzin*, an indigenous catechist, announcing that she had appeared in order to offer spiritual shelter and protection for the oppressed.[47] Soon, a cult surrounding Our Lady of Guadalupe played a powerful role in the simultaneous acceptance and resistance of colonial society, and her image has become an influential symbol of Mexican nationalism. The veneration of Mary, or *Marianismo,* maintains a tremendous impact on the Chicano movement in the United States.[48]

That Guadalupe is represented atop a large serpent is not by accident. In her exchange with Diego *Cuauhtlatoatzin*, it is believed she used the *Nahuatl* word *coatlaxopeuh*, which is pronounced similar to the Spanish word, Guadalupe. Guadalupe literally means "(one) who crushes the serpent."[49] Pictographic representations of serpents correspond to *Quetzalcoatl*, the feathered serpent-god. *Tenochtitlán*'s demise under Spanish forces symbolically mirrors the descent of Mesoamerican spirituality, which was certainly crushed under the weight of Judeo-Christian conversion. It is also noteworthy that Genesis 3:15 prophetically indicates that a woman would step on the serpent's head. Guadalupe's comical exchange with Wonder Woman's fierce vigilantism highlights the violence engrained in the dominant narrative of Christianization. But Guadalupe's evident alliance with the DC hero undermines her archetypal image as spiritual mother of purity and protection. Guadalupe's compliance with the brute force of colonization presents a satiric counterpoint to the veracity of conversion.

Quetzalcoatl's twin pictograph *Ehecatl/Mictlantecuhtli*, *Quetzalcoatl's* serpent pictorial, DC Heroes and their alter egos, and the twofold symbolism of Christ and *Marianismo* collectively function as a repetitive invocation of dualism, a metaphorical communicative device central to Mesoamerican cosmology. Through pictography and Mexican iconography, the *Codex* becomes a Mestiz@ example of reactivating and utilizing *Yancuic Tlahtolli* to critique the colonial past and global present. Though each screen is filled with significant visual imagery that cannot be overlooked, multilingual alphabetic descriptions encircle, overlap, and cover these graphic images. I will now turn my attention to how various handwritten and word-processed lettered characters in the *Codex* likewise work to critique the dominant historical narratives of assimilation.

The alphabetic script in *Codex Espangliensis* intersects various texts from performance artist Guillermo Gómez-Peña, whose publications combine cyberculture and Mestiz@ art. Numerous screens of the *Codex* include references to his *The New World Border* (1996), "a kind of post-Mexican literary hypertext" (ii). Throughout *New World Border* and *Codex Espangliensis*, Gómez-Peña references the collapse of Three Worlds theory, the post-1955 Bandung conference mapping of global social space. The breakdown of the opposition between First and Second Worlds with the disintegration of the Soviet Union makes it possible to imagine beyond the production of the so-called Third World and to define postnational modes of collective identity across the borderlands.

Screen 10/6 poses questions to the reader such as Where exactly is the United States located? In which world are you located? For which world does your art speak? Are you experiencing once again an identity crisis? Has your community been left out of the above categories? Set across from these solitary questions, multiple-choice descriptions materialize, crooked alongside the margin of the right-hand folded screen, as if the script were competing against the material border and confines of the codex:

> First World • A tiny and ever shrinking
> conceptual archipelago from which 80%
> of the resources of the planet are
> administered and controlled.

Second World • aka "Geo-political Limbo."
Greenland, the Antarctic continents, the
oceans, the mineral world and the
dismembered Socialist Block.
Third World • The ex-underdeveloped
countries and the communities of color
within the ex-First World.
Fourth Word • The con-
ceptual place where the
indigenous and deterri-
torialized peoples meet.
It occupies portions of
all the previous worlds.
Fifth World • Virtual
space, mass media, the
U.S. suburbs, the art schools, the malls,
Disneyland,
the White House and La Chingada.
(Screen 10/6)

In *New World Border*, Gómez-Peña explains how the old colonial hierarchy of First World/Third World is being supplanted by the more pertinent notion of the Fourth World, understood as a conceptual place where the indigenous inhabitants of the Americas meet with the displaced, the property-less immigrants, and the exiles (7). Readers of the *Codex* are confronted with transnational flows of labor and human flesh in the "Fourth World," spaces that undermine the racially coded hierarchical dichotomy of Mesoamerica and Europe. Whereas the social and political alliances between the Indian and the Mestiz@ were once severed under U.S. imperial development, now, under monopoly capitalism, these boundaries appear not as complete.[50]

Fourth World multiple spacializations also forward their temporalities, which furthermore compel readers to reside in the early twenty-first century era of late global capitalism while simultaneously inhabiting the sixteenth-century colonial era of Spanish feudalism. Readers are again confronted with an invitation to metaphorically invent and read in reverse, to consider both pre-Columbian and neocolonial forms of prenational territorialization as well as forward to think about newly emerging frontiers and regional logics that revise the dominant narratives of globalization, colony, the border, and ensure the survival of Mestiz@ and other denigrated cultures.

Illustrating such temporalities, transnational corporate imagery of the North American Free Trade Agreement, Disney, and telecommunications reside along savage depictions of "barbarian" Mexicans, Mestiz@s, and Mesoamericans. On screen 15/1, cannibal Aztecs distribute bloody remains of Disney's principle animated character, Mickey Mouse, thereby critiquing Christianization and the civilizing mission under the banner of global colonialism across the Mexico/U.S. borderlands. Disney, a transnational conglomerate, no longer merely signifies the U.S. commercial circuit. The Disney Corporation, like American capitalist development, permeates the world.

For years after the U.S. Congress passed the North American Free Trade Agreement in 1993, debates about the treaty provoked Western rhetorics of xenophobia, border crossing, and crisis that were not too different from the sixteenth-century disputes over the proper role of Mesoamericans under Spanish rule. Legacies of these debates form a thread of images throughout *Codex Espangliensis* with wordplays and blurred distinctions between "fee trade art" and "free art." Stretched across a bloodstained screen 1/15, readers are twice faced with such cognitive dissonance as it is mediated and translated through two languages: "donde radica la diferencia entre el arte de libre comersio y un tratado de libre cultura?" (What is the difference between Fee-Trade art and a Free Art Agreement?). The lingering unanswered questions parallel an unreciprocated challenge that imperialism account for its transactions across borders.

Literary critic Thomas Foster, in "Cyber-Aztecs and Cholo-Punks," suggests that NAFTA represents both misfortune and opportunity

> to the extent that transculture and border crossing could be domesticated as "conservative diplomacy," it also proved that the idea could be reappropriated for less conservative purposes. But that reappropriation could only be accomplished through the admission that the border is no one's exclusive property or territory, neither NAFTA's nor Gómez-Peña's. (48–49)

The rhetorical work of *Codex Espangliensis* therefore highlights the futility of clearly distinguishing between assimilationalist transcultural forms and resistant ones. On one hand, the rhetoric of border crossing can be a subversive and critical act. Conversely, such articulations can be exploitive whether emerging from the political right or the left.[51]

In *The Location of Culture*, Homi Bhabha writes of "the danger that the mimetic contents of a discourse will conceal the fact that the hegemonic structures of power are maintained in a position of authority through a 'shift in vocabulary'..." (241–242). The *Codex* warns of such a shift in diction from geographical colonialism to cultural imperialism, from Cortéz to Free Trade, from Columbus to the Border Patrol, a shift that maintains power structures through a thinly veiled rhetoric of popular culture and advertising. Critically reading such colonial power also provokes a global border consciousness, a strategic departure from the site-specific concept of the México/U.S. borderlands. Gómez-Peña mirrors such a shift to globalize the border when he acknowledges, "...the border is no longer located at any fixed geopolitical site. I carry the border with me, and I find new borders wherever I go."[52] Gómez-Peña's symbolic reversals and expressions across borders subvert the hierarchies of power between opposites. By inventing between cultural paradigms, codex rhetorics enact possibilities beyond them.

Specifically, intermediations between dissonant literacies and divergent reading practices revise the hierarchical configuration of notation/illustration. Strategic border crossing between Western dichotomies works to assert Mesoamerican pictography and Mexican iconography as equally valuable methods of inscription. Readers are physically confronted with pictorial systems that function as a highly complex and equally suitable communicative form. Pictography could even be situated as a type of notation in the Western world, of course, as are charts, graphs, and icons in ideographs. By rereading disparate Mesoamerican rhetorics as equivalent to notation, Western literacy and the invention of alphabetic and syllabic systems become dislodged as the central and normative element of information storage.

The *Codex Espangiensis* supports the idea of writing as a term inclusive of the rich complexity inherent to Mestiz@ symbolization. Writing is no longer limited or reduced to simply those types of signs for which Western scholars deem truly alphabetic. It is precisely through the direct graphic weaving of Mesoamerican pictography with the Western alphabet that readers are confronted with the hierarchical discord between them. To look at pictographs and icons as disembodied, decontextualized systems is to misunderstand and underestimate the communicative power they hold for cultures that continue to produce them. The *Codex* encourages new definitions of writing that depend less on the notion of visible speech and more on the permanency and visibility of particular signs. In his *The Darker Side of the Renaissance: Literacy, Territoriality, and Colonization* (1994), Walter Mignolo defines writing that expands on this idea:

> Semiotically, a graphic sign is a mark on a solid surface made for the purpose of establishing a semiotic. Consequently, a human interaction is a semiotic one if there is a community and a body of common knowledge according to which: (a) a person can produce a visible sign with the purpose of conveying a message (to somebody else or oneself); (b) a person perceives the visible sign and interprets it as a sign produced for a purpose of conveying a message; and (c) that person attributes a given meaning to the visible sign. (78)

Mignolo's definition can account for a variety of Mesoamerican graphic practices, including the pre-Columbian *amoxtli*. Mestiz@ codex rhetorics require such an expanded understanding of graphic interactions, where the links between speech and writing are no longer universal.

Contemporary codices can be understood as communicative devices that are not necessarily subservient to alphabetic or syllabic systems. Thus Mesoamerican pictographs are not an alternative to Western systems. Rather, the Mestiz@ codex rhetorics subversively question how and in what ways Western ideologies of writing are superior alternatives to the plurality of Mesoamerican possibilities. Codex rhetorics embrace the diverse inscription practices of pre-Columbian cultures as fully literate, highly complex, and suitable methods of communication. These new translations of literacy are capable of accounting for both the annotative and illustrative aspects of Mestiz@ activity, thereby providing a view of writing responsive not only to the plurality of other historically non-Western cultures across the Americas and beyond, but also to current trends in visual and digital rhetoric, trends that belatedly call for increased attention to multigenre and multimedia composition practices. More than the act of inclusion, entwining the discontinuity between pictographic and alphabetic worlds into the contemporary Western expression "writing" works to revise the hierarchical frame of definition. Moreover, working directly against an enduring Aristotelian syndrome of marginalizing and subjugating "cultural Others," the new codices provoke analysis of corresponding and coevolutionary histories of inscription as the spreading of color on hard surfaces.

Conclusion

I have argued that the dialectic of oppositions and reversals in Mestiz@ codices resist and revise Western hierarchical categories of assimilation. Each screen fold in the *Codex Espangliensis* works to dislodge colonial power, past and present. This resistance is embedded within symbolic reversals and temporal distinctions between worlds. The strategy I have adapted from Cherríe Moraga and Miguel León-Portilla accounts for how symbolic oppositions and reversals disrupt the hierarchical tensions of European-imposed categories. By inventing between cultural paradigms, the *Codex* enacts variations of *Yancuic Tlahtolli*, graphic and rhetorical variations of Mesoamerican expression. The reactivation of Mesoamerican rhetoric does not aspire to glorify a mythical past but specifically aims to better understand and articulate the present.

Western writing specialists are thus compelled to think about writing practices rhetorically, and how the colonization of languages beginning in the early sixteenth century has lead to limited notions of language as an object to be owned, with a grammar and vocabulary that must be mastered and regulated under some form of European governance. It is too often the case that efforts to clarify alphabetic literacy often overlook the pivotal role of illustration and image within language. In contrast, the view of writing proposed here necessitates and values all that language, including pictography, can accomplish under colonial and neocolonial situations. If, rather than theorizing rhetoric and writing based on the pedagogically vanguard "Composing-East-to-West" trajectory, specialists accept Mestiz@ codices as starting points, we are left with expressions better suited to emerging non-Western rhetorics as well as current material realities in America and beyond.

Consequently, new modes of Mestiz@ historiography imply new ways to interpret history, rhetoric and composition, thereby having substantial implications for both practitioners and writing students. When in history did the Americas become literate, literary, and rhetorical? When did writing begin in North America? According to whose measuring stick? What counts as writing and what does it mean to be literate? What does it mean to be civilized? In the context of these crucial pedagogical questions, in chapter 5, I will examine more closely how writing specialists might read Mestiz@ scripts as a theoretical and historiographical paradigm, as a new vantage point to rethink the relationship between supposedly expanding notions of literacy and composition. The codices evidence precisely what the dominant historical imaginary erases and what English composition lacks: coevolutionary or parallel histories of writing and rhetoric in the Americas. This in turn radically compromises the cultural authority and hegemony of composition's historical emphasis on writing only as alphabetized, visible, and Anglo-European speech.

Rethinking rhetoric and writing from Mestiz@ codex legacies advances a more constructive understanding of parallel writing systems and rationalities in America yet also promotes a critical intervention in the politics of writing instruction in the present. Such an intervention involves a decided departure from the paradigm of alphabetic supremacy. Writing specialists today need to invent far beyond the myths of a Greco-Roman horizon toward its challenges and mutations on a global scale. As writing specialists in the twenty-first century, we need to enact a new politics of rhetorical inquiry that reads colonial history both backward and forward, and aims to significantly revise the dominant narratives of Mesoamerican assimilation.

V

The Spreading of Color: Sacred Scripts and the Genesis of the Rio Grande

We followed the coast day and night; on the following day... we sighted a city or town so large that Seville would not have appeared bigger or better... a very tall tower was to be seen there..

—Juan Díaz, Tulum, Yucatán Peninsula, 1518

In 1518, only a few years before military general Hernán Cortéz and his combatants invaded *Tenochtitlán*, Conquistador Juan de Grijalva lead a colonial expedition to the coastal Maya city of *Tulum*. Juan Díaz, chaplain and conquistador under de Grijalva, recorded one of the only existing firsthand Spanish accounts of the well-populated metropolis with complex painted designs on its buildings. A soaring tower, constructed on the edge of a cliff above the turquoise waters of the Yucatán peninsula, caught his attention. In the European mind of Díaz, *Tulum's* tower was the equivalent of the Torreóns from Seville, fortified towers for protection against enemy invasion. Years later Spaniards would realize that, on the contrary, the tower sheltered a ceremonial altar for burning incense and prayer. Geometric scripts and traces of painted knowledge up and down the walls of the tower presumably align with the prayer rituals. Although these "fortified towers" vary across time and region, as is evidenced by contemporary buon fresco muralist Frederico Vigil's Torreón near the Rio Grande river, the historical link to Mesoamerican, Spanish, and Mexican syncretism are crucial to understanding these painted rituals. By "syncretism," I mean the cautious, perpetual adaptation of multiple and conflicting cultures in a shared expressive context.

This chapter analyzes the aesthetic fusions and border crossings between Mesoamerican and Spanish conceptualizations of internationally renowned Frederico Vigil's most foundational work *The Genesis of the Rio Grande* in northern New Mexico. Here I build upon the concept of *Tlaquilolitztli*, the earliest word for "writing" in the Americas, translated as "the spreading of color on hard surfaces," and thus identify Vigil within the tradition of *Tlaquilo* painters/writers. I first describe the mural itself, its major characteristics and the primary figures of *Malintzin Tenepal* and *Moctezuma Xocoyotzin* in the ritual dance, Los Matachínes. I examine the painstaking process of buon frescos that are traced to their European roots, where clear distinctions between "art" and "writing" are firmly rooted. Fresco historians look to Europe, however, as the analogous Mesoamerican wall-writing practices and traditions have become largely forgotten. Yet the buon fresco style is not exactly "European"; buon fresco traditions emerge from an interregional and cross-cultural Mediterranean system, which includes Egyptian, Asian, Arabic influences as well as its Greco-Italian contributions. Using the tropes of interregional and cross-cultural histories, I analyze Vigil's *Genesis of the Rio Grande* as well as his monumental El Torreón in particular his strategic interweaving of contrastive symbols and figures as they are enacted within colonial structures of power. Specifically I argue that Frederico Vigil's rhetorical exchanges of intermediacy and border crossing work to revise and displace dominant narratives of Spanish, monotheistic and alphabetic assimilation through representations of Los Matachínes, the sacred dance of *Malintzin* and *Moctezuma*. Vigil's ceremonial scripts resist dominant narratives by fusing and embellishing their own local histories.

Frederico Vigil as *Tlaquilo*

Inside El Torreón, the 45-foot tower at Barelas-Albuquerque's National Hispanic Cultural Center, Frederico Vigil diligently hovers over at a draftsman's table, encircled by paints, brushes, and other tools of the buon fresco ritual practice. On the walls surrounding Vigil are Madonnas, Olmec and Aztec spirits, Malintzin and Moctezuma, societal and religious elders, philosophers, scholars, and numerous other figures—pencil sketches, others gleaming with bright colors that soar above him. The mural, like the interplay between Malintzin and Moctezuma, conflates time and space in a structure that privileges "movement" and mutability. Vigil is at work on a monumental production, depicting centuries of IndoHispano history and culture. Vigil argues that "IndoHispano" is a more accurate signifier that emphasizes continuous syncretic interactions between Pueblo Indian and Hispano cultures since the time of the Conquest.

The outside of the adobe-colored Torreón appears modest in size. However, the sky-lit cylinder's concave interior is a vast structure that calls for a sense of reverence and contemplation. Aside from the ceremonial center at Tulum, the tower's history includes ancient traditions from the Spanish Iberian peninsula used by Romans, Visigoths, and Muslims through the early modern era. In the Americas, Spanish colonizers also built these stone defensive structures and watchtowers in Mesoamerica's northern region. Colonial settlers used the Torreón to protect them from Indigenous Nations defending their land.

Vigil completes his masterwork in progress as the city of Albuquerque marked its three-hundredth anniversary in 2006. Vigil's work offers the Albuquerque metropolitan area a powerful new artistic and architectural symbol that incorporates traditions of Mesoamerica, Spanish settlement, Mexico, and IndoHispano cultures of the U.S. southwest borderlands. Since he began this time-consuming and scrupulous work in 2002, Vigil has painted 900 square feet of the 4,300 square feet fresco. The painting includes the ceiling and 45 foot tall interior walls. Near the tower's peak, enormous hands against a cobalt background, seem to reach toward the viewer through a skylight. Halfway down, a Madonna in gold-trimmed vestments stands beside a blazing sun, and nearby, newborn infants are lifted toward the heavens.

The remainder of the fresco, in progress at the time of this publication, is composed of curving walls covered with charcoal outlines. These depict the imagery that will trace millennia of Indigenous and IndoHispano civilizations. Other segments of charcoal sketches focus on local histories of New Mexico, Nuevomexico, Mexico, Nueva España, and the pre-Columbian world. Vigil was raised in Santa Fe, in the barrio along Canyon Road. Today, Canyon Road is one of the most gentrified neighborhoods in the city, with high-scale major galleries selling "southwest-style" artwork imported from either out of state or visiting artists without cultural or historical connections to Pueblo Indian or IndoHispano cultures. During Frederico Vigil's youth, the physical labor of carpentry and masonry eventually lead him to the buon fresco, yet another artistic form of corporeal, gestural, bodily, and tactile challenges. To complete the Torreón project, Vigil relocated from Santa Fe to the Barelas barrio.

The buon fresco first requires applying five layers of plaster made from a mixture of slaked lime and sand. The first 3 layers need 10 days to dry, then an additional 2 layers are added and dried. Vigil paints onto the final fifth layer, known as the *intonaco*, an Italian expression for "finish coat," applied while wet. The artist grinds pigments to a fine powder and brushes them onto wet plaster, following the outlines of his charcoal sketches. The paint is absorbed into the damp wall, resulting in luminous, durable hues. The project's scale allows Frederico Vigil to use a wider range of brushes and strokes, employing his whole arm and back rather than his wrist. Vigil's act of painting/writing is a kinetic gesture in motion, leaving behind a residual energy. Buon fresco technologies are unforgiving; when mistakes occur, the section must be thoroughly scraped off, replastered, and the surface should be repainted. Moreover, the Torreon's immense height and concave walls change perspectives depending on where and how the artist sees his work. More than once, Vigil has stood on the tower's floor after completing ceiling fragments only to realize, after seeing his work from below, that significant revision is needed. Vigil relies on ladders and scaffolding to reach the upper tower, as well as lifts outfitted with a weight bench, on which he reclines as he inscribes painted knowledge on the ceiling. Although Frederico Vigil uses contemporary tools and surfaces to inscribe his fresco, he draws upon a multitude of ancient traditions across the globe that reach back to limestone cave paintings in Spain (15,000 BCE), wall paintings in France (30,000 BCE), as well as pictographic scripts in Brazil (500,000 BCE).

Frederico Vigil learned buon fresco inscription practices in the 1980s from pupils of the great Mexican painter Diego Rivera. It is noteworthy that Rivera's murals in the National Palace in Mexico City, for example, create a visual and verbal structure that corresponds to those of pre- and post-Conquest codices, and they dramatize how Mesoamerican forms confronted and revised European colonizing systems, and continue to do so today. This mural tradition continued through Rivera's pupils, and has been passed on to Vigil's generation.

As I explain in chapter 4, Rivera and his contemporaries merged Mesoamerican pictography and imagery with Western muralist art, four centuries after the Spanish imposition of the art of letters. The Mexican muralist movement also engaged and transformed the "visual rhetoric" of the codices. Muralists working in postrevolutionary Mexico during the 1920s, 1930s, and 1940s politicized the rhetoric of modern art by engaging the visual media of Mesoamerican *Tlaquilolitztli*. In *The Inordinate Eye: New World Baroque and Latin American Fiction* (2006), Lois Parkinson Zamora elaborates on the self-conscious character of Mexican artists:

> The Muralists created icons of national consciousness, and their project was specifically tied to the *indigenista* movement. This pan-American movement generalized the awareness of indigenous cultures during the first decades of the twentieth century, valorizing indigenous traditions and practices and reconstituting the question of cultural inclusiveness. (The self-awareness of Native American and Chicano groups in the United States, beginning in the 1960s and sometimes expressed in murals, is a manifestation of this movement.) No longer was the inclusion of indigenous cultures limited to areas where the indigenous heritage was a defining cultural characteristic; rather, it had become (and remains) an essential element of regional and national self-definition throughout the hemisphere. Virtually all contemporary postcolonial discourse in/about Latin America includes elements engendered y *indigenista* imperatives. (77)

The movement is thus recognized as an effort to incorporate Mesoamerican cultural productions and practices into dominant structures of power. Postrevolutionary murals of the time aimed to advance manifestations of cultural syncretism in order to revise their own national history.

Engagement of the Mesoamerican past also speaks to the present use of the codices as explained in chapter 4. Indo-Hispano artists such as Frederico Vigil, within the shifting continuum of nontribalized indigenous subjectivity, find connections to Mesoamerican rhetorical structures and their *tlacuilos* forebears. The *tlacuilo*, as I have shown, was simultaneously scribe, painter, diviner, recorder of history, and writer/performer of communal knowledge. It is as *tlacuilo* that Vigil conveys local histories and global knowledge. Across Vigil's corpus we find the combined functions of artist and conveyor of communal wisdom, just as we do with other Indo-Hispano and Mexican muralists. Lois Parkinson Zamora elaborates:

> This public role reflects and extends the role of artists in prehispanic Mesoamerica, though the word "artist" is inadequate in this context. The *tlacuilos* and *ah ts'ib* (painter/priests), in central Mexican and Maya cultures respectively, served as scribes for the gods, painting their dispositions in iconographic languages and interpreting their meanings in oral performance. The visual grammar of the codices

> contained and communicated the theological, astronomical, calendrical, and divinatory wisdom of the community, historical and genealogical records, and, in case of the Mayas, the history of their dynasties as well. The pictorial writing of these "painted books" makes no distinction between "text" and "image." Painting and writing combine in colourful pictographic and ideographic structures, as do theological, astronomical, and aesthetic wisdom. (xix–xx)

Despite the harmfully narrow Western separation between "art" and "writing," Frederico Vigil's reactivation of Mesoamerican inscription practices can informs today composers of muralists and codex scripts. Vigil's buon frescos in particular are an example of this de-colonial rhetoric. Mesoamerican *tlaquilolitztli* is not only symbolic but also structural in Vigil's work. His murals never consist of a single scene but are, rather, a multiplicity of structures that speak to the fusions and fissures across Mesoamerican, Mexican, and U.S. territorializations. Vigil's history moves horizontally and vertically, backward and forward, inviting viewers to think with, against, and beyond linear accounts of the pan-American past.

The Genesis of the Rio Grande

Near the center of the buon fresco, a masked figure bows before a preadolescent girl, illuminated by vivid light descending from above. The masked figure, known as Monarca, is adorned in a colorful costume with a mitre-like hat, scarf, ribbons, and shawl that flutter as he submits himself to the child on the left. In one hand Monarca holds a three-pronged Trinitarian wand and in the other hand, a small rattle. Sitting on the left, a fiddler, guitar player, and Pueblo Indian drummer appear performing music, as if accompanying the masked figure and child. The girl, popularly known as La Malinche, is dressed in a First Holy Communion dress, and is the sole figure in the buon fresco with arms held toward the viewer. Both sun and moon are balanced in the sky above.

Behind Monarca, a figure known as Abuela/Abuelo (grandmother, grandfather) faces Malinche. The Abuela is dressed in a grotesque rubber facemask, a felt hat, ragged trousers, and an old knee-length coat. Abuelo carries a coiled whip that appears as though it could unravel at any time. To Malinche's immediate left is La Llorona, a weeping woman carrying her pale, lifeless child; the woman's right arm reaches into the vibrant beams of light that descend upon Malinche.

The juxtaposition of Monarca and Malinche is from a ceremonial drama, Los Matachínes. Many Western traditions consider the Matachínes folk dance as a derivative from medieval European folk dramas that celebrate Christian subjugation of the Moors.[1] This dominant narrative asserts that the Spanish military used the ritual as a vehicle for Christianizing Indigenous Mexicans. Spanish Iberian elements would have eventually merged with Pueblo forms in central Mexico, it is argued, and a hybrid variety of the dance was transmitted to Indians farther north, including Rio Grande valley Pueblos. This narrative would suggest that Frederico Vigil's *Genesis of the Rio Grande* celebrates Monarca willingly submitting to theirown colonial domination, through the ceremonial figure of Malinche.

As performed today in the U.S. borderlands, the Matachínes ritual mirrors centuries of IndoHispano cultural relations and provides a shared rhetorical framework upon which Pueblo and Hispano communities embellish their own local histories. The dance illustrates a distinctive dramatic pattern in the upper Rio Grande valley and is often considered to be identical between both Indian and Hispano groups. While the dominant narrative positions the dance as largely Christian rather than Indigenous, most Pueblos and many IndoHispanos perceive that the ritual was brought from Mexico by the Aztec emperor himself, Moctezuma, who is prominently represented in the dance as El Monarca.[2] This IndoHispano history suggests that in the early sixteenth century Moctezuma appears to the Pueblos of the upper Rio Grande valley to warn them of bearded strangers advancing from the south. First contact would constitute a crushing blow against Indian culture, Moctezuma prophesied, but in time these strangers would learn to respect the Pueblos, and by learning the steps of the ritual dance, the strangers will eventually transform to become like them.[3] As derived from Aztec combat dances, the Matachínes ceremony intertwines symbols of Mesoamerican survival within the historical narrative of colonial defeat. Resisting the framework of Judeo-Christian conversion, the dance furthermore reflects a gradual Spanish Iberian ethnic adaptation toward its present-day American manifestations of Mexican, Chicano, and IndoHispano.

Because the dance is said to suggest the advent of Christianity among Mesoamericans by referring to the conversion or expulsion of the Moors, Frederico Vigil's fresco may symbolically comment on the colonial power of Hernán Cortéz, although he is not characterized in *Genesis of the Rio Grande*. The fresco, like most of Vigil's work, has historical and often contrasting meaning for Indian and Hispano groups. A somewhat intermediary and historically plausible narrative suggests the Matachines dance was brought to the Rio Grande Pueblos via *Tlaxcalan* Mexicans who accompanied the Spanish armed forces advancing from the south. In his *Pueblo Indians of North America* (1970), anthropologist Edward Dozier explains,

> We suggest that these ceremonies were introduced by Mexican-Indians who accompanied the early Spanish exploring expeditions and also came with the colonists. These Indians held no positions of authority and hence provided no threat to the Pueblos. If these Indians presented the ceremonies to the Pueblos, then it is easy to understand why the Pueblos accepted them. (187)

Cultural exchanges between Rio Grande Pueblos and Mexicans were not new by the sixteenth-century conquest, as trade routes had been established across greater Mesoamerica as early as 500 CE.[4] Indeed, Dozier's explanation may help clarify why northern IndoHispano communities so quickly adopted the ceremony, and why Vigil chooses to represent this sacred dance in his own sacred mural scripts.

The upper Rio Grande valley consists of the length of the river that cuts across the state of New Mexico running north to south, distinguishable from the lower Rio Grande valley, which runs along the Texas-Mexico border from El Paso to Brownsville. As explained in prior chapters, New Mexico became New Spain's northern frontier during the sixteenth century, as conquistadors and colonists followed up the river and established missions and settlements along the corridor. The frontier colonial society that developed during the next 300 years involved the mixing of Hispano and Indian bloodlines, and the blurring of cultural and territorial boundaries between them. Despite massive demographic shifts, 19 of the more than 100 Pueblos existing at the time of contact survive well into the twenty-first century.[5] Most of the Rio Grande Pueblos are surrounded by clusters of colonial and subsequent Mexicano settlements that emerged across the New Mexican landscape during four centuries of mutual opposition, growing interdependence, and eventual displacement under U.S. occupation.

In barrios such as Barelas and Atrisco (Albuquerque South Valley), Matachínes performances include several dance sets by Malinche and Monarca, an exchange of wands, a variable combination of choreographic interweavings, crossovers, and reversals between two columns of dancers. The grotesque Abuelo typically functions as a conductor and provides satire throughout the proceedings. Frederico Vigil's fiddler, guitarist, and Pueblo percussionist represent the musical accompaniment for the ritual. The tunes tend to be short, varying from 4 to 20 measures in length, and subject to multiple repetitions. Most are done in duple or triple count and feature conventional harmonies in dominant and tonic chords on the guitar, while the fiddle carries the melodic line.[6] Along the Rio Grande valley, the Matachínes folk dance has been incorporated into the annual ritual calendars of San Ildefonso, Tortugas, Santa Clara, Jemez, Cochiti, Santo Domingo, San Juan, Picuris, and Taos Pueblos and is performed in Albuquerque South Valley barrios such as Alcalde, Bernalillo, Barelas, and Atrisco.

The Matachínes Literature

European references to "matachin dances" date from the sixteenth century. There are two main Western views on the etymology of the term matachin: that it is (1) of Arabic origin, deriving from *mutawajjihin,* which refers to being masked or muted, or (2) of Italian origin, matto, meaning madman or fool.[7] The ritual is assumed to have begun as a sword dance symbolic of combat involving two inter-facing columns of masked dancers and the use of sticks and castanets. The dance became associated with the theme of Moorish-Christian conflict, a type of dance known in Spain as a morisca and in England as morris dances.[8] Some versions of these dances were brought to Mesoamerica along with other forms of Iberian music and drama. Many elements of the dances gradually syncretized into "new" forms in central Mexico and elsewhere along the Spanish frontier, adapting and transforming under the intensely stressful conditions that comprise a borderland "culture of conquest."[9]

Pueblo variations of the Matachínes ritual are reported from Mexico and Arizona for the Tarahumara,[10] Yaqui, Otomi, Ocoroni, Huichol, and Cora Indians.[11] Their common elements include cross-overs and exchanges between two lines of masked dancers who carry rattles and wands, wear high caps with streamers and feathers, and dance to the accompaniment of fiddle, drum, or guitar. Some versions involve down-like figures and/or young boys cross-dressed as La Malinche.[12] Though most scholars maintain that the matachin or morisca is an Old World form, those who have observed the dance in the borderlands nevertheless recognize the significant presence of Pueblo elements.[13]

Folklorist Gertrude Kurath provides, overall, the most complete account of the Western origin and distribution of the Matachínes dance and provides choreographic notations of the San Juan Pueblo and Santa Clara Pueblo versions in her *Music and Dance of the Tewa Pueblos* (1970). This work offers the first comparative treatment of Old and New World morisca elements and choreographic patterns. She identifies the key symbolic elements of moriscas as combat, killing, resurrection, clown, woman disguise, animal, mask, crown, bells, and feathers and provides a table showing their distribution among 14 Old and New World regions (105). Kurath also diagrams 9 basic choreographic patterns, which are distributed differentially across 12 Old and New World examples. Although Kurath's diagrams exclude the Rio Grande valley, her findings nevertheless correspond to what is found in Atrisco-Albuquerque and other regions of northern New Mexico.

Flavia Champe's *The Matachínes Dance of the Upper Rio Grande* (1983) contains the most detailed choreographic description on the Rio Grande Matachínes to date, based upon the San Ildefonso Pueblo version, which Champe claims is the "clearest, longest, and most complete" she has seen (1). Champe compares the major elements of the San Ildefonso dance with those she has observed at other Pueblos, including Taos, San Juan, Santa Clara, Picuris, and Jemez, and in the Hispano villages of Alcalde and Bernalillo. Champe's analysis was done in an era when the ritual was experiencing a severe decline. Fearing the demise of the dance, Champe claims her main purpose is to provide a practical guide for those who would preserve it. The book contains choreographic diagrams of each movement or set as well as selected intervillage comparisons, numerous color photographs, and a vinyl phonograph record of the San Ildefonso music.

Musicologist John Robb adds significantly to the literature on the Rio Grande Matachínes. Robb's main contribution consists of sound recordings and transcriptions of numerous Matachínes tunes and folk dances or dance sets, including 11 from Tortugas and 7 from Taos, as well as some more from other villages.[14] Robb also provides a valuable overview of the greater Southwestern Matachínes tradition and its features among Pueblos and Hispano villages, along with a fairly detailed description of the Tortugas version.

Most Western scholarship on the Matachínes dance deals with questions of European origin, distribution, and selected ethnographic detail. The previous mentioned scholars provide a detailed description of various aspects and versions of the dance, yet no single account is entirely adequate from a rhetorical point of view. For example, even though both Kurath and Champe supply detailed choreographic and musicological descriptions of all the sets within particular versions of the dance, neither imagines the performance as part of a larger inclusive, progressive configuration. Like many Western observers of the ritual, these scholars isolate the collection of movements as the unit of study and analytically ignored the larger historical context—the ceremonial event and its critique of colonial domination—within which each dance is embedded. My intervention will be to interpret these dances within the particular colonialist context of power that created them.

The Matachínes is typically performed more than once for any given occasion, and sometimes several times each day for up to three days. Previous studies of the Matachínes treat the folk dance generically in terms of its presumed meaning, that of commemorating European conquest on Catholic holidays. Sylvia Rodríguez' *The Matachínes Dance: Ritual Symbolism and Interethnic Relations in the Upper Rio Grande Valley* (1996), however, offers a critical departure from previous scholarship by studying specific features of the ceremony in terms of the historical, ecological, and social particularities of communities in northern New Mexico. This involves what Rodríguez calls the "operational, exegetical, and positional levels of analysis, with systematic focus on native explanation and consideration of the symbols in relation to one another and their overall cultural and historical contexts" (15).

Rodríguez offers a "thick description" of Pueblo Matachínes dances in Taos, Picurís, and Arroyo Seco. These three geographically proximate performances are then compared to a southward sequence of seven additional cases along the Rio Grande valley (excluding the Barelas-Atrisco dance variety). Rodríguez' framework is predicated on the proposition that the Matachínes communicates metaphorically about the colonial history and character of IndoHispano relations in the communities that perform it. My analysis follows a similar approach by attempting to decipher, through the investigation of symbols, and rhetorical strategies of resistance encoded in the Albuquerque ritual. It is true that symbols tell about the people who use and create them[15] and my interpretation is akin to Frederico Vigil—such symbolization as a ceremony addresses a larger backdrop of colonial resistance and revision. Through metaphorical exchanges of intermediacy and border crossing, Frederico Vigil's *Rio Grande*/ Matachines sacred rhetorics critique and revise the dominant narratives of conversion and assimilation.

Analysis of Vigil's Malintzin and Moctezuma

> Like the pre-Columbian glyph-making scribes and the modern-day artists inspired by them, I am a *tlacuilo*-like literary and visual thinker, and I have hoped to provide *tlamatinime*-like interpretive performances, decodings, or readings of this dialoguing mixture of difference art forms, not only to give voice to my own fascination and what it has helped produce in me but also to contribute to a new, more universal scholarship grounded, where relevant, in both European/Euroamerican and non-Western aesthetics and philosophies. It is my hope that... [my work], alongside the many essays and manuscripts presently in production on related topics, will consign to distant memory both the exclusion from, or merely tokenistic inclusion of Chicana art in visual studies...(13)

In *Chicana Art: The Politics of Spiritual and Aesthetic Altarities* (2007), Laura Pérez recognizes that visual practices among non-Western cultures involve rhetorical processes that express commentary about cultural relations, as well as about forces that shape local history. Pérez' study pinpoints structures of power that make up local communities and argues that what transpires beneath the surface reveals *tlamatinime*-like masks of power. Tlamatinime-like performances in effect subvert dominant power structures and ensure the survival of Mestiz@ cultures. Such subversion is invented not only in light of a given communal identity but also with references to that local community's history and economy. The following analysis focuses on the hidden meaning embedded in Frederico Vigil's strategic representation of Malinche and Monarca.

Specifically, my analysis examines Vigil's Malinche as an archetypal border crosser through IndoHispano history and memory, as a subversive product of conflicting and intertwining worlds. My rhetorical framework is informed by Gloria Anzaldúa's examination of mestiza consciousness in the borderlands. In her landmark *Borderlands/La Frontera: The New Mestiza*, Anzaldúa writes,

> In a constant state of mental nepantlism, an Aztec word meaning torn between ways, la mestiza is a product of the transfer of the cultural and spiritual values of one group to another. Being tricultural, monolingual, bilingual or multilingual, speaking a patois, and in a state of perpetual transition, the mestiza faces the dilemma of the mixed breed: which collectivity does the daughter of a dark-skinned mother listen to? (25)

Nepantlism, Anzaldúa suggests, is a state of being in a border space, a symbolic space where multiple cultural values intersect. A borderland's identity is furthermore a movement between cultural places, a perpetual transition between worldviews. Inventing from *nepantlism*, from a position of suspension between two contradictory frames of reference, does not fabricate a harmonious union between Mexico and Spain. It instead implies being "torn between ways" (78) and forms new perspectives that do not require linear or hierarchical dichotomies.

Consistently, the ceremonial rhetoric of Vigil's *Origins of the Rio Grande* and the Barelas South Valley Torreón represent key symbols of resistance to colonial domination. The buon fresco's underlying structure entails bilateral oppositions and reversals reflected in the pairing of Malinche and Monarca, Malinche's multifaceted identity, the duality of the sun and moon, and the symmetrical position of "visual" history and memory. Frederico Vigil's sacred arrangements symbolize rhetorical interchanges among paired and opposed personae, between Mesoamerican and Iberian worlds, thereby challenging and revising an assumed IndoHispano trope of Christianization. In fact, most of Vigil's work signifies a constant intervention in the enduring legacy of European colonization. Even the interregional, border crossing, Mediterranean cultural network that invented the European buon fresco, predating the birth of Jesus of Nazareth, likewise complicates and provincializes hierarchical dichotomies of Christian conversion.

Malinche and the "Conversion" of Moctezuma

The oppositional contrast or juxtaposition between Mesoamerican spirituality and Judeo-Christianity is most evident in Vigil's dramatic pairing of Monarca and Malinche. Yet the dominant assumption casts these oppositions and combinations as signs of Mesoamerican submission and assimilation. Indeed, Monarca as the Emperor Moctezuma epitomizes an "Indian god in European clothes"[16] and serves as the mediating symbol and temporal marker for the invasion of *Tenochtitlán*. Malinche, in a white Holy Communion dress, corresponds to some extent to the advent of Catholicism and the Christian conception of virginal purity.

The work's symmetrical formations and crossovers further signify Mesoamerican alignment with and conformation to a Judeo-Christian world system. The expression La Cambiata, from the Spanish verb *cambiar,* means "to exchange one thing for another." In this tradition, Vigil's converted Moctezuma rearranges the order of Aztec and Spanish worlds through symbolic enactments of similarity and contrast. It is noteworthy that the Trinitarian wand doubles as weaponry in a further overlapping of religion and warfare. Under the dominant trope of Moctezuma's conversion, Vigil symbolically evokes the historical conditions of subjugation and conquest that surround Mexico's imposition. The buon fresco ceremonial paintings as a whole would thus constitute a dramatic means by which Mesoamericans commemorate their own colonial defeat. My analysis argues instead that Frederico Vigil's aesthetic production ritually enacts resistance to European conquest and serves as a model for the survival of IndoHispano culture. This counternarrative is encoded and expressed primarily in Vigil's multifaceted figure of Malinche.

Malinche

A closer examination of Malinche effectively thwarts Moctezuma's Christian conversion and the dominant narrative of assimilation. As I explained earlier in the book, Mexican-origin peoples interpret the Virgin Mary through the mediating figure of Señora de Guadalupe/ *Coatlaxopeuh.* The popular folk narrative places the first Mexican apparition of Mary before Juan Diego *Cuauhtlatoatzin*, an Indigenous farm worker and catechist. By 1531, Latin and Castilian had been enforced as the official languages of Catholicism for almost a decade, yet the apparition communicated to Juan Diego in *Nahuatl.* The name Guadalupe derives from the Spanish mispronunciation of *Coatlaxopeuh*, which is pronounced "quatlasupe." Central to the account is the fact that Guadalupe not only affirms Mesoamerican survival but also suggests a European inability to fully translate this survival.

Rather than symbolizing Spanish Christianity, Guadalupe therefore signifies the collective endurance of IndoHispano identity. In "Indigenista Hermeneutics and the Historical Meaning of Our Lady of Guadalupe of Mexico," sociologist Miguel Leatham argues,

> The Virgin of Guadalupe may serve as a symbol of mediation and dialogue between groups of differing status and cultural backgrounds within the church today as in the colonial period. To a large degree, the Virgin can mediate because, according to an Indigenista interpretation, the image of Guadalupe encodes key elements out of Mexico's

> indigenous heritage while also being historically linked to the emergence of a cultural heritage, is given divine sanction, providing an ideological basis for religious empowerment and greater appreciation of the Mexican presence among the "people of God." (36)

Leatham confirms Guadalupe's influence as a rhetorical intervention, a continuous mediation between Catholicism and Mesoamerican spirituality. As the symbolic mother of Mexican cultures, Guadalupe promotes a communal identity forged between worlds. Vigil's work inspires viewers to look forward and backward, from Malinche to surrounding images, personify an oppositional contrast between Mary and Guadalupe. Malinche's embodied exchanges between Iberian and Mesoamerican worlds do not necessitate a rejection of Roman Catholicism, however, but a strategic weaving of Christianity into Aztec local histories. The use of Judeo-Christian symbols in Federico Vigil's work, from Malinche's Holy Communion dress to other Catholic representations, can be understood without the hierarchical baggage of religious conversion.

Vigil's careful negotiation with Catholic imagery is further encoded through the etymology of La Malinche. Malinche is the Aztec name for *Malintzin Tenepal*, a woman born of *Mexica* nobility who was later presented as a servant to Hernán Cortéz in 1519 when his armed forces landed in Veracruz.[17] While one of Cortéz' soldiers had learned a Mayan language variety common to Mexico's eastern coast, his conquistadors were lacking in *Nahuatl* literacy and experienced difficulty communicating with Oaxacan valley populations such as *Tenochtitlán*. *Malintzin's* extensive knowledge of Mayan and *Nahuatl* dialects and customs, her ability to interpret Aztec pictography, and her mastery of Castilian caught the attention of Cortéz. Soon, *Malintzin* became Cortéz' interpreter, advisor, mistress, and mother of his child.[18]

Bernal Diaz del Castillo, the Spanish foot soldier who describes Moctezuma's ritual court dance in his *History of the Conquest of Mexico*, records *Malintzin Tenepal* as a heroine. Her predicament as a servant or slave is overlooked as Diaz praises *Malintzin*, at one point calling her a "most excellent" woman (62). *Malintzin's* ability to assist and advise Cortéz' communiqués with the Mexican intelligentsia shaped the entire military campaign. From the first meeting between Cortéz and Moctezuma's emissaries, efforts were made to establish relations with the Aztec Emperor while secretly recruiting or enslaving Indians less friendly with the Triple Alliance to join forces with

Spain. Without a skilled informant, such rapid negotiations would have been unlikely.

While the Spaniards proudly baptized Malintzin as Doña Marina, the Aztec labeled her La Malinche, literally meaning "captain's mistress." The tragedy of Malinche cannot be ignored, as she represents not only Mesoamerica's first religious convert but also a defector and traitor of catastrophic proportions. Malinche's cultural and sexual "disloyalty" fostered the invasion of *Tenochtitlán*, it is frequently thought, or at least made the Triple Alliance more penetrable for Spanish combatants. In "Chicana's Feminist Literature: A Re-vision Through Malintzin/or Malintzin: Putting Flesh Back on the Object," Norma Alarcón notes:

> ...the myth of Malintzin seeps into our...consciousness in the cradle through...[male] eyes as well as our mothers', who are entrusted with the transmission of culture...All we see is hatred of women. We must hate her too since love seems only possible through extreme virtue whose definition is at best slippery...the pervasiveness of the myth is unfathomable, often permeating and suffusing our very being without conscious awareness. (135)

Contempt for *Malintzin* runs deep, for she is the symbolic perpetrator of Mesoamerica's fall into European subjugation. But Alarcón surmises that *Malintzin's* mythic dimension also connotes the defiled mother of Mestizaje (182). Her bearing of "illegitimate" mixed-blood offspring represents Mexican women as sexually submissive and manipulated by European men through seduction or rape (184). *Malintzine's* descendents may have no alternative, Alarcón suggests, but to harbor an innate disdain buried in Chicana/o collective memory. Even today, "malinchismo" is a derogatory term used to describe Mexicans who express solidarity with Western or Anglo cultures.

Predictably, *Malintzin* as symbolic betrayer would reinforce the dominant narrative of assimilation and conversion. As the first Mexican convert, how appropriate that *Malintzin* would symbolize the role of enticing and ultimately subduing the Aztec emperor! Yet some attempt has been made to vindicate *Malintzin* from her negative mythology.[19] Regardless of the young interpreter's involvement, Spain's rudimentary Christianity and imperial hubris made Mesoamerica's conquest unavoidable. Furthermore, attention to misogyny and sexual slavery underscores *Malintzin's* predicament with Spanish compliance. But even her obedience under Cortéz is questionable considering that *Malintzin's* careful negotiations may have saved Mexico from additional slaughter. Had Cortéz failed in his negotiations his next expedition, perhaps without an interpreter, would likely have shed more Mexican blood. Then too, had Cortéz met with no success, the Smallpox epidemic that raged in *Tenochtitlán* might well have spread throughout the entire Triple Alliance and beyond.[20] The swift destruction of Moctezuma and the capitol city may have salvaged the country.

Furthermore, *Malintzin's* subversion is embedded in her own translations and in the key role she played in convincing Cortéz to employ persuasion rather than additional physical force. Previous training in the Aztec art of discourse at the *Calmecac* conservatory[21] would have prepared *Malintzin* for such tasks. As an interpreter under Cortéz, *Malintzin* engaged her adversaries in multiple translations through multiple languages. But her exchanges and reversals between Spanish to Maya and Maya to Nahuatl forward more than syntactic or semantic transactions between languages. *Malintzin's* strategy also intertwines rhetorical configurations across cultural borders. Her translation of Spanish worldviews into Maya and Nahuatl thought and Maya/Nahuatl views back into Spanish thought promotes a new strategy of invention. Frederico Vigil, like *Malintzin*, invites the crossing of linguistic boundaries and the possibility of "inventing between" the historical memories engrained in each language.

Expanding *Malintzin's* historical act of translation from its linguistic conception to its present-day symbolic and rhetorical potential adds significantly to *Malintzin's* role in Barelas-Atrisco communities. If understood as Mexico's first subversive rhetor in the face of European invasion, *Malintzin* performs Vigil's primary role of revision and resistance. The sexual struggle and predicament of *Malintzin* forms an opposing paradigm against the virginal purity of Guadalupe that in turn counters the Christian Mary. *Malintzin* embodies multiple contradictions and puts them into motion through the ritual's key choreographic motifs. Variable combinations of interweaving, crossovers, and reversals effectively resist the linear and hierarchical configuration of conversion. Thus it is not Moctezuma that is converted but the European model of Christian conversion itself that is undermined and revised through *Malintzin's* dynamic mediation.

Anzaldúa's *nepantlism* as described earlier contributes significantly to my analysis of *Malintzin's* role in Vigil's buon frescos. *Malintzin* is the key mediator between Pueblo and Hispano worlds. Anzaldúa points out that IndoHispanos identify *Malintzin* as,

> A synthesis of the old world and the new, of the religion and culture of the two races in our psyche, the conquerors and the conquered... She mediated between the Spanish and Indian cultures and between Chicanos and the white world. She... is the symbol of ethnic identity and of the tolerance for ambiguity that... people who cross cultures... possess. (29)

Accordingly, *Malintzin* synthesizes Judeo-Christian and Mesoamerican worlds by crossing between them. *Malintzin* demonstrates the tension of this rhetorical interchangeability through repeated sequences of forward and backward steps, alternate turns to the left and right, and continued weaving within and between the opposing rows of danzantes. As Moctezuma mimics *Malintzin's* choreography, they too symbolically "walk out of one culture and into another" (30). By straddling Mesoamerican and Christian cultures, these sacred figures intervene in the overarching historical narrative of assimilation.

Embroidered within these explanations is an IndoHispano account that proposes yet another effective counternarrative to Christian conversion. Some local histories explain that *Malintzin* and Moctezuma's wand doubles as an ancient Aztec feather fan, a marker of Mesoamerican nobility and spirituality.[22] The fans were said to hold feathers from the *Quetzal*, a sacred bird associated with two divine beings. *Xochiquetzal*, meaning "feathered flower," is a goddess of arts and fertility. Every eight years the Aztec held a banquet in her honor where the celebrants wore animal and flower masks. *Quetzalcoatl*, or "feathered serpent," is the Mesoamerican god of human sustenance, self-sacrifice, and rebirth. When Hernán Cortéz arrived in Veracruz, Moctezuma's emissaries presented him with many tributes, including feathered Quetzal fans. After the fall of *Tenochtitlán*, both the bird and the myth of *Quetzalcoatl* came to symbolize Mesoamerican authority and sovereignty. But *Quetzalcoatl* is more overtly implicated in oral history: when Moctezuma first presented the ritual before the Rio Grande Pueblos, he did so while atop the god-serpent.

Moctezuma's wand is itself a symbolic intermediary between divergent worlds. The Trinitarian wand contrasts with colonial weaponry that in turn counters Aztec feather fans. Far from suggesting a cultural utopia, these relations are fraught with tension. Frederico Vigil's strategic oppositions and reversals between these religious symbols reflect Moctezuma disengaging from the hierarchical dichotomy of conversion by legitimizing its alternatives. This tactic is akin to Gloria Anzaldúa's call for a "massive uprooting of dualistic thinking in the individual and collective consciousness" (102). By refusing to designate Roman Catholic theological perspective as the *only* IndoHispano faith heritage, this work rejects conceiving Mesoamerican spirituality as deviant and insufficient. Asserting pre-Columbian spiritualities as enduring and equally suitable frames of reference, then, effectively resists the triumphant narrative of Christian domination.

One of the most visual and dramatic demonstrations of Vigil's intermediation occurs in *The Origin of the Rio Grande*. It could be assumed that the weaving symbolically reenacts "miscegenation" between Spain and Mexico.[23] Preceding acts are thought to portray Moctezuma's conversion and "union" with *Malintzin*. Within this storyline, the figures would certainly reinforce the defeat of Mesoamerican culture and Pueblo subordination to both Christianity and Spanish bloodlines. The buon fresco would celebrate a mixed ancestry of physical violence and religious conquest. But Frederico Vigil's subversive mediations of the Malintzin and Moctezuma allow for another translation. As I've attempted to show, Vigil's work does not commemorate Christian conversion so much as it fuses Catholicism into Mesoamerican legacies. Far from imposing a rejection of Christianity, Frederico Vigil's *Origin of the Rio Grande* enacts a careful negotiation through resistance and adaptation. The Torreón, for example, demonstrates Mesoamerica's strategic intertwining of Catholicism without the hierarchical logic of conversion. In sum, a dominant theme flowing through Frederico Vigil's painstaking creations enacts the exchange and transformation between opposing worlds.

Abuelo

The significant presence and intervention of Mesoamerican symbols produce a fracture in Vigil's visual narrative. In contrast to the serious roles of Malinche and Monarca, striking variation is seen in the personality of the Abuelo. The buon fresco is structured around sacred figures. Yet the Abuelo, dressed in a grotesque rubber facemask, serves as reminder or descendent of Moctezuma's court jesters. The foot soldier Bernal Díaz del Castillo describes them as humpbacked, deformed, and ugly, who plays tricks of buffoonery, comic jestures, exhibiting burlesque behavior (230).

That the irreverent Abuelo is positioned so closely to the "innocent" young Malinche assumes particular significance. Abuelo's close proximity to Malinche offers a hidden satiric counterpoint to the supposed enactment of Moctezuma's Christian conversion. The Abuelo, whip in hand, interrupts the reverent symbols of Moctezuma's assimilation and Malinche's Holy Communion. The transformation of these motifs into a burlesque illustrates how colonial struggle in the borderlands is continually translated and reinterpreted. The unruly vulgarity of the Abuelo alludes to Moctezuma's court jesters who once performed before Cortéz and his conquistadors. Frederico Vigil's reference to this history underscores IndoHispano origins that becomes yet another vehicle for historical revision. As Moctezuma's gift to the Rio Grande valley, present-day Matachines rituals observe European rule while simultaneously offering a hidden strategy to resist it, under the protective facade of compliance. In most of Vigil's sacred murals partake of both Mesoamerican and Spanish elements are present, which are infused with something new through symbolic oppositions and reversals. This strategy of intermediation must also be examined within the larger environmental context of the ceremony, including the fiesta in which it is embedded.

Rio Grande, Malintzin-Moctezuma, and Political Economy

The powerful symbols of *Malintzin* and Moctezuma are both a reflection of and a response to the historical conditions of subjugation and resistance that characterizes Pueblo-Hispano relations and, later, Mexicano-Anglo and Indian-Anglo relations. Thus, Vigil's depiction of *Malintzin* and Moctezuma endures not because of devotion to some "authentic" Mesoamerican tradition but because the ritual continues to hold meaning as colonial relations of power shift across time. Vigil's sacred script plays an important role in the formation of communal and individual subjectivity in the borderlands. The simultaneous embracing of and resistance to Christianization can be understood in the context of present-day environmental struggles along the Barelas-Atrisco Rio Grande river basin.

In 1706, Valle de *Atrisco* was officially incorporated into what is today the city of Albuquerque. The original name of this South Valley community is *Atlixco*, a *Nahuatl* word ("aht-leesh-co"), translated as "place on the water."[24] For generations, *Atlixco* villagers and their

Barelas neighbors relied upon the valley's natural resources for survival. Regional native grasses were critical for grazing sheep and cattle, and the lands were cultivated and irrigated to grow corn, chile, squash, alfalfa, and beans. To honor the water that nourished the fields and brought life to the valley, Barelas-*Atlixco* residents would gather at acequias, naturally formed canals along the Rio Grande, to offer blessings and prayer for an abundant harvest. Today, Barelas-Atrisco, of all the Rio Grande communities in New Mexico, is part of the larger Albuquerque metropolitan center—these townships are one of the most urbanized and integrated into an advanced industrial or, rather, postindustrial economy. Increased performances of the Malintzin-Moctezuma drama along the Barelas-Atrisco riverbeds are not by accident.

The Water Information Network, a South Valley community-based organization, publicly acknowledges the Barelas-Atrisco Matachínes revival as part of this water blessing in its manifesto "Protecting Water and People on the Border" (2003) (54). In collaboration with the Atrisco Land Rights Council and the Barelas-Atrisco South Valley Growers Market, an Indigenous environmental organization, the Water Information Network actively promotes the empowerment and survival of local Mestiz@ culture. The political economy of Barelas-Atrisco has been shaped by centuries of colonial relations, from European conquest and incorporation into a mercantile industry to the present capitalist nation-state. Today, for example, coal and uranium-mining projects throughout New Mexico threaten community sustainability by controlling, exploiting, and polluting natural resources.[25]

For the Water Information Network, the water blessing and Matachínes resurgence correspond with mobilizations around issues of traditional resources and community control:

> Globalization is challenging our ability to survive as a distinct people and culture, and we are forced to labor in an economy that knows no respect for people or the environment...[t]he border areas face a multitude of environmental problems that transcend the limits of international boundaries. We face huge demands for water resources as well as sharp expansion of Mexico's industrial base fueled by NAFTA and global pressures. Environmentally destructive coal and uranium mining activities are located predominantly on Native American lands characterized by high unemployment and depressed economies...We are concerned with the abuses of workers and of human rights associated with U.S. immigration policies, and with the

> poverty and lack of respect for the plight of indigenous people who do not recognize the imposition of the border on their homeland. (55)

This struggle applies easily to the long historical and cultural record of colonial relations in New Mexico, as it does elsewhere across the borderlands, where natural resources are typically the limiting factor. For example, northern New Mexico at large is ranked sixth in production and reserves of coal, oil, and Uranium, and it is the third largest exporter of electricity and copper. Yet all or most of the minerals are shipped to outside plants and economies for processing, refining, and distribution.[26] Unskilled New Mexican labor is used to mine the resources, thereby increasing corporate profit. This economic strategy mirrors the techniques enforced upon Mesoamericans by Europeans interested in mineral deposits. Local Aztec and Inca laborers were forced to strip deposits out of the earth and load it for shipping to the Western imperial center, thereby leaving Mesoamericans and their progeny with stripped mountains and a collapsed economy in the periphery. The Atrisco-Albuquerque ritual occurs at the precise setting where economic changes on farmland and water are intensified.[27] The pressure of intensifying capitalist development provokes the ceremony and other forms of ritual activism throughout much of New Mexico. The Matachínes once clearly referenced Catholic conversion, but today it symbolizes IndoHispano determination to persist against assimilating to the demands of an AngloAmerican global market.

In the Albuquerque South Valley the dance has come out of the danger of extinction in the late 1950s to being a major festival some 30 years later, a fiesta in which the number of performers has more than doubled and ritual organization operates through community status. The Matachínes tradition is linked in native thought to survival of the Pueblo Revolt, Bernalillo's official reconquest origin, and its expressed desire to survive as a community today. By the people's own account, the intertwining of Malinche and Moctezuma symbolizes the community's identity. As in the other cases along the Rio Grande valley, the ceremony currently enjoys a surge of popularity and strong participation.

In addition to the December ritual, South Valley residents conduct the Matachínes each May on the fifteenth in honor of San Ysidro Labrador, the patron saint of farm workers. San Ysidro is invoked for agricultural aid, favorable weather, and prosperous crops. Barelas, Corrales, Alameda, and other Rio Grande communities join

Barelas-Atrisco in annually celebrating the saint. As the local history goes, San Ysidro was instructed by God to stop working in order to observe the Sabbath. The Judeo-Christian tradition regards the Sabbath as a sacred day of blessing and physical rest in a week. The demands of planting seeds, watering the soil, and harvesting crops continually overwhelmed Ysidro, leaving him unable to rest. After being prompted by God three times, Ysidro eventually agreed to observe the Sabbath. In return, an angel was given to labor with Ysidro in the farmlands.[28]

The saint's day conveys gratitude for the land's fertility and offers prayers for future crops. On another level the celebration suggests a bond between divine sacrifice and the sacrifice of living labor. The San Ysidro ceremony affirms Malinche and Moctezuma religious imagery as symbolic intermediaries between Mexican Catholic faith and Barelas-Atrisco labor struggles. It is noteworthy that other upper Rio Grande Matachínes dances have also undergone some form of resurgence since about 1970, preceded by a period of decline.[29] This pattern reflects larger economic and ecological trends that have had comparable impacts on IndoHispano communities located within different rural and urban centers across the borderlands. Vigil's Torreón therefore refers not merely to the Mesoamerican and Spanish past but also to the IndoHispano living present in terms of the tower's rhetorical structure as well as in relation to top-down economic pressures.

Conclusion

I have argued that rhetorical exchanges of intermediacy and border crossing in Frederico Vigil's selected works resist and revise the hierarchical logic of assimilation. Each work contains what historian James Scott calls a "hidden transcript" (5) whereby the subjugated covertly critique the dominant culture. This transcript is embedded within the larger historical narrative of Moctezuma's Christian conversion and *Tenochtitlán*'s defeat under Spanish rule. The strategy I have adapted from Gloria Anzaldúa's *Borderlands/La Frontera: The New Mestiza* accounts for how symbolic oppositions and reversals between Mesoamerica and Spain work to disrupt the hierarchies of power between them. By inventing between cultural paradigms, Malinche and Moctezuma enact possibilities beyond them. In other words, Vigil's IndoHispano ceremonial scripts rearticulate and embrace Catholicism without the material psychological violence of conversion.

Today the dominant power is neither Spain nor Mexico but American neoliberalism, though representing this dominance inside the Torreón is unnecessary. The distinctive adobe ascension is a visual reminder of IndoHispano memory and persisting culture. While capitalist development is not Christianization, it does operate on a related European-imposed axis of progress and assimilation. Conversion to global market demands remains a hidden principle and enacts a similar dichotomous pattern. U.S. dominance is an undeniable horizon against which Vigil's Torreón stands.

The Torreón and National Hispanic Cultural Center offer a counternarrative to downtown Albuquerque's commercial-circuit expansion, which is in close proximity to the pressures of urban development against the resource bases of Barelas, Atrisco, and other long-standing communities across the Rio Grande. Pueblo and Mestiz@ responses alike have not advanced the absolute rejection of Americanization and development. This sentiment is mirrored by advocacy associations such as the Water Information Network, the Atrisco Land Rights Council, and the Atrisco-South Valley Growers Market.[30] In place of a rejection of Americanization, Mestiz@ groups attempt to entwine the cultural values of Pueblo and Mexican communities into gradual economic change. This suggests, for example, resisting pressures to sell water rights in the open marketplace, protecting existing rights, and affirming time-honored communal water uses. Straddling the cultural values of Mestiz@ rural self-reliance and the pressures of urbanization involves revising the dominant narrative of global market demands to reinvent new potential paths of progress and development.

The fusions and border crossings between opposing cultural worlds is dramatically symbolized through Vigil's Barelas Torreón. The buon fresco contrastive symbols and characters are enacted within colonial structures of power that revise and displace the dominant narratives of alphabetic conversion and Spanish assimilation. Vigil's ceremonial inscription practices resist these narratives by fusing and embellishing their own local histories. The ceremony represents the assertion of the community's sense of history and culture, the attachment to its land base, and intertwining faith systems. This assertion is by definition a product of the ongoing fusions and fissures between Spanish-Iberian, Mesoamerican, Pueblo, Mexican, American, and New Mexican local histories. Today, Vigil's buon fresco ceremony is not exclusively European but an ongoing, reinvented rhetorical strategy of resisting and revising the historical narratives of domination as they endure across the U.S. borderlands.

VI

Crossing Borders: Gloria Anzaldúa and the Territories of English Composition

Knowing is what counts. To know one's country and govern it with that knowledge is the only way to free it from tyranny... The European University must yield to the [Latin] American... The history of [Latin] America, from the Incas to the present, must be taught in clear detail and to the letter, even if the archons of Greece are overlooked. Our Greece must take priority over the Greece which is not ours.

—José Martí, 1884, Cuba

We are part of a discipline that is twenty-five hundred years old, and our continuity from Aristotle and the earliest rhetoricians cannot now be doubted by anyone. Our history is its own justification...

—Robert Connors, 1992, United States

The demographics of conference paper proposals, and areas within rhetorical studies today, suggest how much that remains to be done. We received... none on Southwestern Hispanic and Chicana/o topics. What about the rich and growing indigenous Chicano literary traditions that readers are flocking to find? Where are the studies we need of their rhetorical cousins and counterparts?

—C. Jan Swearingen, 1999, Rhetoric, the Polis,
and the Global Village Symposium

Taken together, these epigraphs invite a dialogue on how educators might revise the dominant historical narratives of Western rhetoric and composition. When does the American history of rhetoric begin? What should educators do with rhetorical traditions unique to the

Western Hemisphere, with beginnings suggested by the memories of Mesoamerica rather than of Greece or the Aryan-Germanic Enlightenment? How, when, and under what circumstances might "Indigenous Chicanos" enter the imaginary of composition history? In the present era of heightened immigration, political conflict, diminishing geographical distances and permeable national borders, such questions suggest the need for a more hemispheric articulation of rhetoric and composition. In addition to exploring these questions, this chapter details how the rhetorical strategy scholar Gloria Anzaldúa promotes new directions in rhetoric and composition historical scholarship. I argue that Anzaldúa's mestiza consciousness, if positioned as a new point of origin, would revise and enlarge the frameworks that educators use to study and teach the history of writing and rhetoric in America. This chapter is not a formal proposal for new curricula or course strategies. It instead aims to flesh out promising responses to the inquiry: what curricular and pedagogical possibilities might be enabled by Anzaldúa's mestiza consciousness?

Simply inserting Anzaldúa into a vanguard Western narrative potentially replicates the hierarchy and authority of Eurocentric foundations. Consequently, I employ Anzaldúa's mestiza consciousness as a theoretical paradigm that significantly revises how writing and rhetoric might be studied and taught. In other words, I intend to go beyond merely adding Anzaldúa into existing curricular models of rhetoric and composition by examining how mestiza consciousness supports new frameworks to rethink and revise what is already known in different ways. By inventing from the borderlands of Spanish-Iberian, *Nahuatl*, Afro-Mestizo, and Anglo-American traditions, Anzaldúa articulates a powerful aesthetic where coevolutionary ways of reading history become possible. A coevolutionary approach would not only assist the field in understanding México/U.S. border politics; coevolutionary or parallel histories could also help teachers and students gain a more global understanding of writing and rhetoric across America, the Western Hemisphere, and beyond.

Cuban guerrilla leader and essayist José Martí was a central figure in the struggle for Latin American sovereignty. As quoted above from his renowned article-manifesto, Martí argues for a reconstruction of historical memory, a retelling of America from the intellectual traditions of Mesoamerica, the Andes and emerging admixtures of Indigenous, African, and Iberian cultures. Martí's belief in critical reeducation is aptly summarized by his insistence that teachers of the "European University" cannot "rule new peoples with a singular and violent composition" (337). Rhetoric and composition historians who contemplate Martí's call with seriousness are charged with the task of rethinking the dominant narratives of the field. Approximately a century later, rhetoric scholar and historian C. Jan Swearingen articulates how far writing specialists have yet to go toward understanding the disparate cultural histories and rhetorical practices of Indigenous Chicanos. Even at a time when the field habitually celebrates diversity and multicultural pedagogy, scholarship in rhetoric and composition represents little knowledge about rhetorical ancestries outside Greco-Latin, Medieval, Anglo-Saxon, and Euro-American configurations.

Rhetoric and composition historian Robert Connors, writing at the quincentenary of America's invasion, illustrates the immense rational and political obstacle that composition specialists face in transcending the field's Eurocentric configuration. According to Connors, the linear cultural horizon of the field undoubtedly and triumphantly advances East-to-West across the planet. This inherited narrative covers over and erases local regions and localized moments in time across the globe that provide, among other things, crucial knowledge about the materiality of writing and various cultural transformations under colonial situations. As a largely unquestioned point of departure, the dominant narrative "from ancient Greece to Modern America" advances myopic assumptions about both the nature of writing and those civilizations that collectively maintain the longest cumulative histories of writing and writing instruction in North America.

Even while writing specialists imagine their ethos around a diversity of inclusive theories, the harmfully narrow, racially coded East-to-West narrative endures as an overhanging determinant of the study of written language. Writing and writing instruction have been reduced to phenomena that occur primarily at sites of formalized instruction, often subservient to Anglo-European nation-building. The field's American teleology began not until the establishment of the British colonies and schools in New England, often with Harvard University's "English A" (1874) seminar.[1] This distorted narrative progresses toward twentieth-century open admissions policies in higher education institutions within the United States. It is typically then, when "people of color" (the immense social majority of the Western Hemisphere), belatedly enter this narrative, not as essayists or poets or historians or philosophers, but as lower-division undergraduate students caught in a cycle of "low literacy."[2] I do not doubt the academic contributions of composition and rhetoric scholarship. I have no intention, however, of replicating an almost systematic logic of historical exclusion and erasure. Given the fact that some writing specialists have been inclined to question Western impulses toward the subjugation of "cultural Others"[3] there remains little focus on sustained dialogue and exchange with Indigenous Chicanos or many other groups across the Americas and the Caribbean.

I propose the rhetorical strategy of mestiza consciousness as a necessary corrective to the field's dominant historical narratives. I furthermore invite a shift from merely "talking about" Anzaldúa's fragmented Chicana identity to "inventing and writing from" her conceptual borderlands in order to contemplate how Western rhetorical knowledge can be revised by learning from Mestizo@s who are living in and thinking from colonial legacies. Because mestiza consciousness has been compared to Mary Louise Pratt's "contact zone,"[4] which builds upon the Afro-Cuban rhetorical concept of *transculturación*, I begin by explaining the parallels and differences of these expressions. The distinctions I draw here help further clarify the intervention my dissertation advances through positioning mestiza consciousness as a powerful rhetorical strategy. I then consider the field's first modern canonical incorporation of an Indigenous Mexican, Gloria Anzaldúa, in Patricia Bizzell and Bruce Herzberg's *The Rhetorical Tradition: Readings from Classical Times to the Present* (2001). The manner in which the editors translate Anzaldúa aligns nicely with the strategy of mestiza consciousness, of simultaneously working within and against Western practices. Building on the work of Bizzell and Herzberg, I then advance the prospect that mestiza consciousness promotes a more hemispheric conception of historical scholarship, and reflect upon three possible curricular models: Periodization, Spacialization, and Region versus Nation. Collectively, these frameworks weave the study of rhetoric across and beyond borders.

Mestiza Consciousness and the "Contact Zone"

In her influential "Arts of the Contact Zone" (1991), Mary Louise Pratt describes contact zones as "social spaces where cultures meet, clash, and grapple with each other, often in contexts of highly asymmetrical relations of power, such as colonialism, slavery, or their aftermaths as they are lived out in many parts of the world today" (530). Pratt explains that in order to understand a culture and its communiqués, academics need to perceive them within the layered context of the contact zone. It is noteworthy that due to "highly asymmetrical relations" between two cultures, the dominant culture's perspectives, rules, and conventions of expression are passed off as natural, universal, without provincial limitations. As a result, Pratt argues, descriptions of interactions between people in conversation readily take it for granted that the situation is governed by a single set of principles or norms shared by all participants. Despite whatever power conflicts or systematic social differences might be in play, the common assumption is that all involved are engaged in the same configuration and that the pattern is the same for all participants. Academics must be aware, Pratt notes, when speakers are from different cultures, or when one party exercises authority and another submits to or counters it.

Pratt's contact zone is structured upon the inventive analysis of Caribbean anthropologist Fernando Ortiz, who coined the term *transculturación* in 1940. In his *Cuban Counterpoint* (1947), Ortiz aims to correct a common Western misunderstanding of the complex discursive products and effects that respond to conflict under colonial situations:

> The word *transculturación* better expresses the different phases of the process of transition from one culture to another because this does not consist merely in acquiring another culture, which is what the English word *acculturation* really implies, but the process also necessarily involves the loss or uprooting of a previous culture, which could be defined as a deculturation. In addition, it carries the idea of the consequent creation of new cultural phenomena, which should be called neoculturation. In the end...the result of every union of cultures is similar to that of the reproductive process between individuals: the offspring always has something of both parents but is always different from each of them. (103)

Transculturación accounts for the transformative phases that unfold between two cultures, as they are enacted and understood in the mind of the colonized. Cuba, of course, emerged as a nation after the imperial war between the United States and Spain. In response to the material consequences of imperial conquest, *transculturación* is a strategic creation, a "new cultural phenomena" of inventing between opposing cultures. Ortiz' distinction between *transculturación* and acculturation is crucial, as Western academics often perceive reality through the dominant framework of conversion and assimilation.[5] Ortiz invents from a position of suspension between cultural worlds. *Transculturación*, then, is a creative strategy that correlates directly to three episodes:

1. Western imperial expansion in the Americas and the ensuing campaign to assimilate Mesoamerican, Mestiz@, Latin American cultures;
2. the rational emergence of Mesoamerican and Mestiz@ critical representation in response to European colonial power; and
3. the dynamic, perpetual reformulation of culture between these episodes.

Engaged in processes of *transculturación*, colonized agents select and invent from cultural materials transported by Western global expansion in order to, as Mary Louise Pratt might describe, "speakback" (36). Yet, rhetorical episodes such as Gloria Anzaldúa's *Borderlands*, for example, will be persistently misunderstood, mistranslated, and misappropriated unless comprehended as "new" rationalities and practices that emerge from the conditions created by colonial legacies. For writing specialists in rhetoric and composition, *transculturación* can provide a much-needed corrective to European-centered models of communication and pedagogy as well as the glaring omission of analyzing colonial power in the framework of language studies.

While Mary Louise Pratt builds her contact zone directly from *transculturación* and the rhetorics of colonized areas, she radically shifts her attention to another cultural location:

> Last year one of my children moved to a new elementary school that had more open classrooms and more flexible curricula than the conventional school he started out in. A few days into the term, we asked him what it was like at the new school. "Well," he said, "they're a lot nicer, and they have a lot less rules. But know why they're nicer?" "Why?" I asked. "So you'll obey all the rules they don't have," he replied. This is a very coherent analysis with considerable elegance and explanatory power, but probably not the one his teacher would have given. When linguistic (or literate) interaction is described in terms of orderliness, games, moves, or scripts, usually only legitimate moves are actually named as part of the system, where legitimacy is defined from the point of view of the party in authority, regardless of what other parties might see themselves as doing. Teacher-pupil language, for example, tends to be described almost entirely from the point of view of the teacher and teaching, not from the point of view of pupils and pupiling (the word doesn't even exist, though the thing certainly does). If a classroom is analyzed as a social world unified and homogenized

> with respect to the teacher, whatever students do other than what the teacher specifies is invisible or anomalous to the analysis. This can be true in practice as well. On several occasions my fourth-grader, the one busy obeying all the rules they didn't have, was given writing assignments that took the form of answering a series of questions to build up a paragraph. These questions often asked him to identify with the interests of those in power over him as parents, teachers, doctors, public authorities. He invariably sought ways to resist or subvert these assignments.[6]

For Pratt, *transculturación* in the contact zone is an analytic for American writing teachers to consider student reaction to classroom policies, the politics of following guidelines, why students feel pressures to mimic or absorb to the governing culture of the classroom, and their imaginative ways of negotiating, resisting, or undermining teacher authority. Pratt's fourth-grade teacher-pupil model is certainly noteworthy, though it significantly departs from the context and impetus of Ortiz' *transculturación*. Asymmetrical relationships between all teachers and all students are certainly not necessarily produced by the workings of colonial power. While Pratt compares the colonization of the Americas to the power dynamics between teachers and students, I would simultaneously call attention to the contrasts between them, beginning with a sustained examination of military conquest, genocide, and occupation in Mesoamerica beginning in the early sixteenth century. More to the point, I do not believe that the thinking of Pratt's fourth-grade child can be so easily paired with the thinking of an Afro-Cuban anthropologist. The formalized transmission of alphabetic literacy is unquestionably a powerful counterpart to the imperial domination of the "New World," and Pratt's comparison certainly welcomes further investigation of these ties. In fact, Anzaldúa's work does address classroom conflict and colonial composition pedagogy. In the following section of this chapter, it will be helpful to note how Anzaldúa's classroom experiences and consequent responses are recognizably distinct from Pratt's account above.

Mestiza consciousness and *transculturación* are complex articulations rooted in the lived colonial experiences of Western expansion. Pratt's narrative above is more in tune with power differences that transpire within imperial centers of adolescent schooling. Admittedly, Pratt's model of classroom conflict can share some similarities with mestiza consciousness and *transculturación*. It is useful, however, to avoid conflating Pratt's model with rhetorical strategies that were articulated from the colonial peripheries of

Western civilization. Moreover, due to Pratt's significant attention to fourth grade level instruction and resistance, I am uneasy with coupling Anzaldúa and Ortiz within this framework. The insinuation, even if vague, that juvenile literacy acquisition can help explain Afro-Cuban and Mestiz@ rhetorical resistance is not constructive. It will be helpful for composition specialists to consider the possibility that their colleagues of color and students of color may not find Pratt's equation of colonialism and elementary education to be empowering or enlightening without adequate classroom discussion of these critical issues.

As for comparisons between *transculturación* and mestiza consciousness, I believe some beneficial connections can be drawn. Both respond to the power of European colonial expansion in the twentieth century. Both invent from suspended positions between the hierarchical tensions of opposing cultures. Together, mestiza consciousness and *transculturación* will help teachers and students understand how colonized cultures adapt, resist, and reconstitute Western narratives of assimilation. Ortiz uses *transculturación* in the context of Cuban nation-building in the aftermath of U.S. and Spanish imperialism. Anzaldúa's mestiza consciousness, in partial contrast, looks outside the political boundaries of biological and national mestizaje as they are articulated along the México/U.S. borderlands. In this sense, the properties of mestiza consciousness, while certainly concerned with state powers, invite an augmentation and redefinition of nation-state subjectivity. Fleshing out these similarities and differences will benefit writing classroom inquiry. Part of this analysis might include teachers and students mutually piecing together the fusions and fissures of mestiza consciousness and *transculturación* while making connections between colonial critique and the mediating power of rhetoric. Pedagogical approaches along this line would involve thinking beyond the sentence level, toward broader theoretical frameworks across borders and cultures. Bizzell and Herzberg's recent collection offers a productive step in this direction.

The Rhetorical Tradition: Readings from Classical Times to the Present

Since the European Renaissance and European colonial expansion, the province of ancient Greece has been appropriated as the intellectual cradle of Western civilization.[7] In the tradition of European Enlightenment philosophy, many Western academics claim early

Greek culture as a universal contribution, often obscuring its regional and provincial genesis. It is frequently "forgotten" that persuasion, as it was observed and catalogued by elite male citizens in ancient Greece, is merely one discursive contribution among a global plurality of other cultural possibilities. Although rhetoric and composition scholarship often professes a concern for multiculturalism, the field does not always demonstrate an understanding of historical complexity outside its own disciplinary boundaries. In their second addition of *The Rhetorical Tradition*, Patricia Bizzell and Bruce Herzberg take steps to disengage from this limited cultural horizon by including "rhetorics of color," selections that evidence discursive practices and life experiences from the underside of Western global expansion. The editors pause in response to this act of inclusion, as the presence of "rhetorics of color" dislodges the primacy and normalcy of how the field might conventionally think about the Western rhetorical canon. Here's an excerpt from the preface:

> Because of the increased diversity in our selections, we considered changing the title of the anthology to *Rhetorical Traditions*. We realized, of course, that the singular title could appear to convey a monolithic view of human language-using potential. But upon reflection, we decided that all the writers we included really were working within a common Western tradition, even if reacting against it. (iv)

As for Gloria Anzaldúa, mestiza consciousness certainly does weave within and against Western linguistic and historiographic traditions. The question of whether "non-Western" selections can or should be incorporated into the Western tradition of Athenian rhetoric echoes a predicament of Europe's first encounter with Mesoamerica. In his prologue to "Rhetoric and Moral Philosophy" (1578) in the *Florentine Codex*, Franciscan ethnographer Bernardo de Sahagún writes,

> All nations, however savage and decadent they have been, have set their eyes on the wise and strong in persuading, on men prominent for moral virtues, and on the skilled and the brave in warlike exercises, and more on those of their own generation than on those of others. There are so many examples of this among the Greeks, the Latin, the Spaniards, the French, and the Italians...The same was practiced in this Indian nation, and especially among the Mexicans, among whom the wise, superior, and effective rhetoricians were held in high regard. And they elected these to be high priests, lords, leaders, and captains, no matter how humble their estate. These ruled the states, led the armies, and presided in temples... (1)

The issue of whether Mexican discursive practice can or should be translated into Western understandings of Athenian rhetoric is mired in a colonial double bind. Either Mexican "rhetorics" are so different from Greco-Roman ones that Western thinkers cannot consider them rhetoric proper. Or conversely, to be accepted, Mexican expression must become similar to and absorbed by Western conceptualizations of persuasive speech beginning with the observations of figures such as Aristotle in Athens or Corax in an Athenian outpost—observations that conceivably did not surface until hundreds of years following those of the ancient Mesoamericans.[8] By recognizing Anzaldúa as an entry that works simultaneously with and against Greco-Latin Western rhetoric, Bizzell and Herzberg welcome intellectual analysis beyond this hierarchical dichotomy.

Given the colonial legacy of Western rhetoric instruction in the "New World," the implications of Anzaldúa's inclusion in Bizzell and Herzberg's canon should not be overlooked. Western writing programs in the Americas were first instituted and managed by Spanish and then British immigrants and their Anglo descendents. These transplanted writing programs systematically ignored and marginalized Mesoamerican, American Indian inscription practices. Writing departments, from their colonial origin, have long promoted an education embedded in European traditions. Consequently, the accumulation of knowledge about rhetoric is aligned with the linear narrative of Western history. When confronted with non-Western selections, Bizzell and Herzberg naturally recognize the inadequacy of this limiting framework. The editors elaborate on their diversification of the long-standing canon:

> Thanks to new scholarship, however, we have been able to include more work by men and women of color and white women in this second edition, such as Mary Astell, Maria W. Stewart, Frederick Douglass, Virginia Wolf, and Gloria Anzaldúa. To be sure, much more needs to be done to recover and analyze the diverse components of Western rhetoric. The old canonical "major" names... still loom large. But we believe that a significantly greater number of European and European American women and African American and Hispanic women and men are represented here. We hope that these new additions will, at the very least, point to directions for future scholarship. (iv)

The idea that non-Western selections might also correspond to or parallel other equally valuable traditions would be a fruitful counterpart to the editors' explanation here. African and Mestiz@ voices could be analyzed as simultaneously contributing to dynamic traditions not necessarily accounted for by Western cultural horizons.

Given my investigation of three curricular models in the following section of this chapter, I will briefly underscore how the chronology of *The Rhetorical Tradition* remains organized according to pseudoscientific periodizations that geographically parallel Western global expansion: Classical, Medieval, Renaissance, Enlightenment, Nineteenth Century, Modern, and Postmodern. Classical Rhetoric (c. 470BCE–400CE) covers ancient Greece and imperial Rome with an emphasis on Aristotelian observations and their elaboration by the orator Cicero and educator Quintilian. The Medieval Rhetoric period (400CE–1400) remains tied to the Christian-Byzantine expansion of rhetoric and includes selections from renowned theologian Augustine. Notably, the powerful tool of persuasion was significant to the advent of imperial Roman Christendom. For the Renaissance (1400–1700), the editors attend primarily to the rhetorical practices of Italian and Northern European humanists including Desiderius Erasmus and Francis Bacon.

Bizzell and Herzberg's Enlightenment Rhetoric period (late seventeenth century to eighteenth century) covers the taxonomies, classifications, and debates forwarded by prominent figures such as British philosopher John Locke and Scottish philosophers David Hume and George Campbell. The nineteenth century examines works of European women on both sides of the Atlantic and the rise of Anglo composition practices in North America. The disparate selections of Maria Steward and Sarah Grimké appear alongside Alexander Bain and Adams Sherman Hill. Bizzell and Herzberg in part address the early U.S./African diaspora with abridged selections from ex-slave and abolitionist Frederick Douglass. Finally, the Modern and Postmodern Twentieth Century exemplifies the editor's increased attention to rhetorics of color. Selected passages from Gloria Anzaldúa's *Borderlands* and Henry Louis Gates Jr.'s *Signifying Monkey* are treated under a subheading "Rhetorics of Gender, Race, and Culture."

Given Bizzell and Herzberg's expressed concern with the "increased diversity" (iv) of Western Rhetoric, their low representation of minority selections might have been expanded to include a more inclusive account of influential intellectuals of color. A research trend in African-American women's rhetorics prior to the second edition of *The Rhetorical Tradition* could help expand the field's understanding of human meaning-making practices in nineteenth and twentieth centuries.[9] A substantial amount of rhetorical scholarship is also available on prominent African-American figures like black nationalist Malcolm X, for example, whose revolutionary rhetoric has been analyzed for almost four decades and counting.[10] Selections such as these would further encourage teachers and students to examine the interrelations between rhetoric, resistance, education, sovereignty, and the struggle for human justice. Because in the quote above, Bizzell and Herzberg indicate that they include Hispanic men in their new edition of *The Rhetorical Tradition* (iv), I would encourage them to in fact do so. Available research on the rhetorics of Mestiz@ labor leader Caesar Chavez,[11] who organized one of the first successful farm workers union in North America, is worth consideration here.

It is no coincidence that "rhetorics of color" arrive at a critical stage of Western development in North America. Under this mantle, it is possible to interpret scholars of color as but an addendum to the looming historical progression of Westward expansion and assimilation. Bizzell and Herzberg's description of Anzaldúa's theoretical contribution suggests a possible corrective to this hierarchical narrative. The editors introduce *Borderlands/La Frontera*:

> Anzaldúa pioneers the use of new discursive resources for women writers, particularly women of color, by mixing dialects of English and Spanish, analytic and autobiographical material, and formal and informal genres...a "mestiza rhetoric," with "mestiza" referring not only to the specific racial and cultural mixing that has produced the Mexican American people, but also to a more generalized concept of internal multiplicity, or complex identity, that is expressed in language drawn from a variety of cultural sources. (1583)

Anzaldúa does indeed mix discourses and voices. I have argued throughout this book that mestiza consciousness advances a new rhetorical strategy of inventing between Mesoamerican and Western worlds. Through symbolic exchanges of intermediacy and border crossing, mestiza consciousness resists the European-imposed axis of progress and assimilation. Overlapping and converging disparate worldviews effectively subverts the linear configuration of conversion and assimilation. By inventing from Anzaldúa's conceptual borderlands, we are no longer obliged to compose under the hierarchical construct of Eurocentric designs. In addition to describing Anzaldúa's rhetoric as a "generalized concept of internal multiplicity," I would add that it is also a culturally explicit means of challenging colonial structures of power as they continue to unfold across the Americas.

The Rhetorical Tradition's historical progression runs parallel with the colonial expansion of Western imperialism. Anzaldúa's *Borderlands/ La Frontera*, however, subverts this monolithic trajectory by highlighting and critiquing the colonial powers embedded in this history. Bizzell and Herzberg's chosen selection "How to Tame a Wild Tongue" appropriately addresses moments of colonial conflict and dissonance as they occur at formal sites of literacy instruction. Here's an excerpt from *Borderlands*:

> I remember being caught speaking Spanish at recess—that was good for three licks on the knuckles with a sharp ruler. I remember being sent to the corner of the classroom for "talking back" to the Anglo teacher when all I was trying to do was tell her how to pronounce my name. "If you want to be American, speak 'American.' If you don't like it, go back to Mexico where you belong."
>
> "I want you to speak English. *Pa' hallar buen trabajo tienes que saber hablar el inglés. Qué vale toda tu educación si todovia hablas inglés con un* 'accent,'" my mother would say, mortified that I spoke English like a Mexican. At Pan American University, I, and all Chicano students were required to take two speech classes. Their purpose: to get rid of our accents.
>
> Attacks on one's form of expression with the intent to censor are a violation of the First Amendment.
> *El Anglo con cara de inocente nos arrancó la lengua.*
> Wild tongues can't be tamed, they can only be cut out. (75–76)

Physical retribution for speaking Spanish go hand in hand with the psychological discord created when English dominance is confronted by the countercultural memories infused in Anzaldúa's Spanish admixtures. Her English instructor not only fails to pronounce Anzaldúa properly but also translates her correction as a marker of insubordination. The pedagogical suggestion "go back to Mexico where you belong," whether explicit or implicit, demonstrates yet another mistranslation, one of historic proportions. In 1845, the United States waged war against Mexico in order to expand its slave plantation economy and secure key territories along the Pacific Coast. Inhabitants of Mexico's northern-most regions became officially incorporated into the United States after the signing of the Treaty of Guadalupe Hidalgo in 1848. Several Mexican communities were culturally displaced under this new imperialist era of Western economic and linguistic dominance. It is noteworthy that the English instructor enacts a pedagogical barrier that obscures the violent realities of Mexico's conquest and its aftermath.

As the forces of English literacy instruction colonize from the top down, Anzaldúa encounters family pressures from the bottom up. Anzaldúa's mother explains, "Pa' hallar buen trabajo tienes que saber hablar el inglés. Qué vale toda tu educación si todovia hablas inglés…," which translates as "To find good work you have to know how to speak English. What good is all your education if you speak English with an accent?" Classroom pressures are layered with familial anxiety and market demands to assimilate under the hegemonic discourse of commerce and academic advancement. Refusing to convert her accent, Anzaldúa declares, "El Anglo con cara de inocente nos arrancó la lengua." The Spanish verb *arrancar* refers to the act of uprooting and is frequently applied in agricultural contexts. Anzaldúa's passage in English reads, "The innocent faced Anglo ripped out our tongue." The rejection of taming and subjugating one's own language is a recurring theme throughout *Borderlands/La Frontera.*

In addition to the textual interplay between Castilian Spanish and English, Anzaldúa's writing weaves multiple language varieties and translations between Spanglish, Chicano Spanish, Pachuco, Tex-Mex, Quechua, and *Nahuatl.* By placing herself at the crossroads and thinking between languages, Anzaldúa reinvents and reconstitutes divergent cultural memories through serpentine rhetorics of the border, both real and symbolic. In an earlier passage in *Borderlands*, Anzaldúa addresses the nomadic life of the new mestiza (24–25). Anzaldúa's migratory narrative across "dangerous terrain" enacts a symbolic trespassing, an infraction against European-imposed borders. Regional and historical realities of the México/U.S. border are not obscured but recodified in order to address political struggles of the colonial present. Metaphorically occupying the thin edge of barbwire demonstrates the tension of Anzaldúa's rhetorical interchangeability. This tension is enacted through repeated sequences of linguistic reversals, alternate voices, and continued weaving within and between opposing worldviews. Anzaldúa's textual choreography invites reading practices that graphically weave out of one culture and into another. By straddling Mesoamerican, Spanish, and Anglo-European languages, mestiza consciousness intervenes in the Western narrative of assimilation.

VII

Thinking and Teaching Across Borders and Hemispheres

Expanding Anzaldúa's subversive act of translation from its linguistic conception to its symbolic and rhetorical potential adds significantly to the possibility of new approaches in rhetoric and composition scholarship. Anzaldúa's fusing of Spanish worldviews into English and *Nahuatl* views into Spanish and back again promotes a new strategy of invention. Anzaldúa invites the crossing of linguistic boundaries and the possibility of inventing between the historical memories engrained in each language. Variable combinations of interweaving, crossovers, and reversals at the sentence level correspond with the larger potential of inventing across coevolutionary and parallel cultural histories. Historical memory is no longer limited to the barriers imposed by Western global expansion and its hierarchical configuration of assimilation. If positioned as a point of origin, Anzaldúa's mestiza consciousness would revise and enlarge the frameworks used to account for histories of rhetoric and writing. Anzaldúa's aesthetic and theoretical strategy promotes new frameworks that transform the borders of Eurocentric history. As a result, hemispheric and coevolutionary ways of reading composition and rhetoric become possible.

Frameworks and Models

It is my aim that the issues raised in this chapter add a sense of urgency to the chorus of "minority" academics welcoming Western rhetoric specialists to revise their dominant historical narratives and stretch the boundaries of U.S. composition.[1] Taken together, these appeals make a compelling case for enlarging the frameworks that composition and rhetoric specialists use to study and teach the history of writing. I argue that Anzaldúa's discursive strategies call for rethinking traditional ideas of Western uniqueness and isolation by examining cross-cultural comparisons and connections across the globe. Anzaldúa herself argues for the need to think across cultures and borders and the building of unity between Chicanos, undocumented and displaced laborers, Mexicanos, indigenous communities across all imposed borders, afro-mestizos, and the collective histories of resistance.[2] To invent from this locality, one must gain an understanding not only of the U.S. border, but also of the cultures of greater Mexico, the Caribbean, Mesoamerica, and Africa, and their collective resistance to Western expansion. Anzaldúa's mestiza consciousness emphasizes the need for wider geographic and temporal contexts in order to trace the roots of globalization as well as to understand the trajectory of the United States' rise to global power. The growing presence of this nation across the planet makes it even more crucial to understand the histories and memories of America held by those in its borderlands. At the same time, looking at U.S. history from its colonial peripheries can help writing teachers better understand ideas, movements, economies, and environments larger than the nation-state.

Mestiza consciousness, if positioned at the center of a curriculum, would encourage an unmistakably more hemispheric approach to rhetoric and composition scholarship. Starting with a rhetorical study of borders and racialized identities, for example, composition specialists could expand their analyses across borders and oceans to examine hemispheric patterns of migration, education, identity construction, and state formation. The question is not whether globalization will influence the field. Western rhetoric and composition studies are already directly implicated in globalizing processes. Rather, the question is how the field will proceed and how it might shape the teaching of rhetoric and writing in a global world. Therefore, what would happen to rhetoric and composition history as the writing curriculum moves toward a more inclusive, coevolutionary approach?

In its traditional framework, the curriculum may become a relic of nation-based historiography to be discarded as scholars distance themselves from the project of transmitting national myths and the forming of national citizens. If the curriculum grows, however, how might it transform to reflect a more hemispheric conception of writing and rhetoric across and beyond U.S. borders? As a focal point,

Anzaldúa's mestiza consciousness could suggest the need for undergraduate and graduate level study in coevolutionary, parallel rhetorics. A more hemispheric and global understanding of writing would of course continue to provide opportunity for further study of the European and Anglo-American practices that we learn about from rhetoric and composition history. Radically different, however, would be the transformation of texts such as the *Rhetorical Tradition* as merely one contribution among a plurality of other suitable possibilities. A new curriculum would emphasize connections, comparisons, and interpretive frameworks across and beyond national boundaries. I will now suggest three promising modifications that mestiza consciousness may bring to the curriculum: Spacialization, Periodization, and Region versus Nation.

Spacialization

Where does American composition history begin? For decades the conventional starting points have been limited to the British North American colonies.[3] Anzaldúa's mestiza consciousness would require going further back in time as well as confronting an extended geographic reach. Consequently, teachers could take time to examine the roles writing played within Spanish, Portuguese, French, and Dutch Empires as they expanded to the Western Hemisphere. Texts such as Rolena Adorno's *Guaman Poma: Writing and Resistance in Colonial Peru* and José Rabasa's *Writing Violence on the Northern Frontier: The Historiography of Sixteenth-Century New Mexico and Florida and the Legacy of Conquest* directly address some of these issues. Embracing larger geographies across Mesoamerica when studying writing involves critiquing the hierarchical progression from Greece to Rome to Western Europe to North America. New spacializations would encourage teachers and students to question this linearity by confronting the very colonial invention of the "New World." Rhetoric and writing seminars that embrace new spacializations would benefit significantly from Walter Mignolo's illuminating *The Darker Side of the Renaissance: Literacy, Territoriality, and Colonization*. By carefully investigating the coexisting territorialities of Mesoamerica and imperial Spain, Mignolo promotes a coevolutionary understanding of alphabetic and pictographic cultures, thereby offering a variety of curricular possibilities.

The Darker Side of the Renaissance chronicles the role of writing and writing instruction in Spain's violent campaign of Christianization.

By locating European forms of literacy as a foundation of Mesoamerican subjugation, Mignolo examines how alphabetic writing is linked directly to colonial relations of power. Furthermore, Mignolo examines the role of the Western conception of "the book" in colonial relations, and the numerous connections between writing, social organization, and political control. Starting with the contrasts between Mesoamerican and European writing systems, Mignolo investigates different understandings of books, codices, and *amoxtli* as texts and analyzes linguistic descriptions and mapping techniques in relation to the construction of territorializing cultural space. A primary vehicle for colonizing the cultural space of the Western Hemisphere was its deliberate remapping as a geopolitical periphery of Western civilization:

> Putting the Americas on the map from the European perspective was not necessarily a task devoted to finding the true shape of the earth; it was also related to controlling territories and colonizing the imagination of people on both sides of the Atlantic: Amerindians and Europeans. The spread of European literacy in the New World colonies transmitted a conception of the world projected in European cartography. The spread of cultural literacy in Europe showed the educated European the nature of an unknown continent. Economic expansion, technology, and power, rather than truth, is what characterized European cartography early on, as well as the national cartography of the Americas at a later date. (281)

The emergence of the geographic idea of the New World is formed within a hierarchical imaginary that proclaims one region as "civilized" and the other as "barbarian." Disengaging from this dichotomous frame involves reinscribing and interrogating Mesoamerica and imperial Spain as coexisting territorialities.

To paraphrase Mignolo, the expression "coexisting" shares two implications: coexistence in the Western Hemisphere since conquest, and coexistence in the same graphic space of two territorial descriptions. The first refers to the physical occupation of territories as well as to graphic alternatives to a Mesoamerican conceptualization of space implemented by the Spanish administration and spread by alphabetic literacy. The second refers to a practice perceived during the first century of colonization whereby Mesoamerican territorial descriptions (or mapping) cohabit on the same piece or flat surface on which the territory has been described.[4] By including the diverse Mesoamerican inscription practices such as codices and lienzos,

Mignolo widens intellectual possibilities no longer limited to European documentation or documentation practices. From this cross-cultural moment in the early sixteenth century, Mignolo engages readers in seeing from a fractured, subalternized Mesoamerican perspective to perceive the world as coexisting territorialities within the same conceptual space (246).

In his chapter "The Movable Center: Ethnicity, Geometric Projections, and Coexisting Territorialities," Mignolo focuses on the intersection of European, Aztec, and Inca worldviews of geography. From Europe's point of view, the Americas formed the planet's fourth continent that would become part of a globalized organization in which Europe would later self-proclaim itself as the planetary center during the Germanic Enlightenment. Anahuac, in contrast, is the Aztec spacialization for the region today known as central Mexico. Moreover, this conceptualization of space does not require distinctions between the order of the land, the larger sacred cosmology, and the count of the year. Anahuac interweaves these properties as an articulation that simultaneously reveals history, prophecy, and subsequent behaviors and methods for organizing geographic space. The Incas of the Andes, Mignolo points out, likewise organized space and time along similar lines. Tahuantinsuyu, which can be translated as "the land of the four parts," was the geographical and political center of Cuzco. The four quadrants of Tahuantinsuyu also include "upper" and "lower" celestial components. As a fundamental organizing structure, this perspective likewise does not disconnect spirituality from rationality or the sacred from the spatial.

That all of these sixteenth-century communities organized themselves according to their respective cosmologies is helpful for rhetoric and writing scholars looking for inclusive ways to study and teach rhetoric and composition history. Mignolo's research calls upon new spacializations that challenge composition specialists with the assertion that knowing and writing are informed by territoriality. *The Darker Side of the Renaissance*, which Mignolo admits is heavily influenced by Anzaldúa's mestiza consciousness (13), promotes a classroom strategy for inventing and teaching from divergent spacializations of the New World. American composition pedagogies could build upon cultural memories far more expansive than those suggested by 1874 models of freshman entrance essays at Harvard University. Along with Mignolo's text as a focal point of analysis, a new rhetoric and composition curriculum might examine the *Codex Espangliensis: From Columbus to the Border Patrol*, which I analyzed at length in chapter 4. As I have argued, this revisionist text is understood as a discursive manifestation of Mesoamerican continuity and adaptation in the colonial present. Rhetorical fusions and fissures between different spacializations and divergent writing practices work, like mestiza consciousness, to bridge the separation between Mesoamerican and "Later American" geographies through a subversive narrative that revises hierarchical orders of Anglo-European territorialization. The *Codex* visualizes not America, but many Americas: Mesoamerica and its conquest, an occupied periphery of the Spanish Cross and Crown, Mexican terrain, and U.S. dominance.

Partnering the *Codex Espangliensis* with Mignolo's *Darker Side of the Renaissance* coincides directly with curricular and pedagogical possibilities implied by Gloria Anzaldúa. *Borderlands/La Frontera* likewise invites readers to envision many American spacializations. As a rhetorical strategy, mestiza consciousness straddles the contradictory territorial borders between Aztlán, Anahuac, Nueva España, northern México, and the southwest United States. Aztlán is the mythical homeland of the Aztec, who eventually established the Triple Alliance at *Tenochtitlán* beginning in 1100 ADE, Mesoamerica's most powerful political and administrative center. Anahuac, as described above, is the *Nahuatl* expression for central México before European invasion. Meanwhile, Nueva España refers to the reterritorialization of Mesoamerica as a Spanish imperial periphery. The northern region of México refers to the homestead of the Anzaldúa family cluster that was split in 1848 after the war between the United States and Mexico. After the signing of the Treaty of Guadalupe Hidalgo, the geographic identification of El Norte de México abruptly became the southwestern border region under U.S. occupation. Interweaving and inventing between these territorial borderlands becomes a powerful strategy for resisting the hierarchical tensions among them.

The texts mentioned above support much more hemispheric and expanded spacializations that link neatly to other possible sources for a new composition curriculum. The *National Standards for United States History* (1994), for example, labels the period prior to 1620 as an era when "three worlds meet" (1), thereby encouraging an increased classroom attention to pre-Contact histories of the Americas as well as Africa. Composition courses could be transformed to examine a broader North American spacialization along with Mesoamerican cultures, empires, and trade networks that thrived long before European settlers, their descendents, and the emergence of their higher education institutions. By starting this early in space and time, composition and rhetoric history seminars could examine the roots and legacies of Mesoamerican pictographic record-keeping practices. Elizabeth Boone Hill's *Writing Without Words: Alternative Literacies in Mesoamerica and the Andes* as well as her *Stories in Red and Black: Pictorial Histories of the Aztecs and Mixtecs* would provide helpful accounts in such seminars. Equally useful are Mexican historian Miguel León-Portilla's landmark accounts of *Huehuetlahtolli* instruction at the *Calmecac* conservatories. León-Portilla's *In the Language of Kings: An Anthology of Mesoamerican Literature, Pre-Columbian to the Present* would be especially insightful for professors and students who seek a greater understanding of diverse inscription conventions beyond alphabetic and syllabic systems as they are studied today. These new spacializations, moreover, would not be limited to investigating some territories while overlooking others.

A curriculum might, for example, consider various West African kingdoms and civilizations that were altered by contact with European as well as Arab traders. Recast as the geographic space where Europeans, Africans, and First Nations Peoples converged, the regional colonies that eventually formed in North America would thus be interpreted as a complex and often-troubled legacy of cultural conflict and domination. This will motivate deeper classroom analysis of the fact that higher education institutions and composition programs in the United States do not exist in a cultural vacuum, without cultural roots or limitations. Western writing programs are instead embedded in a historical web of transatlantic imperialism and colonial trade. Conventional composition texts that cover early U.S. history could be paired with Latin American and African philosopher Lewis Gordon's *Her Majesty's Other Children: Sketches of Racism from a Neocolonial Age* to better understand how race, racism, and identity emerge from colonialism. This trend of widening horizons and moving further back in time suggests that a more hemispheric approach to rhetoric and composition that is aligned with Walter Mignolo's proposal for reinscribing coexisting territorialities. Collectively, these sources offer multiple spaces and starting points for new narratives that generate, analyze, and contest American histories of rhetoric and writing.

A new curriculum might also feature greater consideration of North America's role beyond its national borders. Highlighting American political, diplomatic, and military activities abroad would also help teachers imagine a more coevolutionary past of writing and rhetoric. Especially in response to the September 11 attacks and the U.S. intervention and occupation of Afghanistan and Iraq, composition specialists could underscore past events that might correspond to contemporary situations. Stressing prior U.S. military interventions in México and Central America, for example, will further call into question the naturalized progression and expansion of Western power, rhetoric, and writing conventions across the globe. By starting with a wide-angle, transatlantic, or hemispheric view of contact and colonialism, the curriculum would be more responsive to the role of writing and rhetoric within larger spatial and globalizing processes. The 1846 war against México or the Spanish-American war of 1898, for example, could be viewed as significant stages of U.S. nation-building and hemispheric involvement.

If the curriculum were thoroughly rethought through mestiza consciousness, then composition's usual coverage of Anglo-American history would also be revised. As noted in the *National Standards for World History*, between 1750 and 1914, "the history of the United States...was not self-contained but fully embedded in the context of global change" (203). Addressing this connectedness involves sustained attention to spacializations outside the nation-state imaginary and a continuous engagement with the ways that North American political and economic developments impact world events. This is the first and perhaps most fundamental of the new changes implied by mestiza consciousness.

It could be argued that from early on, events in the peripheries of the United States have always corresponded to its center. As historian Paul Gagnon writes, American history "should make it plain that the bell tolled for us when the Portuguese began African slave-trading in 1444, when the French invaded Saigon in 1859, when the Japanese humiliated Czar Nicholas in 1905, [and] when Franz Ferdinand was assassinated in 1914" (46). At the same time, from the Columbian exchange onward, North American organisms, products, and political ideas have initiated important transformations around the world. Simultaneous with these two-way global connections, and partly because of them, the Americas and the Caribbean have experienced parallel developments that provide opportunities for coevolutionary comparisons. The trajectory of the United States as a European settler society that subjugated Mexicans and other indigenous groups, imported African slaves, industrialized, and built universities and colleges unified by monolingual composition instruction should be compared to the experiences of other cultures that were forged during the advent of Western expansion.

A variant of this geographic opening of composition and rhetoric would be to use a number of non-American societies as comparative focal points, thus incorporating a sustained transnational dialogue or multinational conversation throughout the curriculum. Historian Carl Guarneri suggests three reference groups appropriate for such comparisons:

> 1. other European "white settler societies" in Latin America, Canada, Australia, and South Africa that confronted aboriginal groups and moved from colonial status to independent nationhood;
> 2. western European nations that forged transatlantic connections with the United States and underwent similar political, social, and industrial trends; and
> 3. the new political and industrial world powers of the twentieth century, Japan and Russia.... The early national history of the United States, for example, suggests striking parallels with the strife-torn and dependent situation of developing nations in Asia and Africa. (48)

Perhaps composition history teachers may not have immediate access to past or contemporary materials on Asia, Africa, Japan, or Russia. But localizing such coevolutionary comparisons by focusing on First Nations Peoples within the United States is likewise a useful approach. Malea Powell's "Blood and Scholarship" and Scott Lyons' "Rhetorical Sovereignty" are reference points closer to the field that are especially helpful for teachers and students to begin thinking within, against, and across national borders.

Periodization

When did composing practices begin in the Americas? What should educators do with rhetorical traditions unique to the Western Hemisphere, with beginnings suggested by the memories of Mesoamerica rather than of Greece or the Aryan-Germanic Enlightenment? A second possible curricular development implied by mestiza consciousness involves greater attention to periodizing composition and rhetoric history. Anzaldúa's rhetorical border crossings would link familiar Western events and movements to counterparts elsewhere, thereby revising traditional chronologies "from Ancient Greece to Modern America" while simultaneously promoting new ones. Rethinking periodization includes a deeper historical outline that is no longer restricted to the pseudoscientific division of time into the categories of Classical, Medieval, Renaissance, Enlightenment, Nineteenth Century, Modern, and Postmodern. The critique implied here is not of Patricia Bizzell and Bruce Herzberg's organization of *The Rhetorical Tradition*, but of the field's dominant historical narrative limits thinking otherwise across time. Liberation philosopher Enrique Dussel's *The Invention of the Americas: Eclipse of "the Other" and the Myth of Modernity* effectively articulates a new paradigm of temporal sequences that break from these virtually unquestioned chronological categories. Dussel forwards the argument that although these dominant periodizations are undoubtedly European occurrences, they originate in dialectical relationship with Europe's colonial peripheries. Moreover, Dussel persuasively disengages from Western Europe's reductionist horizon by affirming a more hemispheric and planetary perspective of chronology and culture.

In *The Invention of the Americas* Dussel forwards the thesis that modernity is a conceptual by-product of Western Europe's emergence as an imperial global center, thereby creating what he defines as the Eurocentric fallacy:

> Modernity appears when Europe organizes the initial world-system and places itself at the center of world history over against a periphery equally constitutive of modernity. The forgetting of the periphery, which took place from the end of the fifteenth, Hispanic-Lusitanian century to the beginning of the seventeenth century, has led great thinkers of the center to commit the Eurocentric fallacy in understanding modernity. Because of a partial, regional, and *provincial* grasp of modernity, the postmodern critique and Habermas's defense of modernity are equally unilateral and partially false. The traditional Eurocentric thesis, flourishing in the United States, modernity's culmination, is that modernity expanded to the barbarian cultures of the South undoubtedly in need of modernization. One can only explain this new-sounding but age-old thesis by returning to medieval Europe to discover the motives which produced modernity and permitted its dissemination. (9–10)

The Eurocentric fallacy refers to the West hierarchically expanding into a world "in need" of Europe's self-described supreme characteristics such as alphabetic literacy. Organizing world chronology that moves according to this logic, from Antiquity to the Middle Ages to Modernity and Postmodernity, is a construct that deforms localized periodizations across the planet. A revised curriculum in rhetoric and writing with Dussel's thesis in mind would first welcome classroom discussion of the Eurocentric fallacy and its potential implications for the field. With a greater awareness of Eurocentrism as Dussel articulates it, teachers could also develop a more detached stance toward postmodern theory as it applied to composition classrooms.[5] A primary pedagogical lesson, that the discipline's long-held periodizations are related to the geopolitics of Western expansion, would assist teachers and students as they together sort out the parallel histories of the field and colonial subjugation.

A new curriculum that accepts analysis of the Eurocentric fallacy might also point toward progressive directions for composition teachers searching for new ways to study and teach the interrelations between writing, rhetoric, empire, and the myth of modernity. Reading and critiquing these colonial relations is crucial, as Dussel asserts that modernity obscures its own domination and violence. The myth of modernity is described as follows:

> 1. Europe is more developed; its civilization is superior to others (major premise of all *Eurocentrism*).
> 2. A culture's abandonment of its barbarity and underdevelopment through a civilizing process implies, as a conclusion, progress, development, well-being, and *emancipation* for that culture. According to the *fallacy of development* [developmentalism], the more developed culture has already trod this path of modernization.
> 3. As a first corollary, one defends Europe's domination over other cultures as a *necessary*, pedagogic violence (just war), which produces civilization and modernization. In addition, one justifies the anguish of the other culture as the necessary price of its civilization and expiation for its culpable immaturity.
> 4. As a second corollary, the conquistador appears to be not only *innocent*, but meritorious for inflicting this necessary, pedagogic violence.
> 5. As a third corollary, the conquered victims are culpable for their own violent conquest and for their own victimization... (66, italics in original)

This constructive examination can be placed directly aside the field's foundational claim that rhetoric and writing hierarchically advance East-to-West across the globe from ancient Greece to imperial Rome to the Germanic Enlightenment only to triumphantly develop in eighteenth-century British American settler societies. Rethinking rhetoric and composition pedagogy in light of these colonial periodizations is a vital new direction for a curriculum based on Anzaldúa's mestiza consciousness.

Dussel's proposal furthermore disengages from the periodization and ideological framework of modernity altogether. In a chapter titled "Amerindia in a Non-Eurocentric Vision of World History," Dussel refuses the Eurocentric deformation of Mesoamericans and affirms the Western Hemisphere as a continent humanized in its totality prior to European conquest and subjugation. Dussel offers an archaeologically and historically plausible reconstruction beginning with the birth of agriculture and cities in Mesoamerican as well as parallel developments in Mesopotamia, Egypt, China, and the Pacific Ocean region. Arguing that these cultures do not serve merely as an ancient era anteceding European culture but as pillars of world history in their own right (75), Dussel invites a new consciousness for periodizing the globe. In his account of the Western Hemisphere, Dussel affirms native articulations for the expanse of the continent: the *Cemanáhuac* of the Aztec, the *Abya Yala* of the *Cunas* of Panama, and the *Tahuantinsuyu* of the Incas (81). Classroom inquiry that begins with these cultural legacies alone will denaturalize Anglo-American dates of origin for rhetoric and composition, thereby welcoming productive analysis of nonwhite, non-Western communicative practices.

Here's an example: Dussel examines the *Tupi-Guaraní*, who inhabited the Amazon forests in the Paraguay region, noting how their existence revolved around a belief in the word as a sacred governing structure for all life. The *Guaraní* affirmed words as a person's initial nucleus, with what is translated as the "word-soul" forming a person's essence. When each *Guaraní* would receive a name, the community would interpret and celebrate the naming ritual through ceremonial dance. To paraphrase Dussel, words founded and made stand each human existence as it "opened-in-flower" at birth, guiding the nature of social organization (85). The communitarian and economic system of the *Guaraní* depended upon the word, as it provided the means to calculate achievement and crisis depending on its formation. Dussel continues,

> How could one ever express all this to the conquistador of the Rio de la Plata...Those *barbarian*, indigenous peoples...deeply worshiped the eternal, sacred, historical word among the tropical forests. To know their world, one would have had to know their tongue, their word, and to have lived it. To dialogue with them, one would have to

> inhabit their world...so beautiful, profound, rational, ecological, developed, and human...However, when the conditions for such conversation were not even in place, as occurred among the Eurocentric conquistadores, conversation became impossible, as did any argumentation in a *real communication community*. (87)

A new curriculum might counter the ideological construct of modernity by embracing new periodizations that no longer obscure First Nations peoples from the realm of history, rhetoric, and composition. The field might then avoid pedagogies embedded within the hierarchical logic of modernity and its theoretical extensions. Dussel's proposal of "transmodernity," an amplified rationality that recognizes and affirms the reason and humanity of the colonized, can lead to promising new pedagogies of cross-cultural dialogue.

As a deliberate strategy to promote dialogue no longer constrained by descendents of the American Puritan colonies, a new curriculum might engage teachers and students in metaphorically joining the much larger conversation of writing and rhetoric across the Western Hemisphere. Coevolutionary, hemispheric periodizations and starting points could welcome further studies of the *Guaraní* or the Aztec. A constructive curriculum would not reduce the *Guaraní* word-soul or the Aztec *Huehuetlahtolli* as mere "alternatives" to, for example, British American belletristic traditions at Harvard University. Classroom discussion might instead envision these as coexisting episodes in the larger study of communicative practice and human meaning making potential. Part of this project involves reprovincializing modernity and its periodizations by placing them in a center-periphery system that is itself a consequence of European conquest. Using Dussel's *The Invention of the Americas*, a new curriculum might integrate composition and rhetoric history into the conceptual schema of World-System theory. A graduate level course designed with this in mind might ask teachers and students to situate U.S. composition history within global interpretive constructs such as the rise of European modernity and Western planetary colonization.

World-System theory was introduced by social scientist Immanuel Wallerstein in his *The Modern World System: Capitalist Agriculture and the Origins of the European World Economy in the Sixteenth Century* (1974), which remains highly influential among world historians and historical sociologists. World-System theory traces the development of an integrated world economy since the fifteenth century. This economy was dominated by the wealthy and powerful core nations of Western Europe and gradually brought distant regions on its periphery into dependence upon a capitalist market. Broadly applied to rhetoric studies, this approach would organize analyses around the dominant periodizations of Christianization, the Civilizing Mission, Development/Modernization, and Global Market. Christianization, as I point out in earlier chapters, refers to the wide-scale Spanish campaign that colonized Mesoamerica beginning in the early sixteenth century. While the Spanish Empire and its imperial reign eventually seceded, the legacies of this ex-colonial power endure. The Civilizing Mission is linked to Spanish invasion and is primarily associated with the subsequent advances by the British Empire and French colonization in North America and Africa. Development/Modernization refers to a critical stage of national expansion that commenced with the war against México in the mid-nineteenth century. The present-day era of globalization, Global Market, is supported by nation-states but is largely driven by transnational corporate entities. Although this era is often characterized by heightened immigration, political conflict, diminishing geographical distances and permeable national borders, World-System theory would affirm that these phenomena link to and transpire within prior eras. When applied to composition's fixation with U.S. history, a World-System approach could begin with North America as an outpost on the world periphery, increasingly enmeshed in the web of colonization, mercantilism, and the slave trade.

In the 1890s, when the frontier was officially closed, the U.S. commenced its national expansion in other territories. For the twenty-first century, a World-System approach demonstrates that composition can be effectively analyzed as it is implicated in the global periodization and rise of Western imperialism. After independence, it could be argued that the United States embarks upon a course followed by other peripheral states as it consolidates national institutions, develops export production, industrializes and exerts control over its own region through formal composition instruction and other methods. Rhetoric and writing courses based on Dussel's Eurocentric fallacy and Wallerstein's World-System scaffolding would thoroughly trace North America's trajectory from the periphery to the center of the world system, or as historian Michael Adas puts it, "from settler colony to global hegemon" (1692).

Inventing new curricular possibilities "from settler colony to global hegemon" can help practitioners revise the dominant narrative "from Ancient Greece to Modern America." The distinction between these two trajectories is noteworthy: one calls explicit attention to the advance of colonial power across borders and oceans whereas the other too often passively inscribes itself within a triumphant imperial mythology. In this light, the conventional body of knowledge referred to as rhetoric and composition history can potentially be reexamined as part of a larger dominant narrative that displaces older, localized spacializations and periodizations across the globe. To return to the epigraph of writing specialist Robert Connors on the nature of rhetoric and composition history,

> We are part of a discipline that is twenty-five hundred years old, and our continuity from Aristotle and the earliest rhetoricians cannot now be doubted by anyone. Our history is its own justification...[6]

While this passage certainly does not mirror the views of all rhetoric and composition practitioners, it is unfortunate that more historical scholarship has not specifically and directly challenged Connors' assertions. Structuring one's scholarly horizon around Connors' idea of Western chronological continuity severely undermines possibilities of building an intellectually expansive curriculum. Pedagogies that support Connors' lineage shut out other worldviews and voices from participating in the disciplinary conversation thereby undermining the ability of diverse scholarly projects to intervene in effective center-periphery dialogue. New curricula in the twenty-first century will need to build not upon the myth of a linear Greco-Roman genealogy but upon the reality that the immense cultural majority of women and men living in the Western Hemisphere do not now nor have they ever shared Connors' emotional and rational attachment to ancient Greek rhetoricians.

Anzaldúa's mestiza consciousness, Dussel's Eurocentric fallacy, and Wallerstein's World-System theory collectively argue for a more coevolutionary curricular perspective, one that welcomes inter- and transregional periodizations. New innovative studies could adapt chronological groupings from *The Global Past*, a current world history textbook that divides the period between 1500 and 1900 in the Western Hemisphere into nine thematic chapters, most spanning two or more centuries: "Oceanic Explorations and Contacts, 1405–1780," "Early European Colonialism, 1500–c. 1750," "The American Exchange, 1492–c. 1750," "The African Slave Trade, 1441–1815," "Revolutions in Europe, the Americas, and Asia, 1543–1895," "The Global Industrial Revolution, c. 1770–1905," "Modern Nationalism around the Globe, 1816–1920," and "Imperialism around the Globe,

1803–1949" (1). These thematic chapter titles suggest numerous possibilities in reimagining periodizations across regions for a new writing curriculum. By clustering research and teaching according to these or similar categories, composition specialists may be more inclined to analyze how writing and rhetoric are implicated in and consequences of trade, border crossing, and globalization.

In *Rethinking American History in a Global Age*, historian Daniel Rodgers theorizes beyond the Western Hemisphere to propose a new global history. Rodgers organizes five broad periodizations according to Western colonial episodes themselves rather than their chronology. First, European exploration opened an "age of outpost settlements" coexisting and struggling with native societies. Then, stretching from the last quarter of the seventeenth century to the last quarter of the eighteenth, an "age of commercial Atlantic Empires" tied these American settlements to European capitals, the slave coast of Africa, and the West Indian colonies in dense networks of trade. The third great periodization, sparked by the American and French Revolutions and continuing beyond the American Civil War, was an "age of revolutionary nation-building." By the late nineteenth century, problems of industrialization and immigration challenged nations to develop the political means to control the excesses of capitalism; thus began an "age of social politics" that encompassed American Progressivism and the New Deal and lasted through the 1940s. The most recent phase according to Rodgers is the "age of the world hegemony of the United States," extending from World War II and the Cold War to the present era. Rodgers' proposal would challenge compositionists to teach from longer periodizations and to cluster topics, such as Spanish Christianization and British colonialism, which rhetoric and composition historical scholarship often overlooks entirely.[7]

A curriculum implied by Gloria Anzaldúa's mestiza consciousness would take up more extensive and fruitful periodizations by also turning specifically to Mestiz@ historical legacies. In "A General Survey of Chicano/a Historiography," Antonio Ríos-Bustamante offers five historical paradigms, all of which are strongly contested among Chicano scholars, and two of which I will mention here. First is the *Indigenista* period, which begins with Native American creation origins. For Mestiz@s like Gloria Anzaldúa whose individual and communal identities are largely indigenous, a Mesoamerican perspective of sacred origins is vital. Through continually evoking *Coatlicue*, *Malintzin*, and other Aztec goddesses or icons, mestiza consciousness not only accepts but affirms the validity of

Mesoamerican spirituality as an origin of Mexican cultures. Also within this period is the Bering Straits theory, which stretches between 15,000 and 100,000 AD (255). Beginning with the presence of prehistoric Asiatic migrations, this starting point would further underline the historic movement of peoples and intellectual traditions across regions and cultures.

Other corresponding approaches in the *Indigenista* period commence with the rise of Mesoamerican cultures in the Valley of Oaxaca. This trajectory would involve the examination of *Olmec* glyphs, the earliest known evidence of North American writing between 650–700 BCE. Even prior to the rise of glyphic documentation, *Olmecan* record-keeping practices emerged as early as 1500 BCE.[8] A similar approach would examine the arrival of the twelve Chichimec nations in the valley of Mexico from Aztlán in 1100 ADE, based directly upon the migration narratives recorded in the Mesoamerican codex manuscripts. The pre-Columbian *amoxtli* not only chronicle the historical origin of Mexican peoples, they provide a glimpse of a civilization that advanced *Huehuetlahtolli*, highly complex writing and rhetoric practices unique to the Western Hemisphere.

Ríos-Bustamante's second historical paradigm of Chicano historiography is the Colonial Period, which is divided into three stages spanning from 1521 to 1810. The Early Conquest, which ranges from 1521 to 1640, marks the period of Western contact and colonization (255). As I have explained in previous chapters, this early wave of violence saw the near total destruction of Mesoamerican writing practices and other pre-Columbian ways of life. As the older *amoxtli* were burned and colonial-era codices were rewritten, the Mestiz@ codex evidences the conflicting scripts and rhetorics of Mesoamerican pictography, Castilian Spanish, and an alphabetized *Nahuatl*. By investigating writing and rhetoric from these points of origin, a curriculum could be more responsive to the realization of coevolutionary developments and changes in diverse writing practices over time. To quote again from Cuban writer José Martí,

> Knowing is what counts. To know one's country and govern it with that knowledge is the only way to free it from tyranny . . . The European University must yield to the [Latin] American . . . The history of [Latin] America, from the Incas to the present, must be taught in clear detail and to the letter, even if the archons of Greece are overlooked. Our Greece must take priority over the Greece which is not ours. (114)

Becoming familiar with and "knowing" Mesoamerican periodizations will help rhetoric and composition historians denaturalize the dominant historical narrative, "from Ancient Greece to Modern America." A countercurriculum might instead imagine writing and rhetoric emerging "from Mesoamerica to Later America." Taking up Martí's challenge, teachers would work forward from volumes like the *Popul Vuh: The Mayan Book of the Dawn of Life*, or Miguel León-Portilla's *In the Language of Kings: An Anthology of Mesoamerican Literature, Pre-Columbian to the Present.* Popular episodes in the field such as the 1911 formation of the National Council of Teachers of English would be understood as merely one moment within a larger, coevolutionary hemisphere.

Embracing coevolutionary periodizations of rhetoric and writing would moreover highlight the necessity to accept nonwhite and non-Western peoples as active agents in writing practices long before the 1970s opened admissions policies in America institutions. To return to Patricia Bizzell and Bruce Herzberg's periodizations in *The Rhetorical Tradition*, across a 2,000-year dominant historical narrative, an analysis of racial subjectivity does not appear until late in the twentieth century. The editors position the subheading "Rhetorics of Gender, Race, and Culture" under the mantle of Postmodernism, which is itself a Western-specific configuration. Obviously, people of color did not first appear in world history as students in need of literacy instruction from Anglo-American composition specialists. Rather than suspending an analysis of race and ethnicity until the U.S. post–civil rights era, a new curriculum might interrogate the racialization of identity across time.

Seminars that take up Bizzell and Herzberg's canon could examine the rhetorics of race and culture as they apply to Germanic romanticism and the Aryanizing of ancient Greek males. Senegalese historian Cheikh Anta Diop's *The African Origin of Civilization: Myth or Reality* (1983) forwards the crushing assertion that ancient Egyptians are black Africans, not European, and that the civilization of ancient Greece is indebted to knowledge that was borrowed and perhaps even stolen from Egypt. Significantly adding to such analysis are the debates surrounding Martin Bernal's *Black Athena: The Afroasiatic Roots of Classical Civilization* (1987), which examines the history of anti-Semitism in Western Europe and North America, especially in colleges and universities. Bernal argues that the historical paradigm that classical scholars use to discuss the value of Greek civilization and its origins is directly and indirectly influenced by racism and

European chauvinism. The ancient Greeks themselves believed that their culture had arisen around 1500 BCE by Egyptians and Phoenicians who "civilized" the native inhabitants. This paradigm, which Bernal calls the "Ancient Model," was displaced after the eighteenth century by various versions of the "Aryan model," in which Greek civilization was seen as the result of an invasion from the north that had taken over local Aegean or pre-Hellenic cultures. Egyptian influence was denied, Bernal argues, and Greek civilization was seen as the finest moment of human achievement, the cradle of Western civilization.

This denial of Egyptian influence on Greek civilization corresponds to the general devaluation of Egypt as well as its detachment from sub-Saharan African cultures. Since it is not historically plausible that Greeks are the biological progenitors of the immense majority of composition practitioners, this research promotes further inquiry into the relationship between race and rhetoric long before Bizzell and Herzberg's Postmodern periodization. Carol Lipson and Roberta Binkley's recent *Rhetoric Before and Beyond the Greeks* is ideal for helping researchers and teachers further investigate a wider cultural history by including Egyptian as well as Near Eastern traditions.

A broader focus on race and the colonization of identity would investigate its close link with economy, gender, slavery, and migration systems, all of which cut across national borders. Keith Gilyard's *Race, Rhetoric, and Composition*, the recent edited collection *African American Rhetoric(s)* and the earlier *Race Rhetoric, and the Postcolonial* would offer valuable perspectives in such teaching and research. Running a thread on race through the rhetoric seminar would likewise examine slavery, the slave trade, and emancipation in global contexts. Thus, teachers could introduce related comparative topics such as the history of racial categories,[9] attitudes, and practices regarding racial admixtures, racial claims, and barriers to citizenship, and theories of internal colonialism. As composition teachers recognize that North American racism is a local phase of a global problem, they could begin to understand the varied ways that racial categorizing has framed struggles over group identity and liberation around the world.

A hemispheric, coevolutionary approach to race and rhetoric studies would encourage discussion of wide-angle, sequential connections and comparisons over time. While I have no difficulty with the schemas mentioned thus far, it is important to note that Anzaldúa's serpentine rhetorics in *Borderlands/La Frontera* do not advocate the stability of clear chronological scaffolding. Conversely, mestiza consciousness is more concerned with generating competing cultural memories, overlapping timetables, and conflictive narrations. Despite her fractured storytelling, however, I do not perceive Anzaldúa's work in political opposition to a project of a corrective, decolonial historiography. For Anzaldúa, material history and the respect for that history are quite central to mestiza consciousness; it is the linear and hierarchical thinking of dominant Western narratives that *Borderlands* writes against. An alternate approach to the ones advocated by Antonio Ríos-Bustamante, Daniel Rodgers, and José Martí could involve starting from Anzaldúa's own work as an introduction to history, thereby weaving a disjointed chronological narrative that cycles both forward and in reverse.

A reperiodization of rhetoric and composition in this spirit would also work by starting with the *Codex Espangliensis: From Columbus to the Border Patrol.* The *Codex* is ideal for revealing sixteenth-century colonial struggles in accessible ways for twenty-first century students and teachers. Crossing the chronological barriers between Mesoamerica and Later America would promote parallel analyses of pictographic inscription practices in *Tenochtitlán* and contemporary American writing programs in ways that revise hegemonic orders of Anglo-European history. By layering the period of the Spanish colonial conquest with the present period of late global capitalism, classroom inquiry can also benefit from a much more historically informed discussion of globalizing processes as well as various strategies of resistance. The Aztec's *Nepantla*, Anzaldúa's mestiza consciousness, Walter Mignolo's coexisting territorialities, Fernando Ortiz' transculturation, and Enrique Dussel's transmodernity are only a few expressions that would set rhetoric and composition historical scholarship toward new directions along these lines.

Teachers in the field could easily adjust a writing curriculum by organizing thematic courses with somewhat parallel chronologies, often alternating between canonized historical accounts like James Berlin's *Rhetoric and Reality* and counternarratives from *Borderlands/ La Frontera* and the *Codex Espangliensis.* If composition history is reorganized to address larger coevolutionary topics, one could expect much longer, chronologically overlapping thematic units that combine segments on colonialism, trade, slavery, and industrialization that may receive little attention in traditional rhetoric and composition seminars. Teachers and students adopting strong thematic approaches must be willing to rethink James Berlin's decade-by-decade chronology of writing instruction in twentieth-century colleges for a more intensive study of key historical developments connecting the parallel timelines of economy and colony across the Americas and beyond. Comparisons under this design would not work to confuse culturally contrastive episodes such as Mary Louise Pratt's fourth-grade child and Fernando Ortiz's transculturation in "Arts of the Contact Zone." Rather, comparative approaches might envision twentieth-century American literacy instruction as merely one culturally specific experience within a hemispheric plurality of others.

A chronology that charts North America's initially small-world significance over four centuries, for example, would provide a necessary corrective to the field's endlessly repeated claim that English composition instruction is unique to the American nation-state. But using rhetoric courses to trace America's rise to globalism would not reproduce another ideological justification for U.S. dominance in the tradition of Francis Fukuyama's hierarchical "end of history."[10] Francis Fukuyama, professor of public policy and author of *The End of History*, argues that we have reached the end because there is a powerful movement toward the emergence and ultimate stability of capitalist democracies. In this paradigm, hierarchical neoliberalism is the solution. Paraphrasing Fukuyama, communities have a natural leaning toward hierarchies. Course strategies in English composition could scrutinize such triumphant global narratives of United States, stories that feed the notion that world history has culminated in the collapse of communism and the victory of Western, democratic, capitalist institutions. Celebratory narratives simply reinforce the myth of an isolationist America. As historian Michael Adas argues, while one face of "exceptionalism" has traditionally separated the United States from all other societies, the other has presented America as the world's "last, best hope" and promoted its global civilizing mission (1698).

Region versus Nation

Fukuyama's dominant narrative brings me to the third and final model that would accompany a more coevolutionary curriculum, one that involves a detached stance toward Anglo-European nation-building. Alfred Arteaga's edited collection *An Other Tongue: Nation and Ethnicity in the Linguistic Borderlands* interrogates the tensions of identification between Region and Nation. By questioning the processes of subjectivity that transpire under the nation-state, *An Other Tongue* helps teachers and students understand the key role rhetoric plays in the push and pull struggle for self-definition under colonial situations. And as mestiza consciousness poetically illustrates, Mestiz@ rhetorics mediate and cross hierarchical distinctions between nationality, region, ethnicity, and colonial status. Undoubtedly, the history of European writing instruction in the Western Hemisphere is closely related to the project of building and preserving the nation.[11] The field's dominant historical progression "from Ancient Greece to Modern America" is perhaps pedagogically framed as a Western epic in which nations form and triumphantly expand. Such courses, and the curricula in which they are located, might easily suggest that the national is the normative scale of the narrative and the nation-state is its most stable character. Rhetoric and writing are birthed in Greece only to effortlessly and naturally expand to the New World, thereby ensuring state-sanctioned democracy and freedom for all within its pathway. Often, such scholarship teaches that the North American composition experience is unique, without subjecting such claims to careful scrutiny or consulting colonial histories.[12]

Arteaga's *An Other Tongue* challenges these assumptions by reconstructing national subjectivity from the perspectives of the colonized. Recognizing that capital and human flesh shift across nation-state boundaries, without loyalty, Arteaga interrogates this fracture, opening it for its intellectual potential. Mexican-origin Mestiz@s are Arteaga's prime example of a "new" subjectivity that intermixes multiple nationalities as one would code-switch and weave between languages. Interlingualism and transnationalism operate hand in hand to critique hierarchical powers of the U.S. nation-state. Because Anglo-American conversations on nationalism have not recognized ancient cultures and historical agency of First Nations Peoples, Chicanos, and Mestiz@s, Arteaga suggests that the national is in need of severe modification. A vanguard national order directs Western expansion across the globe:

> History is a narrative made story with plot, with telos, with heroes and villains. The United States locates itself at the climax and terminus of the trajectory of Western Civilization that began at the original Eden. The move West, from Eden to the thirteen colonies, traces not only the spatial relocation but, more importantly, the historical development of civilization proper, through Greece and Rome, the English "re"naissance, and peaking at the American naissance of Adam Jr. Egypt, the rest of Africa, and the "Orient," of course, are ignored. And according to Western cartography, the West does not stop at Appalachia; there is a manifest destiny civilization was destined to move as far West

as possible, to the edge of that ultimate boundary with the East, to that ultimate "shining sea." (23)

The dominant historical narrative displaces American Indians as noble inhabitants of a distant past, an operation that rhetoric scholar Malea Powell has called second-wave genocide.[13] On the national level, American Indians exist as a nostalgic story, not as living humans with active agency today. Mestiz@s, meanwhile, are welcomed to appear in this nationalist narrative *a*historically, if and when they do appear. Just as Spanish is made to appear after English, Mestiz@ intellectual legacies and cultural issues are limited to occurrences that transpire only recently, within a Western-imposed axis of development and assimilation through state-sanctioned democracy.

Arteaga elaborates on the ways in which European and U.S. nationalisms work to displace and deform Mestiz@ subjectivity. Because Anglo nationalism totalizes, speaks in a universal voice, and ignores colonial power, the complexities of Mestiz@ cultural and regional subjectivity are obscured:

> Chicanos are foreign immigrants and illegal aliens. The Immigration and Naturalization Service (INS) and the Texas Rangers attest to that. Present-day Chicanos are divorced spatially from Mexicans south of the border, temporally from the *Californio*, and racially from the Indian. Chicanos are divorced from the Southwest and read, instead, as an immigrant labor force. Not the noble savage Indian nor the genteel *Californio* Spaniard, the Chicano is the pest, is the bracero who had the audacity to stay and have children in gangs and on welfare. (27)

Composition and rhetoric seminars that interrogate this dominant narrative could research Mestiz@ legacies by researching from the ancient *Olmec* in the Valley of Oaxaca. Another approach would place discussions of contemporary Mexican migrations within a wider hemispheric dialogue about asymmetrical and dependent economies. Along with immigration, the national mythology of self-determination and freedom might likewise be placed in a wider transregional dialogue on how "freedom" has been articulated and interpreted from other various regional perspectives in the Western Hemisphere.

Studying the complex play of national and regional subjectivities created by movement and immigration, whether voluntary or forced, is a powerful way the curriculum might construct a position in between views of the nation and global views that are themselves part of a larger inquiry. One might imagine coevolutionary rhetoric courses examining the nation much more as a site than a subject, located as a focal point in between local, regional, continental, and global processes. The idea here is that the nation-state is not necessarily the most significant entity of inquiry. A writing curriculum that centers on coevolutionary and parallel processes like oceanic trade, migration, and industrialization would feature several scales of rhetorical analysis, from the local to the global.

Just as the United States has never been separate from the world, its individuals and local communities have been enmeshed in networks of trade, migration, and culture that continually cross borders. In an age of electronic communication, planetary travel, and global sweatshops, the notion of interconnection is slowly becoming more concrete for academics in rhetoric and composition. To examine these connections in meaningful ways, a coevolutionary approach to writing and rhetoric would trace regional developments like English instruction at Harvard College in the 1840s with and against national events such as America's territorial war against Mexico and global trends like the escalation of the transatlantic commercial circuit. Such comparative approaches would support a running dialogue between the ethnic and economic history of specific regions as well as larger patterns emerging from studies of trade, industrialization, warfare, and migration.

A sustained classroom discussion on writing and rhetoric in relation to regional location from Arteaga's *An Other Tongue* might help teachers denaturalize the linguistic subordination of Spanish as well as all non-English language systems that are inscribed in the American landscape. The multidiscursive memories of linguistically and racially subjugated writers would be subversively fused into nationalist histories and pedagogies of composition in America. Arteaga presents a poetic expression that is akin to Gloria Anzaldúa's mestiza consciousness, which together inspire new curricular possibilities for rhetoric and writing. From José Antonio Burciaga's "Poema en tres idiomas y caló" in *Undocumented Love* reads,

Poema en tres idiomas y caló
Españotli titlan Englishic,
titlan nahuatl titlan Caló
Qué locotl!
Mi mente spirals al mixtli,
buti suave I feel cuatro lenguas in mi boca.

Coltic sueños temostli
Y siento una xóchitl brotar
from four diferentes vidas...

I yotl recordotl el tonatiuh
en mi boca cochi
cihuatl, nahuatl
teocalli, my mouth
micca por el English
e hiriendo mi español,
ahora cojo ando en caló
pero no hay pedo
porque todo se vale,
con o sin safos.
Poem in Three Idioms and Caló
Spanish between English
between Nahuatl, between Caló.
How mad!
My mind spirals to the clouds
so smooth I feel four tongues in my mouth.
Twisted dreams fall
and I feel a flower bud
from four different lives...

I remember the sun
in my mouth sleeps
woman, Nahuatl
temple my mouth,
killed by the English
and wounding my Spanish,
now I limp walk in fractured Spanish
But there is no problem
for everything is valid
with or without safeties.[14]

Burciaga's lines graphically illustrate the convergence of four available means of identification between nation and region. Hierarchical orders of U.S. nationalism are fused with a logic that crosses linguistic borders from Spanish and English to *Nahuatl* and *Caló*, and back again. By suspending inquiry between opposing languages and national memory, teachers and students are invited to consider an invention of subjectivity that builds upon the lived colonial experiences of the borderlands. The motivation here is not to discover authentic truth about Mestiz@s or Mesoamerica but to foster a plural dialogue that would itself severely alter the terms of the larger conversation about rhetoric, composition, and the Americas.

Mestiz@, Mesoamerican, and American Indian expressions are not to be merely included into canonized patterns of researching and teaching. These diverse intellectual legacies furthermore work to significantly revise hierarchical assumptions of U.S. nationalism. Moreover, thinking through Mestiz@ and Mesoamerican knowledges as a strategy for revising political hierarchies might also call into question nationalist ideas about race and gender. For example, classroom discussion of gender would analyze beyond the feminisms that emerge as theoretical extensions of modernity, exclusive to First World, nationalist, and individualist articulations. The idea here is to decenter nationalist concepts of gender and race by placing them in dialogue with local regional perspectives across the borderlands.

Some seminars might start with traditional questions about national identity and development. What exactly does it mean to be American? What is unique and exclusive about composition history? If the nation is a spatial organization that justifies hierarchy, what other models are available? But by contextualizing U.S. nationalism and pairing it with and against other nationalisms, a curriculum could aim to produce nuanced comparisons that break from the hierarchical dichotomy of "the West and the rest." New courses in the curriculum would interrogate myths of American and Western isolationism, from specific claims about the frontier to the more general notion that Americans are exempt from trends elsewhere in the world. One crucial aim of this approach would be to illuminate how writing and rhetoric in the Western Hemisphere have been enmeshed in historical networks and forces much larger and older than the U.S. nation-state. Another could be to develop a more constructive sense of the differences within and beneath a national subjectivity. Culturally divergent ideas about American citizenship could be compared to other articulations of national identity such as Zapatista sovereignty,[15] Quebecois separatism,[16] and even neo-Nazi nationalism.[17] As teachers rethink composition in the U.S. within a broader spectrum of nations, regions, and subjectivities, the tendency will be to comprehend North American events as variations of coevolutionary, hemispheric developments, and to focus teaching and research on such processes and movements.

To impart this sense of constructedness, a curriculum would research the tensions between various regional and national versions of history. Does national identity involve commitment to a set of rules and principles that are "beyond" race and ethnicity? Are the "true" rhetors of world history the ones who descend, as Alfred Arteaga metaphorically explains, only from Eden or the 13 colonies? Placed in a global context, these tensions can be seen as a North American variant of a national struggle between racial inclusion and exclusion that shapes other countries across the planet.[18] Another way to rethink the field's nationalism might be to examine composition history centered on other forms of subjectivity, such as allegiances to region, language, culture, faith, ethnicity, family, and gender. Thus, teachers would come to appreciate the multiple identities and solidarities that coexist with national identity, even as those solidarities are in conflict. Ideally, by incorporating these diverse perspectives into its readings and discussions, the new curriculum would demonstrate some of the connections between composition's "domestic multiculturalism" and a more hemispheric, transregional, and transnational plurality.

One benefit of stressing these connections is avoiding the limits of concealing entire communities and cultures in the discussion of the monolithic, disembodied historical narrative "from Ancient Greece to Modern America." Decade-by-decade accounts of writing instruction in nineteenth-century colleges in the United States, for example, will not, by themselves, clarify these connections. Furthermore, making meaningful local-global linkages in the curriculum involves more than "giving voice" to first-year undergraduate student autobiographies as an addendum to a seemingly overwhelming and unchanging Eurocentric teleology. A curriculum could moreover address these problems by embracing local histories as a new point of origin. In the following passage from *Race, Rhetoric, and the Postcolonial*, Gloria Anzaldúa notes,

> So for me, writing has always been about narrative . . . some are master narratives, and some are outsider narratives. There's that whole struggle in my writing between the dominant culture's traditional, conventional narratives about reality and about literature and about science and about politics; and my other counter narratives as a mestiza growing up in this country, as an internal exile as an inner exile, as a postcolonial person, because the Mexican race in the United States is a colonized people. My ancestors were living life on the border. The band was part of the state of Tamaulipas, Mexico, and then the United States bought it, bought half of Mexico, and so the Anzaldúas were split in half. (48)

Through this local articulation of the ties between narrative and colonization, region and nation, Anzaldúa illuminates how the act of writing is caught up in larger historical processes of frontiers and the expansion of global capital. From this perspective, a dialogue about the history of rhetoric and writing could extend beyond eighteenth- and nineteenth-century formations of early English departments in New England. Learning about the practice of inventing and writing from Anzaldúa's conceptual borderlands implies confronting the continual struggle for self-defined adaptations of subjectivity over and against globalizing forces of Western colonialism. Continuing from the same passage, Anzaldúa illustrates how, after the war against México and the forging of the militarized border, local human relationships are skewed by displacements of material and discursive power:

> The Anzaldúas with an accent, which is my family, were north of the border. The Anzalduas without an accent stayed on the other side of the border, and as the decades went by we lost connection with each other. And so the Anzaldúas and the Anzalduas, originally from the same land, the state of Tamaulipas in the nation of Mexico, all of a sudden became strangers in our own land, foreigners in our own land. We were a colonized people who were not allowed to speak our language, whose ways of life were not valued in this country. Public education tried to erase all of that. So here I am now, a kind of international citizen whose life and privileges are not equal to the rights and privileges of ordinary, Anglo, white, Euro-American people. My narratives always take into account these other ethnicities, these other races, these other cultures, these other histories. There's always that kind of struggle. (48)

Understanding the experiences explained here would help rhetoric and composition teachers to reflect on colonialism and its various stages of domination, from military occupation to subsequent hegemonies of writing instruction. Through comparative biographies or representative accounts of First Nations peoples, Mestiz@, African slaves, colonists, and other figures, teachers of a new curriculum could better understand how writing and rhetoric have always been caught up in the crossing of borders and the transformation of history. Incorporating the perspectives of such lives into the curriculum would engage teachers and students in material history while raising their awareness of the many regions and experiences that have informed the practice of writing across North American territories.

Writing specialists could reframe rhetoric history courses into larger regional or ecological units. Built around the México/U.S.

borderlands, seminars could incorporate comparisons, contacts, border migrations, as well as U.S. interventions and influences in México, Latin America, the Caribbean, and Canada. Casting a wider hemispheric net, the rhetoric history course might pursue a strategy for the entire Western Hemisphere "from an Other tongue," as Alfred Arteaga puts it. Drawing upon Latin American Subaltern Studies scholarship, which illustrates how North and South America share common histories,[19] such a course could trace parallel developments in the colonial, independence, and national periods as well as analyze borderland and international relations issues.

Alternatively, some seminars may choose the Atlantic Basin as their primary geographic context. Peter Linebaugh's *The Many-Headed Hydra: The Hidden History of the Revolutionary Atlantic*, for example, largely reframes the early colonial era and American slavery as episodes in Atlantic history, which serves as an excellent synthesis for composition history teachers to draw upon. However, Morris Young's scholarship on Asian American rhetorics and the colonial history of English instruction in Hawaiian schools could help educators invent and write from yet another side of the continent.[20] Teachers could use a Pacific Rim approach to contrast or complement the Atlantic focus with its own discussion of colonization, trade, and labor systems. In either case, composition and rhetoric historians would fuse wider regional contexts as settings and reference points into the nationalist chronicle of composition programs in universities and colleges.

Another possibility would be to select an aspect of North American history that is inherently international and build around it as the main theme or special angle. A seminar-long emphasis on the México/U.S. border, war, migration, or trade would ensure that U.S. composition and rhetoric could be studied from a sustained viewpoint of interaction that stresses America's participation in rather than isolation from the movement of rhetorical knowledge, labor, and human flesh across borders. An emphasis on international relations, for example, could bring North American intervention more consistently into the course. Teachers could situate westward expansion in a global arena by understanding rhetorics surrounding episodes like the fall of *Tenochtitlán* or the Trail of Tears as international and transnational phenomena. Exploring U.S. international involvements could help the field better understand the United States' war against México or the American occupation of Japan from multiple perspectives. Examining the ways that domestic and international policies interact can illuminate how racial thinking fosters imperialism or how labor movements influence migration and immigration policies. The expanding reach of American influences overseas after the mid-nineteenth century can be demonstrated through episodes such as the colonization of the Hawaiian Islands, thereby challenging the persisting myth of North American isolationism. Considering the impact of America's influence abroad in the twentieth and twenty-first centuries, rhetoric courses would raise important questions about the nature of hegemony, empire, and globalization. Especially after the events of September 11, 2001, peripheral perspectives of the United States are vital. For all kinds of rhetoric courses, whether focused on history or not, disparate cultural views can provide informative alternatives to Anglo-American hegemonic perspectives. As Enrique Dussel's *The Invention of the Americas* metaphorically implies, those who view North America from the "outside" reveal patterns and expressions evidently hidden to "insiders" about colonial power and imperialism.

Another fundamentally hemispheric, transregional subject is trade. Historians have shown the enormous impact of cross-cultural exchange in altering daily life as well as long-term patterns related to population and the global distribution of power. Rather than becoming simply an addendum to Western rhetoric and composition history, a central strategy could follow economic flows of production and exchange, thereby providing a lens through which to view a global perspective in line with Dussel's transmodernity. Beginning with the exchanges following the Spanish conquest of Mesoamerica, for example, a course could trace the political struggles and social changes of early America through the development of international trade routes. The focus would not be sugar, tobacco, or cotton themselves, but the rhetorics and legal documents that are fastened to these commodities and operations across the Atlantic. The theme of trade connects directly with issues related to colonialism, the border, labor systems, the national and world economy, and foreign policy—all inherently hemispheric and coevolutionary subjects.

The models explained here, Spacialization, Periodization, and Region versus Nation are three possible curricular variations that could be derived from Gloria Anzaldúa's new mestiza consciousness. These modifications to the Western rhetoric and composition curriculum would equally emphasize connections, comparisons, and interpretive frameworks across and beyond national boundaries, thereby embracing a more hemispheric perspective, both literally and symbolically. Each model works to form a new curriculum that would seriously examine the ways in which writing and rhetoric are historically coupled with the material conditions of colonial subjugation as well as tactics of resistance and cultural survival.

Conclusion

This chapter provides three broad suggestions for how Anzaldúa's rhetorical strategy invites a more coevolutionary and expansive configuration of the curriculum. While some will read these suggestions as most appropriate for upper-division and graduate level seminars, the changes I outline here would impact all levels of teaching and research in the field. Furthermore, by sorting out concepts such as colonialism, imperialism, and Westernization in the context of global border crossing, teachers and students of composition could aim to grasp more fully the scope and limits of American power in a world in which, on the one hand, the United States is the sole remaining superpower, and on the other, its influence is constrained by competing global forces. Analyzing these changing relations will help rhetoric and composition scholars better understand their place in the world. Also in the new curriculum, teachers could be welcomed to examine the notion of the United States as an imperial power, whether in the traditional sense of ancient Rome or nineteenth-century Great Britain or perhaps in other ways. In either case, a curriculum in rhetoric and composition need not be limited to a legacy of Western assimilation, and writing specialists do not have to presume that all curricular and pedagogical possibilities emerge "from Ancient Greece to Modern America."

As a corrective to the field's dominant historical configuration, I have proposed a shift from "talking about" rhetoric and writing from the perspective of those in the imperial center and their followers to "inventing and writing from" the conceptual Mestiz@ borderlands implied by Gloria Anzaldúa's mestiza consciousness. The powerful rhetorical practices evidenced in *Borderlands/La Frontera*, if positioned as a new beginning, work to adapt and transform colonial histories resulting in unique discursive configurations. Western contributions to rhetoric and composition would not be discarded in the new curriculum. Instead, Mestiz@ rhetorics call for a monumental rereading and revising of composition and rhetoric history—this time not so much for what it collectively declares, but for what it too often conceals: the limits of an enduring Eurocentric teleology and its consequent dominant narrative of assimilation.

Notes

1 Mestiz@ Scripts and the Rhetoric of Subversion

1. The expression "mestizaje" is a highly contested semantic marker associated with Mexican nationalism and Jose Vasconcelos' *La Raza Cósmica* (1945), which forwards an elitist assumption of "mixed-blood" peoples. Some additional readings are
   De Castro, Juan. *Mestizo Nations: Culture, Race, and Conformity in Latin American Literature*. Tucson: University of Arizona Press, 2002.
   Miller, Marilyn Grace. *Rise and Fall of the Cosmic Race: The Cult of Mestizaje in Latin America*. Austin: University of Texas Press, 2004.
   Swarthout, Kelly. *Assimilating the Primitive: Parallel Dialogues on Racial Miscegenation in Revolutionary Mexico*. New York: Peterlang, 2004.
2. "Hispanic" is a bureaucratic invention for census purposes. For this reason, some Mestiz@s prefer other identifiers. Still, "Hispanic" is commonly used today, both inside and outside the community.
3. U.S. Census Bureau. "Census 2000 Brief, March 2001, and National Population Estimates." U.S. Census Bureau, Population Division, Ethnic & Hispanic Statistics Branch, 2006.
   http://www.census.gov/population/www/socdemo/hispanic/ho06.html. Accessed January 17, 2008.
4. The phrase as a collective cultural expression is inspired by "Indo-Hispano," from the work of New Mexican writers E.A. Mares, Tomás Atencio, and Enrique Lamadrid. I recommend the following publications for a further explanation of Indo-Hispano cultures:
   Lamadrid, Enrique. "Luz y Sombra: The Poetics of Mestizo Identity." *Nuevo México Profundo: Rituals of an Indo-Hispano Homeland*. Santa Fe: Museum of New Mexico Press, 2000. 1–11.
   Lamadrid, Enrique. *Hermanitos Comanchitos: Indo-Hispano Rituals of Captivity and Redemption*. Albuquerque: University of New Mexico Press, 2003.
5. Grosfoguel, Ramon, Nelson Maldonado-Torres, and Jose David Saldivar, eds. *Latin@s in the World-System: Decolonization Struggles in the 21st Century U.S. Empire*. Boulder, CO: Paradigm, 2006.

Simal, Begoña. "'The Cariboo Café' as a Border Text: The Holographic Model. Rodopi." *Perspectives on Modern Literature, Literature and Ethnicity in the Cultural Borderlands*. Ed. Jesus Benito and Anna Maria Manzanas. Kenilworth, NJ: Rodopi Press, 2007.

6. Geertz, Clifford. *The Interpretation of Cultures: Selected Essays*. New York: Basic Books, 1973. 5.
7. Raymond Williams, as cited in Hebdige, Dick. *Subculture: The Meaning of Style*. London: Routledge, 1979. 6.
8. Keali'Inohomoku, Joann. "Hopi and Hawaiian Music and Dance: Responses to Cultural Contact." *Musical Repercussions of 1492: Encounters in Text and Performance*. Ed. Carol Robertson. Washington: Smithsonian Institution Press, 1992. 429–450.
9. Schiappa, Edward. "Did Plato Coin Rhêtorikê?" *American Journal of Philology* 111 (1990): 157–170.
10. León-Portilla, Miguel, and Earl Shorris, eds. *In the Language of Kings: An Anthology of Mesoamerican Literature, Pre-Columbian to the Present*. New York: W.W. Norton, 2001. 73.
11. Santiago, Deborah, and Sarita Brown. *Federal Policy and Latinos in Higher Education*. Washington, DC: Pew Hispanic Center, 2004. 6.
12. Landa, Diego de. *Yucatan Before and After the Conquest*. 1566. Trans. William Gates, New York: Dover, 1978. 2.
13. Murphy, James, ed. *A Short History of Writing Instruction: From Ancient Greece to Modern America*. 2nd ed. Mahwah, NJ: Laurence Erlbaum, 2001.
14. Abbott, Don Paul. "The Ancient Word: Rhetoric in Aztec Culture." *Rhetorica* 5.3 (1987): 251–264.

II New Consciousness/Ancient Myths

1. See page 99. Anzaldúa, Gloria. *Borderlands/La Frontera: The New Mestiza*. 1987. San Francisco: Aunt Lute Books, 1999. 19.
2. Alarcón, Norma. "Anzaldúa's *Frontera* Inscribing Gynectics." *Displacement, Diaspora, and Geographies of Identity*. Ed. Lavie Smadar and Ted Swedenburg. Durham: Duke University Press, 1997. 364.
3. Carrasco, David. *Religions of Mesoamerica: Cosmovision and Ceremonial Centers*. San Francisco: Harper and Row, 1990.
4. Anzaldúa, Gloria. *Borderlands/La Frontera: The New Mestiza*. 1987. San Francisco: Aunt Lute Books, 1999. 19.
5. The following publications are helpful for further reading on applying Anzaldúa to the politics of identity formation:

   Adams, Kate. "Northamerican Silences: History, Identity, and Witness in the Poetry of Gloria Anzaldúa, Cherríe Moraga, and Leslie Marmon Silko." *Listening to Silences: New Essays in Feminist Criticism*. Ed. Elaine Hedges and Shelly Fisher Fishkin. New York: Oxford University Press, 1994. 130–145.

Barnard, Ian. "Gloria Anzaldúa's Queer Mestisaje." *MELUS* 22.1(1997): 35–53.

Fowlkes, Diane. "Moving from Feminist Identity Politics to Coalition Politics through a Feminist Materialist Standpoint of Intersubjectivity in Gloria Anzaldúa's *Borderlands/La Frontera: The New Mestiza.*" *Hypatia* 12.2 (1997): 105–124.

Raisin, Judith. "Inverts and Hybrids: Lesbian Rewritings of Sexual and Racial Identities." *The Lesbian Postmodern.* Ed. Laura Doan. New York: Columbia University Press, 1994.

6. García, Alma, ed. *Chicana Feminist Thought: The Basic Historical Writings.* New York: Routledge, 1997.

Grewal, Inderpal. "Autobiographical Subjects and Diasporic Locations: *Meatless Days* and *Borderlands.*" *Scattered Hegemonies: Postmodernity and Transnational Feminist Practices.* Ed. Inderpal Grewal and Caren Kaplan. Minneapolis: University of Minnesota Press, 1994. 231–254.

Hedley, Jane. "Nepantilist Poetics: Narrative and Cultural Identity in the Mixed-Language Writings of Irena Klepfisz and Gloria Anzaldúa." *Narrative* 4.1 (1996): 36–54.

Keating, AnaLouise. "Writing, Politics, and las Lesberadas: Platicando con Gloria Anzaldúa." *Frontiers* 14.1 (1993): 105–130.

Lugones, María. "On *Borderlands/La Frontera*: An Interpretive Essay." *Adventures in Lesbian Philosophy.* Ed. Claudia Card. Bloomington: Indiana University Press, 1994.

Wright, Melissa. "'Maquiladora Mestizas' and a Feminist Border Politics: Revising Anzaldúa." *Hypatia* 13.3 (1998): 114–131.

7. Anzaldúa, Gloria. "To(o) Queer the Writer—Loca, Escritora y Chicana." *Inversions: Writing by Dykes, Queers and Lesbians.* Ed. Betsy Warland. Vancouver: Press Gang, 1991. 249–263 (252).

8. Hames-Garcia, Michael. "How to Tell a Mestizo from an Enchirito®: Colonialism and National Culture in the Borderlands." *diacritics* 30.4 (2000): 102–122.

9. Mignolo, Walter. *Local Histories/Global Designs: Coloniality, Subaltern Knowledges, and Border Thinking.* Princeton: Princeton University Press, 2000. 228.

10. Hernández-Avila, Inés. "The Flowering Word." *American Language Review* 4.3 (May 2000): 1.

León-Portilla, Miguel. *Huehuetlahtolli: Testimonios de la Antigua Palabra.* 1988. 2nd ed. Mexico City: Fondo de Cultura Económica, 1992. 13.

11. Anzaldúa, Gloria. *Borderlands/La Frontera: The New Mestiza.* 1987. San Francisco: Aunt Lute Books, 1999. 77–79.

12. Sánchez, Rosaura. *Chicano Discourse: Socio-Historic Perspectives.* Houston: Arte Publico Press, 1994. 103–108.

13. Anzaldúa, Gloria. *Borderlands/La Frontera: The New Mestiza.* 1987. San Francisco: Aunt Lute Books, 1999. 239.

14. Mignolo, Walter. *The Darker Side of the Renaissance: Literacy, Territoriality, and Colonization.* Ann Arbor: University of Michigan Press, 1995. 40–41.

III Mestiz@: A Brief History, from Mexicatl to Chican@

1. Tedlock, Dennis, ed. *Popul Vuh: The Mayan Book of the Dawn of Life.* Charmichael, CA: Touchstone Books, 1996. 5–6.
2. Tedlock, Dennis, ed. *Popul Vuh: The Mayan Book of the Dawn of Life.* Touchstone Books, 1996.
3. León-Portilla, Miguel, and Earl Shorris, eds. *In the Language of Kings: An Anthology of Mesoamerican Literature, Pre-Columbian to the Present.* New York: W.W. Norton, 2001. 675.
4. Ríos-Bustamante, Antonio. "A General Survey of Chicano/a Historiography." *Voices of a New Chicana/o History.* Ed. Refugio Rochín and Dennis Valdés. East Lansing: Michigan State University Press, 2000. 254–255.
5. Carrasco, David. "Reimagining the Classic Heritage of Mesoamerica: Continuities and Fractures in Time, Space, and Scholarship." *Mesoamerica's Classic Heritage: From Teotihuacán to the Aztecs.* Ed. David Carrasco, Lindsay Jones, and Scott Sessions. Boulder: University Press of Colorado, 2000. 1–18.
   Ascher, Marcia. *Mathematics Elsewhere: An Exploration of Ideas Across Cultures.* Princeton: Princeton University Press, 2002.
   Ascher, Marcia. *Code of the Quipu: A Study in Media, Mathematics, and Culture.* Ann Arbor: University of Michigan Press, 1981.
6. Carrasco, Davíd. *Gods and Symbols of Ancient Mexico and the Maya.* New York: Thames and Hudson, 1993.
7. Carrasco, Davíd. *Aztec Ceremonial Landscapes.* Boulder: University Press of Colorado, 1999.
8. Carrasco, Davíd. *Aztec Ceremonial Landscapes.* Boulder: University Press of Colorado, 1999.
9. Carrasco, Davíd. *Aztec Ceremonial Landscapes.* Boulder: University Press of Colorado, 1999.
10. *Ramirez Jose Fernando, Cuadro Historico-geroglifico de la Peregrinacion de los Tribus Aztecas (No. 2). Imprenta de Jose Mariano Fernandez de Lara, Mexico City, 1858.*
11. Maiz, Apaxu. *Looking For Aztlán: Birthright or Right for Birth?* East Lansing, Michigan: Sun Dog Press, 2004.
12. Carrasco, Davíd. *Aztec Ceremonial Landscapes.* Boulder: University Press of Colorado, 1999.
13. Carrasco, Davíd, and Eduardo Matos Moctezuma. *Moctezuma's Mexico: Visions of the Aztec World.* Boulder: University Press of Colorado, 1992.
14. Carrasco, Davíd. *Religions of Mesoamerica: Cosmovision and Ceremonial Centers.* San Francisco: Harper and Row, 1990.
15. Carrasco, Davíd. *Mesoamerica's Classic Heritage: From Teotihuacán to the Aztecs.* Boulder: University Press of Colorado, 2000.
16. Carrasco, Davíd. *Mesoamerica's Classic Heritage: From Teotihuacán to the Aztecs.* Boulder: University Press of Colorado, 2000.

17. Carrasco, Davíd. *Aztec Ceremonial Landscapes*. Boulder: University Press of Colorado, 1999.
18. Carrasco, Davíd, and Eduardo Matos Moctezuma. *Moctezuma's Mexico: Visions of the Aztec World*. Boulder: University Press of Colorado, 1992.
19. Carrasco, Davíd, and Eduardo Matos Moctezuma. *Moctezuma's Mexico: Visions of the Aztec World*. Boulder: University Press of Colorado, 1992.
20. Torquemada, Juan. *Monarquía Indiana*. 1615. Ed. Miguel León-Portilla. Mexico City: Universidad Nacional Autónoma de Mexico, Instituto de Investigaciones Filológicas, 1977. 32.
21. Duran, Fray Diego. *The Aztecs*. New York: Orion Press, 1964.
22. Torquemada, Juan. *Monarquía Indiana*. 1615. Ed. Miguel León-Portilla. Mexico City: Universidad Nacional Autónoma de Mexico, Instituto de Investigaciones Filológicas, 1977. 32.
23. Díaz del Castillo, Bernal. *The History of the Conquest of Mexico*. 1568. Trans. J.M. Cohen. Baltimore: Penguin Books, 1963. 83.
24. Gruzinski, Serge. *The Aztecs: Rise and Fall of an Empire*. New York: Harry N. Abrams, 1992. 37.
25. Duran, Fray Diego. *The Aztecs*. New York: Orion Press, 1964.
26. Sahagún, Bernardino. *Codex Florentine Book 12: The Conquest of Mexico*. Trans. with notes by Arthur J.O. Anderson and Charles E. Dibble. Provo: University of Utah Press. 1982.
27. Carrasco, Davíd, and Eduardo Matos Moctezuma. *Moctezuma's Mexico: Visions of the Aztec World*. Boulder: University Press of Colorado, 1992.
28. Manuel Gonzales documents that thousands of Mesoamericans were sacrificed at the stake for their beliefs and resistance.
    Gonzales, Manuel. *Mexicanos: A History of Mexicans in the United States*. Bloomington: Indiana University Press, 1999. 15.
29. Crown of Spain, "The Laws of Burgos." *Indian Labor in the Spanish Indies*. Boston: D.C. Heath and Company, 1966. 26.
30. Himmerich y Valencia, Robert. *The Encomenderos of New Spain*. Austin: University of Texas Press, 1991. 4.
31. Chamberlain, Robert Stoner. "Pre-Conquest Labor Practices." *Indian Labor in the Spanish Indies*. Boston: D.C. Heath and Company, 1966. 3.
32. Himmerich y Valencia, Robert. *The Encomenderos of New Spain*. Austin: University of Texas Press, 1991. 11.
33. Simpson, Lesley Byrd. "On the New Laws." *Indian Labor in the Spanish Indies Boston*. D.C. Heath and Company, 1966. 7.
34. Simpson, Lesley Byrd. "On the New Laws." *Indian Labor in the Spanish Indies Boston*. D.C. Heath and Company, 1966. 20.
35. Simpson, Lesley Byrd. "On the New Laws." *Indian Labor in the Spanish Indies Boston*. D.C. Heath and Company, 1966. 7.
36. Kurlansky, Mark. *Cod: A Biography of the Fish That Changed the World*. New York: Penguin Books, 1998.
37. Saragoza, Alex. "Recent Chicano Historiography: An Interpretive Essay." *Aztlán* 19.1 (1990): 1–77. 51.

38. Gonzales, Manuel. *Mexicanos: A History of Mexicans in the United States.* Bloomington: Indiana University Press, 1999. 15.
39. The long tradition of Sephardim amongst Mexican-origin peoples continues to influence particular circles of Mestiz@ subjectivity today. The following publications are helpful for further reading:

    Atencio, Tomas. *The Sephardic Legacy in New Mexico: A Prospectus.* Albuquerque: Southwest Hispanic Research Institute, University of New Mexico Press, 1987.

    Gitlitz, David. *Secrecy and Deceit: The Religion of the Crypto-Jews.* Albuquerque: University of New Mexico Press, 1996.

    Jacobs, Janet Liebman. *Hidden Heritage: The Legacy of the Crypto-Jews.* Berkeley: University of California, 2002.

    Sanchez, Dell. *Sephardic Destiny: A Latino Quest.* Niles, IL: Mall, 2003.

    Stavans, Ilan, ed. *The Scroll and the Cross: 1000 Years of Jewish-Hispanic Literature.* New York: Routledge, 2003.
40. Gruzinski, Serge. *The Aztecs: Rise and Fall of an Empire.* New York: Harry N. Abrams, 1992. 109.
41. Menchaca, Martha. *Recovering History, Constructing Race: The Indian, Black, and White Roots of Mexican Americans.* Austin: University of Texas Press, 2001.
42. Acuña, Rodolfo. *Occupied America: The Chicano's Struggle Toward Liberation.* New York: Pearson Longman, 2004. 30.

    Chávez, Fray Angelico. *My Penitente Land: Reflections on Spanish New Mexico.* Norman, University of Oklahoma Press, 1979.
43. Manuel, Espinosa, J., ed. *The Pueblo Indian Revolt of 1598 and the Franciscan Missions in New Mexico: Letters of the Missionaries and Related Documents.* Norman: University of Oklahoma Press, 1988.
44. Manuel, Espinosa, J., ed. *The Pueblo Indian Revolt of 1598 and the Franciscan Missions in New Mexico: Letters of the Missionaries and Related Documents.* Norman: University of Oklahoma Press, 1988.
45. Folsom, Franklin. *Indian Uprising on the Rio Grande: The Pueblo Revolt of 1680.* Albuquerque: University of New Mexico Press, 1996.
46. Ortiz, Simon. *A Ceremony of Brotherhood, 1680–1980.* Albuquerque: Academia, 1981.
47. Ortiz, Simon. *A Ceremony of Brotherhood, 1680–1980.* Albuquerque: Academia, 1981.
48. Espinosa, Aurelio Macedonio. *The Folklore of Spain in the American Southwest: Traditional Spanish Folk Literature in Northern New Mexico and Southern Colorado.* Norman: University of Oklahoma Press, 1990. 161–162.
49. Espinosa, Aurelio Macedonio. *The Folklore of Spain in the American Southwest: Traditional Spanish Folk Literature in Northern New Mexico and Southern Colorado.* Norman: University of Oklahoma Press, 1990. 160–161.
50. Gandert, Miguel. *Nuevo Mexico Profundo: Rituals of an Indo-Hispano Homeland.* Albuquerque: Museum of New Mexico Press, 2000. 1–10.

51. Gandert, Miguel. *Nuevo Mexico Profundo: Rituals of an Indo-Hispano Homeland*. Albuquerque: Museum of New Mexico Press, 2000.
52. Ortiz, Simon. *A Ceremony of Brotherhood, 1680–1980*. Albuquerque: Academia, 1981.
53. Gandert, Miguel. *Nuevo Mexico Profundo: Rituals of an Indo-Hispano Homeland*. Albuquerque: Museum of New Mexico Press, 2000.
54. Ortiz, Simon. *A Ceremony of Brotherhood, 1680–1980*. Albuquerque: Academia, 1981.
55. Espinosa, Aurelio Macedonio. *The Folklore of Spain in the American Southwest: Traditional Spanish Folk Literature in Northern New Mexico and Southern Colorado*. Norman: University of Oklahoma Press, 1990.
56. Altman, Ida. *The Early History of Greater Mexico*. Upper Saddle River, NJ: Prentice Hall, 2003.
57. Krauze, Enrique. Mexico, *Biography of Power: A History of Modern Mexico, 1810–1996*. New York: Harper Collins, 1997.
58. Merrell, Floyd. *The Mexicans: A Sense of Culture*. Boulder: Westview Press, 2003.
59. Krauze, Enrique. *Mexico, Biography of Power: A History of Modern Mexico, 1810–1996*. New York: Harper Collins, 1997.
60. Merrell, Floyd. *The Mexicans: A Sense of Culture*. Boulder: Westview Press, 2003.
61. Merrell, Floyd. *The Mexicans: A Sense of Culture*. Boulder: Westview Press, 2003.
62. Krauze, Enrique. *Mexico, Biography of Power: A History of Modern Mexico, 1810–1996*. New York: Harper Collins, 1997.
63. Rock, Rosalind. "'Pido y Suplico': Women and the Law in Spanish New Mexico, 1697–1763." *New Mexico Historical Review* 65.2 (April 1990): 159.
64. Vigil, Maurilio. "The Political Development of New Mexico Hispanas." *The Contested Homeland: A Chicano History of New Mexico*. Ed. Erlina Gonzales-Berry and David Maciel. Albuquerque: University of New Mexico Press, 194.
65. Gonzales, Manuel. *Mexicanos: A History of Mexicans in the United States*. Bloomington: Indiana University Press, 1999. 77–78.
66. Gonzales, Manuel. *Mexicanos: A History of Mexicans in the United States*. Bloomington: Indiana University Press, 1999. 79.
67. Diego Vigil, James. *From Indians to Chicanos: The Dynamics of Mexican-American Culture*. Prospect Heights, IL: Waveland Press, 1998.
68. Rosales, F. Arturo. *Chicano! The History of Mexican American Civil Rights*. Houston: Arte Público Press, 1996. 88–92.
69. Acuña, Rodolfo. *Occupied America: The Chicano's Struggle Toward Liberation*. New York: Pearson Longman, 2004.
70. Benton, Thomas Hart, ed. *Abridgment of the Debates of Congress, 1789–1850*. 16 vols. New York: Putnam, 1857–1861.
71. Gerard, Lewis. "Wah-To-Yah and the Taos Trial." Palo Alto, CA: American West Publishing Company, 1968.

72. Torrez, Robert. "A Pardon for the Rebels of the Revolt of 1847." *The Albuquerque Tribune.* Saturday March 16, 2002. Section C 1–3.
73. Acuña, Rodolfo. *Occupied America: The Chicano's Struggle Toward Liberation.* New York: Pearson Longman, 2004. 28–29.
74. Doña Ana County Historical Society. *The Treaty of Guadalupe Hidalgo, 1848: Papers of the Sesquicentennial Symposium, 1848–1998.* Las Cruces, New Mexico: Yucca Tree Press, 1999.
75. Doña Ana County Historical Society. *The Treaty of Guadalupe Hidalgo, 1848: Papers of the Sesquicentennial Symposium, 1848–1998.* Las Cruces, New Mexico: Yucca Tree Press, 1999.
76. Rosales, F. Arturo. *Chicano! The History of Mexican American Civil Rights.* Houston: Arte Público Press, 1996. 88–92.
77. Gonzales, Manuel. *Mexicanos: A History of Mexicans in the United States.* Bloomington: Indiana University Press, 1999. 73.
78. Diego Vigil, James. *From Indians to Chicanos: The Dynamics of Mexican-American Culture.* Prospect Heights, IL: Waveland Press, 1998.
79. Rosales, F. Arturo. *Chicano! The History of Mexican American Civil Rights.* Houston: Arte Público Press, 1996. 88–92.
80. Acuña, Rodolfo. *Occupied America: The Chicano's Struggle Toward Liberation.* New York: Pearson Longman, 2004. 272–273.
81. Rosales, F. Arturo. *Chicano! The History of Mexican American Civil Rights.* Houston: Arte Público Press, 1996. 104–105.
82. Acuña, Rodolfo. *Occupied America: The Chicano's Struggle Toward Liberation.* New York: Pearson Longman, 2004.
    Diego Vigil, James. *From Indians to Chicanos: The Dynamics of Mexican-American Culture.* Prospect Heights, IL: Waveland Press, 1998.
    Gómez-Quinones, J. *Mexican Students por La Raza: The Chicano Student Movement in Southern California, 1967–1977.* Santa Barbara: Editorial La Causa, 1978.
    Rosales, F. Arturo. *Chicano! The History of Mexican American Civil Rights.* Houston: Arte Público Press, 1996.
83. Gonzales, Manuel. *Mexicanos: A History of Mexicans in the United States.* Bloomington: Indiana University Press, 1999. 196–201.
84. Gonzales, Manuel. *Mexicanos: A History of Mexicans in the United States.* Bloomington: Indiana University Press, 1999. 193–195.
    Anaya, Rudolfo A., and Francisco Lomelí, eds. *Aztlán: Essays on the Chicano Homeland.* Albuquerque: Academia/El Norte, 1989.
85. Rendon, A. *Chicano Manifesto.* New York: Macmillan, 1971.
    Muñoz, C. *Youth, Identity, Power.* New York: Verso, 1989.
    Gómez-Quinones, J. *Mexican Students por La Raza: The Chicano Student Movement in Southern California, 1967–1977.* Santa Barbara: Editorial La Causa, 1978.
86. Siméon, Rémi. *Dictionary of Nahuatl or Mexican.* Mexico City: Siglo Veintiuno America Nuestra, 1977. 271.
87. Acuña, Rodolfo. *Occupied America: The Chicano's Struggle Toward Liberation.* New York: Pearson Longman, 2004.

Gómez-Quinones, J. *Mexican Students por La Raza: The Chicano Student Movement in Southern California, 1967–1977.* Santa Barbara: Editorial La Causa, 1978.

88. Rosales, F. Arturo. *Chicano! The History of Mexican American Civil Rights.* Houston: Arte Público Press, 1996. 183.
89. Acuña, Rodolfo. *Occupied America: The Chicano's Struggle Toward Liberation.* New York: Pearson Longman, 2004.

    Diego Vigil, James. *From Indians to Chicanos: The Dynamics of Mexican-American Culture.* Prospect Heights, IL: Waveland Press, 1998.

    Gómez-Quinones, J. *Mexican Students por La Raza: The Chicano Student Movement in Southern California, 1967–1977.* Santa Barbara: Editorial La Causa, 1978.
90. Rosales, F. Arturo. *Chicano! The History of Mexican American Civil Rights.* Houston: Arte Público Press, 1996.
91. Acuña, Rodolfo. *Occupied America: The Chicano's Struggle Toward Liberation.* New York: Pearson Longman, 2004.
92. Gonzales, Manuel. *Mexicanos: A History of Mexicans in the United States.* Bloomington: Indiana University Press, 1999. 230.
93. Arrom, Sylvia. *The Women of Mexico City, 1790–1857.* Stanford, CA: Stanford University Press, 1985.

    Dore, Elizabeth. "The Holy Family: Imagined Households in Latin American History." *Gender Politics in Latin America.* Ed. Elizabeth Dore. New York: Monthly Review Press, 1997.

    Kuznesof, Elizabeth. "Sexual Politics, Race and Bastard Bearing in Nineteenth Century Brazil: A Question of Culture or Power?" *Journal of Family History* 16.3 (1991): 241–282.

    Safa, Helen. "Female-Headed Households in the Caribbean: Deviant or Alternative Form of Family Organization?" *Latino(a) Research Review* (Spring/Winter 1999): 16–26.
94. Herrera-Sobek, Maria. "Introduction." *Reconstructing a Chicano/a Literary Heritage: Hispanic Colonial Literature of the Southwest.* Ed. Maria Herrera-Sobek. Tucson: University of Arizona Press, 1993. xx.

    Apodaca, Maria Linda. "The Chicana Woman: An Historical Materialist Perspective." *Latina/o Thought: Culture, Politics, and Society.* Ed. Francisco Vásquez and Rodolfo Torres. New York: Rowman and Littlefield, 2003. 27–50.

    Alma García, ed. *Chicana Feminist Thought: The Basic Historical Writings.* New York: Routledge, 1997.
95. Rosales, F. Arturo. *Chicano! The History of Mexican American Civil Rights.* Houston: Arte Público Press, 1996. 174.
96. Mares, E.A. "Once a Man Knew His Name." *The Unicorn Poem & Flowers and Songs of Sorrow.* Albuquerque: West End Press, 1992. 34–36.
97. Ortiz, Alfonso. *The Tewa World: Space, Time, Being, and Becoming in a Pueblo Society.* Chicago: University of Chicago Press, 1969. 13–14.
98. Simpson, Lesley Byrd. *Many Mexicos.* 4th ed. Berkeley: University of California Press, 1966.

IV Codex Scripts of Resistance: From Columbus to the Border Patrol

1. Boone Hill, Elizabeth. "Glorious Imperium: Understanding Land and Community in Moctezuma's Mexico." *Moctezuma's Mexico: Visions of the Aztec World*. Ed. David Carrasco and Eduardo Matos Moctezuma. Boulder: University Press of Colorado, 2003. 159.
2. Hill, Elizabeth Boone, and Walter Mignolo, eds. *Writing Without Words: Alternative Literacies in Mesoamerica and the Andes*. Durham: Duke University Press, 1994.

   Cifuentes, Barbara. *Letters Over Words/Voices*. Mexico City: Centro de Investigaciones y Estudios Superiores en Antropologia Social, 1998.

   Fischer, Steven R. *A History of Writing*. London: Reaktion, 2001.
3. Duverger, Christian. *Mesoamerica: Art and Anthropology*. Mexico City: Conaculta, 2000.
4. Mexican anthropologist Bonfil Batalla claims that indigenous civilization, along with its distinctive traits and ways of thinking, was established between approximately 2000 BCE and 1500 BCE. Mesoamerican hieroglyphic writing has been dated back to around 500 BC, with pictographic forms appearing much earlier.

   Bonfil Batalla, Guillermo. *México Profundo: Reclaiming a Civilization*. Trans. Philip A. Dennis. Austin: University of Texas Press, 1996.

   It is noteworthy that Mesoamerican writing practices are possibly the only system created anywhere in the world that does not owe its existence to the concept of writing developed by the ancient Egyptians and Samarians. In his *A History of Language* (1999), linguist Steven Fischer confirms this uniqueness: "Surprisingly, only three main script traditions have effectively guided the course of written language: that of Egypt and Samaria, here termed Afro-Asiatic writing; that of China, or Asiatic writing; and that of Mesoamerica" (89).

   Molina, Alonso. *Vocabulary in Spanish and Mexican*. 4th ed. Ed. Miguel León-Portilla. Mexico City: Porría Editorial, 1970. 120.
5. León-Portilla, Miguel. "Have We Really Translated the Mesoamerican Ancient Word?" *On the Translation of Native American Literatures*. Ed. Brian Swann. Washington, DC: Smithsonian Institute Press, 1992. 317.
6. León-Portilla, Miguel, and Earl Shorris, eds. *In the Language of Kings: An Anthology of Mesoamerican Literature, Pre-Columbian to the Present*. New York: W.W. Norton, 2001. 73
7. Quiñones Keber, Eloise, ed. *Codex Telleriano-Remensis: Ritual, Divination, and History in a Pictorial Aztec Manuscript*. Austin: University of Texas Press, 1995.

   Also, in her *Stories in Red and Black: Pictorial Histories of the Aztecs and Mixtecs* (2000), historian Elizabeth Hill Boone confirms, "...women, too, were learned in this art. Both boys and girls were trained in the *Calmecac* where such skills were taught" (27).

8. León-Portilla, Miguel. *Huehuetlahtolli: Testimonios de la Antigua Palabra.* 1988. 2nd ed. Mexico City: Fondo de Cultura Económica, 1992.
9. León-Portilla, Miguel, and Earl Shorris, eds. *In the Language of Kings: An Anthology of Mesoamerican Literature, Pre-Columbian to the Present.* New York: W.W. Norton, 2001. 230.
10. Carrasco, Davíd. *The Imagination of Matter: Religion and Ecology in Mesoamerican Traditions.* Oxford: BAR International Series, 1989.
11. León-Portilla, Miguel. *Pre-Columbian Literatures of Mexico.* Trans. Grace Lobanov and Miguel León-Portilla. Norman: University of Oklahoma Press, 1986. 117.
12. Carrasco, Davíd. *Religions of Mesoamerica: Cosmovision and Ceremonial Centers.* San Francisco: Harper and Row, 1990. 81.

    León-Portilla, Miguel, and Earl Shorris, eds. *In the Language of Kings: An Anthology of Mesoamerican Literature, Pre-Columbian to the Present.* New York: W.W. Norton, 2001. 16–17.
13. Brotherston, Gordon. *Painted Books from Mexico: Codices in UK Collections and the World They Represent.* London: British Museum Press, 1995. 10.
14. León-Portilla, Miguel. *Huehuetlahtolli: Testimonios de la Antigua Palabra.* 1988. 2nd ed. Mexico City: Fondo de Cultura Económica, 1992.
15. León-Portilla, Miguel. *Los Antiguos Mexicanos a Traves de Sus C.* Cultura Económica, 1961. 60–65.
16. León-Portilla, Miguel, and Earl Shorris, eds. *In the Language of Kings: An Anthology of Mesoamerican Literature, Pre-Columbian to the Present.* New York: W.W. Norton, 2001.
17. León-Portilla, Miguel. *The Ancient Mexicans.* Mexico City: Fondo de Cultura Economica, 1995. 66.
18. In *Aristotle and the American Indians*, Lewis Hanke analyzes some of the sixteenth-century Western Rhetorical strategies of racial prejudice that are still used today in naming and interpreting Mexicans and other indigenous cultures, what is now understood as *Indianism*. In what was to be called the "Great Debate," some Europeans idolized and romanticized "native" peoples as the "Noble Savage," a peaceful yet "simple" people. Meanwhile, others worked to demonize Mexican cultures. At the heart of this discourse was a Christian bias that Aztec and Mayan religious practices were "ancient idolatries and false religions with which the devil was worshiped until the Holy Gospel was brought to this land" (47).

    Hanke, Lewis. *Aristotle and the American Indians: A Study in Race Prejudice in the Modern World.* Bloomington: Indiana University Press, 1959.
19. Romano, Susan. "Tlaltelolco: The Grammatical-Rhetorical Indios of Colonial Mexico." *College English* 66.3 (January 2004): 264–265.
20. Leibsohn, Dana. "The Paradise Garden Murals of Malenalco: Utopia and Empire in 16th Century Mexico." *Americas* 51.3 (1995): 433–435.
21. Mignolo, Walter. "Afterward: Writing and Recorded Knowledge in Colonial and Postcolonial Situations." *Writing Without Words: Alternative Literacies*

in *Mesoamerica and the Andes*. Ed. Elizabeth Boone Hill and Walter Mignolo. Durham: Duke University Press, 1994. 299.

22. Brotherston, Gordon. *Painted Books from Mexico: Codices in UK Collections and the World They Represent*. London: British Museum Press, 1995. 17.
23. Hill, Elizabeth Boone, and Walter Mignolo, eds. *Writing Without Words: Alternative Literacies in Mesoamerica and the Andes*. Durham: Duke University Press, 1994.

    Cifuentes, Barbara. *Letters Over Words/Voices*. Mexico City: Centro de Investigaciones y Estudios Superiores en Antropologia Social. 1998.
24. Eckmann, Teresa. *Chicano Artists and Neo-Mexicanists: (De)constructions of National Identity*. Albuquerque: University of New Mexico Press, 2000. 19.
25. Cumberland, Charles. *Mexico: The Struggle for Modernity*. New York: Oxford University Press, 1972. 228.
26. Mignolo, Walter. *The Darker Side of the Renaissance: Literacy, Territoriality, and Colonization*. Ann Arbor: University of Michigan Press, 1995. 76.
27. García Icazbalceta, Joaquín. *Nueva Colección de Documentos Para la Historia de México*. Vol. 2. Mexico City: Salvador Chavez Hayhoe, 1941. 204.
28. Abbott, Don Paul. "The Ancient Word: Rhetoric in Aztec Culture." *Rhetorica* 5.3 (1987): 251–264.
29. Glass, John. "A Survey of Native Middle American Pictorial Manuscripts. *Handbook of Middle American Indians*. Vol. 14. Ed. Robert Wauchope and Howard Cline. Austin: University of Texas Press, 1975. 23.

    Cline, Howard. "Selected Nineteenth-Century Mexican Writers on Ethnohistory." *Handbook of Middle American Indians*. Vol. 13. Ed. Robert Wauchope and Howard Cline. Austin: University of Texas Press, 1973. 374–377.
30. See

    Aguilera, Carmen, ed. *El Tonalamatl de Aubin*. Tlaxcala: Gobierno del Estado, 1981.

    Chavero, Alfredo. *Antiguedades Mexicanas publicadas por la Junta Colombina de México en el cuarto centenario del descubrimiento de América*. Mexico City: Oficina Tipográfica de la Secretaría de Fomento, 1892.

    Ehrle, Franz, ed. *Il manoscritto messicano caticano 3738, ditto il Códice Ríos, riprodotto in fotocromografia a spese di sua eccellenza il duca di Loubat per cura della Biblioteca Vaticana*. Rome: Stablimento Danesi, 1900.

    Nuttall, Zelia, ed. *Codex Nuttall*. New York: Dover, 1975.

    Peñafiel, Antonio. *Códice Mixteco: Lienzo de Zacatepec*. Mexico City: Secretaria de Fomento, 1900.

    Trovar, Juan, ed. *Codice Ramirez*. Mexico City: Editorial Leyenda, 1944.
31. Paul Radin's *Sources and Authenticity of the Ancient Mexicans*. Berkeley: University of California. 17.1 (1920): 1–150.

32. Robertson, Donald. *Mexican Manuscript Painting of the Early Colonial Period: The Metropolitan Schools.* New Haven: Yale University Press, 1959. 62–65.
33. Nicholson, Henry B. "Pre-Hispanic Central Mexican Historiography." *Investigaciones Contemporáneas Sobre Historia de México.* Mexico City: El Colegio de México, 1971. 33, 81.
34. León-Portilla, Miguel. "Have We Really Translated the Mesoamerican Ancient Word?" *On the Translation of Native American Literatures.* Ed. Brian Swann. Washington, DC: Smithsonian Institute Press, 1992. 313–338.
35. León-Portilla, Miguel. *Huehuetlahtolli: Testimonios de la Antigua Palabra.* 2nd ed. Mexico City: Fondo de Cultura Económica, 1992. 43–55.
36. Hernández-Avila, Inés. "The Flowering Word." *American Language Review* 4.3 (May 2000): 1.

    León-Portilla, Miguel. *Huehuetlahtolli: Testimonios de la Antigua Palabra.* 1988. 2nd ed. Mexico City: Fondo de Cultura Económica, 1992. 13.
37. Primarily, the Codices Mendoza and Azcatitlan illustrate the great Aztec migration narrative toward *Tenochtitlán*. The following publications are facsimiles of the original manuscripts:

    Berdan, Frances, and Patricia Reiff Anawalt. *The Codex Mendoza.* 4 vols. Berkeley: University of California Press, 1992.

    Barlow, Robert. "Codex Azcatitlan." *Journal de al Societe des Americanistes* 38 (1949): 101–135.
38. In the aftermath of the early conquest, the codices were given names of those who "discovered," purchased, or otherwise collected them, which explains the names *Laud*, *Féjérváry*, *Selden*, *Bodley*, *Zoche*, *Egerton*, and so on.
39. Arciniegas, Germán. *Why America?: 500 Years of a Name: The Life and Times of Amerigo Vespucci.* Trans. Harriet de Onís. Bogotá, Colombia: Villegas Editores, 2002.
40. Alarcón, Norma. "Anzaldúa's *Frontera*: Inscribing Gynectics." *Displacement, Diaspora, and Geographies of Identity.* Ed. Lavie Smadar and Ted Swedenburg. Durham: Duke University Press, 1997. 44.
41. This stylistic device is reminiscent of Powell's "rhetorics of survivance" (400).

    Powell, Malea. "Rhetorics of Survivance: How American Indians Use Writing." *College Composition and Communication* 53.3 (February 2002): 396–434.
42. Carrasco, Davíd. *Religions of Mesoamerica: Cosmovision and Ceremonial Centers.* San Francisco: Harper and Row, 1990. 137.
43. Boone Hill, Elizabeth. *Stories in Red and Black: Pictorial Histories of the Aztecs and Mixtecs.* Austin: University of Texas Press, 2000. 27.
44. Boone Hill, Elizabeth. *Stories in Red and Black: Pictorial Histories of the Aztecs and Mixtecs.* Austin: University of Texas Press, 2000. 232–233.
45. Boone Hill, Elizabeth. *Stories in Red and Black: Pictorial Histories of the Aztecs and Mixtecs.* Austin: University of Texas Press, 2000. 18.
46. Carrasco, Davíd. *Religions of Mesoamerica: Cosmovision and Ceremonial Centers.* San Francisco: Harper and Row, 1990. 126–127.

47. Carrasco, Davíd. *Daily Life of the Aztecs: People of the Sun and Earth.* London: Greenwood Press, 1998. 244.
48. Nieto, Consuelo. "The Chicana and the Women's Rights Movement." *Chicana Feminist Thought: The Basic Historical* Writings. Ed. Alma García. New York: Routledge, 1997. 208.
49. Starr-LeBeau, Gretchen. *In the Shadow of the Virgin: Inquisitors, Friars, and Conversos in Guadalupe, Spain.* Princeton: Princeton University Press, 2003.
50. Lamadrid, Enrique. "Luz y Sombra: The Poetics of Mestizo Identity." *Nuevo México Profundo: Rituals of an Indo-Hispano Homeland.* Santa Fe: Museum of New Mexico Press, 2000. 1–11.
51. In *Border Matters*, José David Saldívar argues that theoretical abstractions such as "subaltern" "Fourth World," and border crossing result in a shift to dematerialize the actual geography and materiality of border (158). The problem with such rhetoric, Saldívar warns, stems from cutting off the trope of the border from its lived experience and therefore may reproduce a detached logic of exaggeration and stereotyping.

    Saldívar, José David. *Border Matters: Remapping American Cultural Studies.* Berkeley: University of California Press, 1997.
52. Gómez-Peña, Guillermo. *The New World Border.* San Francisco: City Lights, 1996. 5.

V The Spreading of Color: Sacred Scripts and the Genesis of the Rio Grande

1. Dozier. Edward. *The Pueblo Indians of North America.* New York: Holt, Rinehart, and Winston, 1970.

    Foster, George. *Culture and Conquest: America's Spanish Heritage.* New York: Viking Fund, 1960.

    Ricard, Robert. *The Spiritual Conquest of Mexico: An Essay on the Apostolate and Evangelizing Methods of the Mendicant Orders in New Spain.* Berkeley: University of California Press, 1966.
2. Gandert, Miguel. *Nuevo Mexico Profundo: Rituals of an Indo-Hispano Homeland.* Albuquerque: Museum of New Mexico Press, 2000. 1–10.
3. Gandert, Miguel. *Nuevo Mexico Profundo: Rituals of an Indo-Hispano Homeland.* Albuquerque: Museum of New Mexico Press, 2000. 1–10.
4. Fields, Virginia, and Victor Zamudio-Taylor. *The Road to Aztlán: Art from a Mythic Homeland.* Los Angeles: Los Angeles County Museum of Art, 2001.
5. Schroeder, Albert. "Pueblos Abandoned in Historic Times." *Handbook of North American Indians.* Vol. 9. Ed. Alfonso Ortiz. Washington, DC: Smithsonian Institution Press, 1979. 236–254.
6. Robb, John. *Hispanic Folk Music of New Mexico and the Southwest: A Self-Portrait of a People.* Norman: University of Oklahoma Press, 1980.
7. Forrest, John. *Morris and Matachín: A Study in Comparative Choreography.* Sheffield, England: CECTAL, 1984. 34–35.

8. Kurath, Gertrude. "Mexican Moriscas: A Problem in Dance Acculturation." *Journal of American Folklore* 62.244 (1949): 94.
   Kurath, Gertrude. "The Origin of the Pueblo Indian Matachínes." *El Palacio* 64.9–10 (1957): 259–264.
9. Foster, George. *Culture and Conquest: America's Spanish Heritage.* New York: Viking Fund, 1960.
10. Bennett, Wendell, and Robert Zing. *The Tarahumara: An Indian Tribe of Northern Mexico.* Chicago: University of Chicago Press, 1935.
11. Robb, John. "The Matachínes Dance-A Ritual Folk Dance." *Western Folklore* 20 (1961): 87–101.
12. Kurath, Gertrude. "Mexican Moriscas: A Problem in Dance Acculturation." *Journal of American Folklore* 62.244 (1949): 87–106.
13. Robb is consistent in his emphasis upon the Matachínes' Iberian source and character, whereas Edward Dozier proposes a fusion of independently similar Old and New World forms in greater Mexico (187).
14. Robb, John D. *Hispanic Folk Music of New Mexico and the Southwest: A Self-Portrait of a People.* Norman: University of Oklahoma Press, 1980.
15. Or, as Geertz argues, symbols "present the sociological mind with bodied stuff on which to feed" (23).
    Geertz, Clifford. *The Interpretation of Cultures.* New York: Basic Books, 1973.
16. Dozier. Edward. *The Pueblo Indians of North America.* New York: Holt, Rinehart, and Winston, 1970. 31.
17. Carmack, Robert, Janine Gasco, and Gary Gossen, eds. *The Legacy of Mesoamerica: History and Culture of a Native American Civilization.* New Jersey: Prentice Hall, 1996. 448–449.
18. Castro, Rafaela. *Chicano Folklore: A Guide to the Folktales, Traditions, Rituals and Religious Practices of Mexican Americans.* New York: Oxford University Press, 2001.
19. Moraga, Cherríe. "From a Long Line of Vendidas." *Feminist Studies/Critical Studies.* Ed. Teresa de Laurentis. Bloomington: Indiana University Press, 1986. 174–175.
20. Lenchek, Shep. "La Malinche - Harlot or Heroine?" *El Qjo Del Lago* (December 1997): 1.
21. León-Portilla, Miguel, and Earl Shorris, eds. *In the Language of Kings: An Anthology of Mesoamerican Literature, Pre-Columbian to the Present.* New York: W.W. Norton, 2001.
22. Torres, Larry. *Six Nuevomexicano Folk Dramas for Advent Season.* Albuquerque: University of New Mexico Press, 1999. 137–140.
23. Torres, Larry. *Six Nuevomexicano Folk Dramas for Advent Season.* Albuquerque: University of New Mexico Press, 1999. 137–140.
24. Cobos, Ruben, ed. *Dictionary of New Mexico and Southern Colorado Spanish.* Bilingual ed. Santa Fe: Museum of New Mexico Press, 2003.
25. For additional information on coal and uranium mining projects and processing plants, see Pulido, Laura. *Environmentalism and Economic Justice: Two Chicano Struggles in the Southwest.* Tucson: University of Arizona Press, 1996.

26. Harben, Peter. "Modern Times and Trends in Industrial Minerals." *Applied Mineralogy.* Ed. M. Pecchio. Sao Paulo, Brazil: International Congress on Applied Mineralogy, 2004.
27. Herrera, Esteban. *Water Resources Issues in New Mexico.* Albuquerque: New Mexico Academy of Science, 1998.
    Lovato, Phil. *Las Acequias del Norte: The Community Ditch Systems of Northern New Mexico.* Taos, New Mexico: Four Corners Regional Commission, 1974.
    Report of the Upper Rio Grande Working Group. *The Course of Upper Rio Grande Waters: A Declaration of Concerns.* Albuquerque: Southwest Hispanic Research Institute, 1985.
    Rivera, José. *The Acequias of New Mexico and the Public Welfare.* Albuquerque, New Mexico: Southwest Hispanic Research Institute, University of New Mexico, 1996.
28. Boyd, Elizabeth. *New Mexico Santos: Religious Images in the Spanish New World.* Santa Fe: Museum of New Mexico Press, 1995.
29. Rodríguez, Sylvia. The Matachínes Dance: Ritual Symbolism and Inter ethnic Relations in the Upper Rio Grande Valley. Albuquerque: University of New Mexico Press, 1996. 46–47.
30. Report of the Upper Rio Grande Working Group. *The Course of Upper Rio Grande Waters: A Declaration of Concerns.* Albuquerque: Southwest Hispanic Research Institute, 1985.

VI Crossing Borders: Gloria Anzaldúa and the Territories of English Composition

1. Please see the following canonical works:
    Berlin, James A. *Rhetoric and Reality: Writing Instruction in American Colleges, 1900–1985.* Carbondale: Southern Illinois University Press, 1987.
    Berlin, James A. *Writing Instruction in Nineteenth-Century American Colleges.* Carbondale: Southern Illinois University Press, 1984.
    Bizzell, Patricia, and Bruce Hertzberg. *Negotiating Difference: Cultural Case Studies for Composition.* Boston: Bedford Books, 1996.
    Brereton, John C. *The Origins of Composition Studies in the American College, 1875–1925: A Documentary History.* Pittsburgh: University of Pittsburgh Press, 1995.
    Connors, Robert. "Writing the History of Our Discipline." *An Introduction to Composition Studies.* Ed. Erika Lindemann and Gary Tate. New York: Oxford University Press, 1991. 49–71.
    Kitzhaber, Albert R. *Rhetoric in American Colleges, 1850–1990.* Dallas: Southern Methodist University Press, 1990.
    Miller, Richard E. "Composing English Studies: Towards a Social History of the Discipline." *College Composition and Communication* 45 (May 1994): 164–179.

North, Steven. *Making of Knowledge in Composition: Portrait of an Emerging Field.* Upper Montclair, NJ: Boynton/Cook, 1987.

2. Please see the following publications:
   Lewiecki-Wilson, Cynthia, and Jeff Sommers. "Professing at the Fault Lines: Composition at Open Admissions Institutions." *College Composition and Communication* 50 (1999): 438–462.
   Shaughnessy, Mina. *Errors and Expectations: A Guide for the Teaching of Basic Writing.* New York: Oxford University Press, 1977.
   Yancey, Kathleen Blake. "Looking Back as We Look Forward: Historicizing Writing Assessment." *College Composition and Communication* 50.3 (1999): 483–503.
3. Bizzell, Patricia, and Bruce Hertzberg. *Negotiating Difference: Cultural Case Studies for Composition.* Boston: Bedford Books, 1996.
   Olson, Gary. "Encountering the Other: Postcolonial Theory and Composition Scholarship." *Journal of Advanced Composition* 18.1 (1998): 45–55.
4. Bartholomae, David, and Anthony Petrosky. *Ways of Reading: An Anthology for Writers.* 6th ed. Boston/New York: Bedford/St. Martin's, 2002.
5. Ortiz's strategy of transculturation in particular counters the assumptions of British anthropologist Bronislaw Malinowski. For additional information, see
   Asad, Talal. "The Concept of Cultural Translation in British Social Anthropology." *Writing Culture: The Poetics and Politics of Ethnography.* Ed. James Clifford and George Marcus. Berkeley: University of California Press, 1986. 141–164.
6. Pratt, Mary Louise. "Arts of the Contact Zone." *Ways of Reading: An Anthology for Writers.* Ed. David Bartholomae and Anthony Petrosky. Boston: Bedford Books, 2002. 530.
7. Bernal, Martin. *Black Athena: Afroasiatic Roots of Classical Civilization.* 2 vols. New Brunswick: NJ: Rutgers University Press, 1987.
   Dussel, Enrique. "Europe, Modernity, and Eurocentrism: The Semantic Slippage of the Concept of Europe." *Nepantla: Views from South* 1.3 (2000): 465–478.
8. León-Portilla, Miguel, and Earl Shorris, eds. *In the Language of Kings: An Anthology of Mesoamerican Literature, Pre-Columbian to the Present.* New York: W.W. Norton, 2001.
9. Ladon-Billings, Gloria. "For Colored Girls Who Have Considered Suicide When the Academy's Not Enough: Reflections of an African-American Woman Scholar." *Learning from Our Lives: Women, Research and Autobiography in Education.* New York: Columbia Teacher's College, 1997.
   Logan, Shirley Wilson. ed. *With Pen and Voice: A Critical Anthology of Nineteenth-Century African-American Women.* Carbondale: Southern Illinois University Press, 1995.
   Royster, Jacqueline Jones. "When the First Voice You Hear Is Not Your Own." *College Composition and Communication* 47 (1996): 329–340.
10. Benson, Thomas W. "Rhetoric and Autobiography: The Case of Malcolm X." *Quarterly Journal of Speech* 60 (1974): 1–13.

Condit, Celeste Michelle, and John Louis Lucaites. "Malcolm X and the Limits of the Rhetoric of Revolutionary Dissent." *Journal of Black Studies* 23 (1993): 291–313.

Epps, Archie, ed. *Malcolm X and the American Negro Revolution: The Speeches of Malcolm X*. London: Peter Owen, 1968.

Illo, John. "The Rhetoric of Malcolm X." *Columbia University Forum* 9 (1966): 5–12.

11. Hammerback, John C., and Richard J. Jensen. *The Rhetorical Career of Cesar Chavez*. College Station: Texas A&M University Press, 1998.

VII Thinking and Teaching Across Borders and Hemispheres

1. Banks, Adam. *Race, Rhetoric and Technology: Searching for Higher Ground*. Urbana, IL: National Council of Teachers of English/Lawrence Erlbaum Associates, 2005.

Canagarajah, A. Suresh. *A Geopolitics of Academic Writing*. Pittsburgh: University of Pittsburgh Press, 2002.

Gilyard, Keith. *Let's Flip the Script: An African American Discourse on Language, Literature, and Learning*. Detroit: Wayne State University Press, 1996.

Lyons, Scott Richard. "Rhetorical Sovereignty: What Do American Indians Want from Writing?" *College Composition and Communication* 51.3 (February 2000): 447–468.

Pough, Gwendolyn. "Personal Narrative and Rhetorics of Black Womanhood in Hip-Hop." Rhetoric and Ethnicity. Ed. Keith Gilyard and Vorris Nunley. Portsmouth, NH: Heinemann, 2004.

Powell, Malea. "Blood and Scholarship: One Mixed-Blood's Dilemma." *Race, Rhetoric, and Composition*. Ed. Keith Gilyard. Portsmouth, NH: Heinemann-Boynton/Cook, 1999.

Richardson, Elaine. *African American Literacies*. New York: Routledge, 2003.

Royster, Jacqueline Jones. *Traces of a Stream: Literacy and Social Change among African American Women*. Pittsburgh: University of Pittsburgh Press, 2000.

Young, Morris. "Standard English and Student Bodies: Institutionalizing Race and Literacy in Hawai'i." *College English* 64.4 (March 2002): 405–431.

2. See page 108.

3. Berlin, James A. *Rhetoric and Reality: Writing Instruction in American Colleges, 1900–1985*. Carbondale: Southern Illinois University Press, 1987.

Berlin, James A. *Writing Instruction in Nineteenth-Century American Colleges*. Carbondale: Southern Illinois University Press, 1984.

Brereton, John C. *The Origins of Composition Studies in the American College, 1875–1925: A Documentary History*. Pittsburgh: University of Pittsburgh Press, 1995.

Connors, Robert. "Writing the History of Our Discipline." *An Introduction to Composition Studies*. Ed. Erika Lindemann and Gary Tate. New York: Oxford University Press, 1991. 49–71.

Kitzhaber, Albert R. *Rhetoric in American Colleges, 1850–1990*. Dallas: Southern Methodist University Press, 1990.

Miller, Richard E. "Composing English Studies: Towards a Social History of the Discipline." *College Composition and Communication* 45 (May 1994): 164–179.

North, Steven. *Making of Knowledge in Composition: Portrait of an Emerging Field*. Upper Montclair, NJ: Boynton/Cook, 1987.

4. Mignolo, Walter. *The Darker Side of the Renaissance: Literacy, Territoriality, and Colonization*. Ann Arbor: University of Michigan Press, 1995. 246–247.
5. Olson, Gary, and Sidney Dobrin, eds. *Composition Theory for the Postmodern Classroom*. Albany: State University of New York Press, 1994.

Schilb, John, and Patricia Harkin, eds. *Contending with Words: Composition and Rhetoric in a Postmodern Era*. New York: Modern Language Association, 1991.

6. Robert Connors, "Writing the History of Our Discipline." *An Introduction to Composition Studies*. Ed. Erika Lindemann and Gary Tate. New York: Oxford University Press, 1991. 49–71.
7. Murphy, James. *A Short History of Writing Instruction: From Ancient Greece to Twentieth Century America*. New York: Hermagoras Press, 1990.

Brereton, John C. *The Origins of Composition Studies in the American College, 1875–1925: A Documentary History*. Pittsburgh: University of Pittsburgh Press, 1995.

Connors, Robert. "Writing the History of Our Discipline." *An Introduction to Composition Studies*. Ed. Erika Lindemann and Gary Tate. New York: Oxford University Press, 1991. 49–71.

Crowley, Sharon. *The Methodical Memory: Invention in Current-Traditional Rhetoric*. Carbondale: Southern Illinois University Press, 1990.

Miller, Richard E. "Composing English Studies: Towards a Social History of the Discipline." *College Composition and Communication* 45 (May 1994): 164–179.

North, Steven. Making of Knowledge in Composition: Portrait of an Emerging Field. Upper Montclair, NJ: Boynton/Cook, 1987.

8. Winter, Marcus. *Oaxaca: The Archeological Record*. México: Minutiae Mexicana, 1989. 128.
9. Wade, Peter. *Race and Ethnicity in Latin America*. New York: Pluto Press, 1997.
10. Fukuyama, Francis. *The End of History and the Last Man*. New York: Free Press, 1992.
11. Connors, Robert. "Writing the History of Our Discipline." *An Introduction to Composition Studies*. Ed. Erika Lindemann and Gary Tate. New York: Oxford University Press, 1991. 49–71.

Mignolo, Walter. *The Darker Side of the Renaissance: Literacy, Territoriality, and Colonization.* Ann Arbor: University of Michigan Press, 1995. 40–41.

Nebrija, Antonio de. *Gramática Castellana. Salamanca.* 1517. London: Oxford University Press, 1926.

Ohmann, Richard. *English in America: A Radical View of the Profession.* New York: Oxford University Press, 1976.

Rama, Angel. *The Lettered City.* Trans. John Charles Chasteen. Durham: Duke University Press, 1996.

12. Crowley, Sharon. *The Methodical Memory: Invention in Current-Traditional Rhetoric.* Carbondale: Southern Illinois University Press, 1990.

    Lunsford, Andrea. "The Nature of Composition Studies." An Introduction to Composition Studies. Ed. Erika Lindemann and Gary Tate. New York: Oxford University Press, 1991.

13. Powell, Malea. "Blood and Scholarship: One Mixed-Blood's Dilemma." *Race, Rhetoric, and Composition.* Ed. Keith Gilyard. Portsmouth, NH: Heinemann-Boynton/Cook, 1999.
14. Burciaga, José Antonio. "Poema en tres idiomas y caló." *Undocumented Love.* San José: Chusma House, 1992. 39–41.
15. Zermeno, Sergio. "State, Society and Dependent Neoliberalism in Mexico: The Case of the Chiapas Uprising." *Politics, Social Change and Economic Restructuring in Latin America.* Ed. William Smith and Roberto Korzeniewicz. Miami: North-South Press, 1997. 123–147.
16. Tremblay, Gaëtan. "Is Quebec Culture Doomed to Become American?" *Canadian Journal of Communication* 17.2 (1992): 134–138.
17. Lewis, Rand. *The Nazi Legacy: Right-Wing Extremism in Postwar Germany.* New York: Praeger, 1991.
18. Greenfield, Liah. *Nationalism: Five Roads to Modernity.* Cambridge, MA: Harvard University Press, 1992.
19. Rodríguez, Ileana. "Introduction."*Latin American Subaltern Studies Reader.* Ed. Ileana Rodríguez. Durham: Duke University Press, 2001.
20. Young, Morris. "Standard English and Student Bodies: Institutionalizing Race and Literacy in Hawai'i." *College English* 64.4 (March 2002): 405–431.

Glossary

A

Abya Yala: Panamanian expression to replace the European name for North and South America, declared by the III Continental Summit of Indigenous Nations and Pueblos in March 1992

Achtontli: Great-grandfather, ancestor

Acicamatl: To understand

Afro-Olmec: Speculation that the ancient Olmec were of Mende African descent, having arrived in the Mexican Gulf as early as 100,000 BCE

Alvarado Tezozomoc, Fernando Texcocan: Author of the *Crónica Mexicayotl*, a 1598 chronicle of Aztec imperial history in central Mexico, written in both *Nahuatl* and Spanish

Altepepan: At the city

Altepetl: Literally, "water/mountain"; the *Nahua* unit of communal identity or group

Amatl: Paper made from tree bark, used for *amoxtli*

America: European name for the Western Hemisphere beginning in 1507; the only continent on the planet named after a man

Amoxcalli: Library

Amoxoaque: Those who interpret and publicly perform the *amoxtli* through oratory, chants, song, and sometimes choreographed dance. A visual, multimodal, collective, and interactive form of communication

Amoxtli: Collaborative, pictographic, "painted books" of Mesoamerica; reinvented today in Mexico and the United States

Anahuac: Land basin of the Pacific and Gulf coastal regions, also references the Valley of Mexico

Arawak: Generalization for the first American Indians to encounter Spanish-Iberian sailors

Atlantic: European name for the body of water east of Portugal

Atolli/Atole: Drink made of corn

Aztec: Derivative of *Aztecatl*, meaning "the *Mexica* who migrated from *Aztlán*"; "*Aztec*" conflates all complex and distinct cultures of central Mesoamerica, though present-day scholarly use of "*Aztec*" refers specifically to the *Mexica*

Aztlán: Legendary homeland of the Aztec according to the codices Boturini, Telleriano-Remensis, Aubin, Crónica Mexicáyotl, and Historia Tolteca-Chichimeca; Some Chicana's and Chicano's adopt Aztlán as metaphor and symbol of civil rights struggle, political activism, and open recognition of Indigenous ancestry

Aymara: Language system of the Aymara people in the Andes. Over one million speakers today

C

Calmecac: System of conservatories for advanced study in writing, astronomy, statesmanship, theology, mathematics, and other areas. The *Calmecac* system was not an Aztec importation, but an education network influenced by the preceding 10,000 years of cultural and intellectual development in the Valley of Oaxaca

Calmanani: Architect

Carib: People who lived in the Lesser Antilles islands, after whom the Caribbean Sea was named

Caxtiltecatl: Spaniard

Chicana/Chicano: A self-identifier asserting respect for the Indigenous roots of Mexican American people. A Spanish derivative of an older *Nahuatl* root, *Mexitli* ("Meh-shee-tlee"), which is part of the dual expression *Huitzilopochtli/Mexitli,* point to the legendary *Mexica* migration from Aztlán to the Valley of Oaxaca

Chicomoztoc: "At the seven caves." The legendary origin of the Aztecs, *Tepanecs*, *Acolhuas*, and other *Nahuatl*-speaking Mesoamericans, as recorded in the 1530 *Codex Boturini* and the 1550 *Historia Tolteca-Chichimeca*

Cihtli: Grandmother. Plural: *Cicihtin*

Chocolatl: Chocolate

Cholula: An urban center in Anahuac, dating to 700 BCE by the Olmec

Cihuatl: Woman. Plural: *Cihauh*

Cihuayao: Woman Warrior

Clovis Man: American English name for remains, 9500 BCE

Codex (Latin): See *Amoxtli*

Colli: Grandfather. Plural: *Coltin*

Conetl: Child. Plural: *Coconeh*

Cortéz, Hernán: Initiated the brutal conquest of the Aztec Empire and surrounding civilizations; killed 3000 *Cholultecas* and 245,000 Aztecs; millions died of chicken pox

Cuauhtémoc: "Eagle that descends," the last Aztec ruler. His capture on August 13, 1521 reportedly ended the Spanish conquest

Cuicatl: Song

Cuitlahuac: Moctezuma's successor as ruler, mounted resistance to the Spaniards

E

Ehecatl: Wind, air

Escuela Tlatelolco: A nonprofit, community-based private school established in Denver Colorado, 1970

Esperanza Peace and Justice Center: A nonprofit community-centered organization established in San Antonio, Texas

G

Globalization: Generalization referring to post–World War II unregulated economic processes, such as the rise of transnational corporate entities that function across cultural and political borders. Some scholars, author included, place the advent of globalization at 1492 CE

H

Hernandez v. Texas: Supreme Court recognizes Mexican Americans as a separate cultural group distinct from Caucasians, paving the way for Latino Americans to use legal means against discrimination

Huehuetlahtolli: Ancient word, discourse of the Ancients, "proper" discourse; wisdom, legacy, tradition, and culture passed down through the generations

Huitzilihuitl: Hummingbird feather

Huitzilopochtli: "Hummingbird on the left." Aztec war deity, principal *Mexica* sun god and god of war

I

Ihcuiloa: To write

Ihcuilotic: It is written

Imperialism: The domination of one group of territories by another group. Imperialist countries exploit less "developed" countries by extracting more raw materials and completed products than they put in. This form of domination is also seen as a recent stage of unregulated "late-global-capitalism" with certain specific features, including the decrease of free competition and the increasing power of monopolies

In Ttlilli, In Tlapalli: Metaphor for books that translates literally as "the black [ink], the red [ink]" and also implies knowledge or wisdom

Intzalan: Between

In Xochitl, In Cuicatl: "Flower and song." An inclusive expression for what Western minds identify as art, literature, rhetoric, poetics, and inscription

L

Ladino: Spanish speaker in Southern Mesoamerica, of Mestizo or Spanish descent

Languages: 170 languages were spoken in Mexico prior to Spanish Invasion; by the late twentieth century, only 62 languages survive

Latina/Latino: An inclusive generalization for North American, Central American, South American, and often for Caribbean peoples living in the United States

Liberation Theology: Latin American movement, emerging in the 1970s. A form of spiritual activism that aims to unite with the struggles of the poor and oppressed while fighting for social justice

M

Malintzin: Prepubescent girl given to Conquistadors by the *Tabascans*; fluent in *Nahuatl*, Quechua, and Spanish, *Malintzin* was translator and mistress of Hernán Cortéz

Mapa de Cuauhtinchan: 1580 *Chichimec* document that records historical information from the twelfth through the fifteenth centuries

Mati: To know

Maya: People of southern Mexico and Central America

Mesoamerica: One of the planet's five regions of early urban development. The region comprises Central America and most of Mexico. Olmec, Teotihuacan, Toltec, the Maya, and the Aztec

Metzli: Moon

Mexica: Last of the seven tribes to migrate from Aztlán to the Valley of Mexico—the Aztec homeland according to oral tradition and some pictographic documentation. Atecas. *Mexica* group of *Nahuatl* speakers who rose to military and political prominence

Mexicatl: Mexican

Mexicayotl: Mexican culture

Mictia: To kill

Mictlan: The Aztec underworld, where the bulk of people were thought to arrive after a passage through nine levels. The realm of a male and female death god, *Mictlantecuhtli* and *Mictlancihuatl*

Mictlantecuhtli: "Lord of Death" *Mictlantecuhtli* ruled over Mictlan, the Underworld, which was divided into nine layers. Travel through *Mictlan* was highly dangerous and often accompanied by a dog, undertaken by those who had died a natural death

Mixtec: Inhabitants of the south of Mexico. The Mixtecs were highly skilled goldsmiths and scribes who the Aztecs employed to create much of their jewelry and write many of the painted books

Moctezuma II: Aztec ruler at the time of the Spanish conquest

Monequiltia: To love

Mopopolhuilia: To forgive

Museo de las Culturas Afromestizas: Museum in the state of Guerrero, Mexico. Research focuses on indigenous traditions of Afromestizo cultures in the Atlantic and Pacific coasts of Mexico

N

Nahuatl: A lingua franca across early Mesoamerica, including northern regions up to Canada and as far south as Panama. *Nahuatl* still spoken in Mexico, the United States, and other regions

Nantli: Mother. Plural: *Nantin*. Reverential: *Nantzintli*

Nemachtiloyan: School

Nepantla: Feeling in between, or "the space between two oceans"

Neocolonialism: System in which former colonial countries are controlled by former colonizers and international institutions like the International Monetary Fund, even though the countries have gained formal independence. Developed countries can often control the economies of their former colonies and other so-called third world nations

Netzahualcoyotl, Tlatoani of Texcoco: *Acolhua*, another *Nahuatl*-speaking culture settled in the eastern part of the Valley of Mexico, settling on the eastern side of *Lake Texcoco*

Nixtamalli: Corn paste for tortillas and tamales

Nocenyeliz: My family

Nochtli: Cactus

Nopal: Cactus

North American Free Trade Agreement: 1994 agreement between the United States, Canada, and Mexico to eliminate tariffs and other fees in order to support unregulated trade between the three countries

O

Olmec: An ancient Aztec culture on the Mexican gulf coast; the first to develop glyphic scripts, the 260-day calendar, and ceremonial centers; precursors to Maya civilization

Ometeotl: The dual she/he deity, supreme god and creator souls
Operation Wetback: From 1954 to 1958, U.S. government deports 3.8 million people of Mexican descent, including legal citizens; thousands of citizens are also arrested and detained
Oquichtli: Male. Plural: *Oquichtin*
Oztotl: Cave

P

Pactia: To give pleasure
Pahpiani: Medicine specialist
Pahti, or *Pahtia*: To cure
Pahtli: Medicine
Papalotl: Butterfly
Pochtecatl: Merchant
Pohua: To count, to read
Population Decline: 40 million in 1491 down to 10 million by 1650.

Q

Quechua: Language spoken in numerous ways by 10 million people throughout South America, including Peru, South-western Bolivia, southern Colombia and Ecuador, north-western Argentina and northern Chile; language of the Inka Empire
Quetzalcoatl: The plumed serpent god of the Toltecs and Aztecs, called Kukulkán by the Maya.
Quipu or *Khipu*: Recording devices used in the Inca Empire and its predecessor societies in the Andean region. A quipu usually consisted of colored spun and plied thread or strings from llama or alpaca hair or cotton cords with numeric and other values encoded by knots in a base 10 positional system. Quipus may have just a few strands, but some have up to 2,000 strands. Khipus represented a binary system capable of recording phonological or logographic data.
Quiyahuitl: Rain
Quizaliztli: Migration

S

Sephardic Crypto-Judaism: Beginning in 1492, migrated to Central America in the attempt to escape the Spanish Inquisition; today, there are roughly 40,000 Mexican Sephardic Jews throughout the United States southwest and various regions of Mexico

T

Tabascans: Civilization at the base if the Yucatan Peninsula; gave Spanish Conquistadors 20 slave girls to avoid further fighting with Cortéz' battalion

Tahtli: Father. Plural: *Tahtin*. Reverential: *Tahtzintli*

Tahuantinsuyu: "Land of the four quadrants"; the Incan geographical and political center of Cuzco. The quadrants of Tahuantinsuyu also include "upper" and "lower" celestial components as a fundamental organizing spiritual and special structure

Tecuhtli: Lord. Plural, reverential: *Tecuhtzintli*

Telpochcalli: "House of the Young," taught history, religion, military arts, agriculture

Temachtiani: Teacher. Plural: *Temachtianimeh*. Reverential: *Temachticatzintli*

Templo Mayor: "Great Temple" of *Tenochtitlán* was the largest Aztec pyramid and represented the physical and spiritual center of their world. It was rebuilt and enlarged several times and had twin shrines at the top dedicated to Tlaloc and *Huitzilopochtli*

Tennamiqui: To kiss

Tenochtitlán: The Aztec capital at the time of the Spanish conquest; the name of the large capital city built on an island in Lake Texcoco where the Aztecs ruler lived and the Great Temple was located. It was the center of the Aztecs world to which all tribute was brought

Tentli: Edge, border

Teocalli: Temple

Teopixqui: Priest/Philosopher. Plural: *Teopixque*

Teotihuacános: (100 BCE–900 ADE) architects of the pyramids near modern-day Mexico City; the template for civilization adopted by Aztecs, other *Nahuatl*-speaking cultures, and the Maya

Tepec: Hill

Tepehuani: Conquistador

Tepetl: Mountain, volcano

Tequipanoa: To labor

Testimonio: Autobiographical witnessing, often associated with and supporting international human rights, solidarity movements, and liberation struggles

Ticitl: Healer, matrifocal

Tlacamatli: Obeyance

Tlacatilia: Conception

Tlacatl: Male

Tlahtoa: To speak

Tlahtoani. King. Plural: *Tlahtoanime*

Tlahtocayotl: Kingdom, nation

Tlaloc: Aztec rain god. It is one of the many gods that existed before the Aztecs and which was later incorporated into the pantheon of gods

Tlamachtilli: Student. Plural: *Tlamachtiltin*

Tlamatinime: Philosopher/priests, women and men study and perform *Huehuetlahtolli*, understood as *Tlaolli*: Corn

Tlaquilolitztli: One of the earlier known expressions for "writing" in the Western Hemisphere, translated as "the spreading of color on hard surfaces"

Tlaquiloque: Trained to inscribe and compose the *amoxtli*

Tlatelolco: North of *Tenochtitlán*, home of the Plaza of Three Cultures; one of the last places defended by the Aztec against Spanish Invasion

Tlatimine: Teacher/priests at the *Calmecac* system

Tlatquitl: Patrimony

Tlaxcalmana: To make bread

Tlaxcalteca (also *Tlaxcalans*): "Place of the tortillas"; A *Nahuatl*-speaking culture inhabiting the Kingdom of Tlaxcala; Allies to Conquistador Hernán Cortés and his Spanish combatants during the invasion of *Tenochtitlán*

Tlazohtla: To love

Toltec: The last dominant Mesoamerican culture before the Aztecs

Toltecatl: Wise one, knowledgeable

Tonalpoalli: Calendar system

Tonantzin: Lunar mother goddess. The Basilica of Guadalupe is built upon *Tonantzin's* ceremonial site, suggesting spiritual syncretism between Mesoamerican and Roman Catholic faith systems

Tonehua: To suffer

Treaty of Guadalupe-Hidalgo: Ending the U.S. war against Mexico, officials sign, in which Mexico looses nearly half its territory, including modern-day California, most of Arizona and New Mexico, and parts of Colorado, Nevada, and Utah.

Triple Alliance: Founded in 1428, the largest Mesoamerican political entity: *Tenochtitlán*, Tetzcoco, and Tlacopan

Tulum: Mayan word for fence or wall. May have been formerly known as *Zama*, meaning city of Dawn

Turquoise: Prized blue-to-green mineral used to decorate masks and jewelry

X

Xi: Name of the Olmec people; infrequently referred to as the Afro-Olmec

Xihuitl: Herb, leaf, year

Xinachtli: Seed

Xochitl: Flower

Xochiquetza: Goddess of flowers and love

Y

Yancuic: New, fresh

Yancuic Tlahtolli: New discourse, new traditions, new knowledge; contemporary communications in *Nahuatl*, Spanish, English, Spanglish, and other discourses

Yeccaqui: To understand, to comprehend

Yectenehua: To bless, to sanctify

Yectli: Good, beautiful

Yollotl: Heart

Yucatán: Homeland of the first Maya, who eventually migrated to Guatemala, Belize, Honduras, El Salvador, and other provinces of Mexico

Z

Zapatistas: Movement, fighting for social reform, political reform, and indigenous rights; engaged in armed rebellion in 1994 to coincide with the implementation of the North American Free Trade Agreement

Zazanilli: Narrative

Bibliography

Abbott, Don Paul. "The Ancient World: Rhetoric in Aztec Culture." *Rhetorica* 5 (1987): 251–264.

———. *Rhetoric in the New World: Rhetorical Theory and Practice in Colonial Spanish America*. Columbia: University of South Carolina Press, 1996.

Acuña, Rodolfo. *Occupied America: The Chicano's Struggle Toward Liberation*. New York: Pearson Longman, 2004.

Adas, Michael. "From Settler Colony to Global Hegemon: Integrating the Exceptionalist Narrative of the American Experience into World History." *American Historical Review* 106 (2001): 1692–1720.

Adorno, Rolena. *Guaman Poma: Writing and Resistance in Colonial Peru*. Austin: University of Texas Press, 1986.

Aguilera, Carmen, ed. *El Tonalamatl de Aubin*. Tlaxcala: Gobierno del Estado, 1981.

Alarcón, Norma. "Anzaldúa's *Frontera*: Inscribing Gynectics." *Displacement, Diaspora, and Geographies of Identity*. Ed. Lavie Smadar and Ted Swedenburg. Durham: Duke University Press, 1997.

———. "Chicana's Feminist Literature: A Re-Vision through Malintzin/or Malintzin: Putting Flesh Back on the Object." *This Bridge Called My Back: Writings by Radical Women of Color*. Ed. Cherríe Moraga and Gloria Anzaldúa. New York: Kitchen Table: Women of Color Press, 1981. 182–190.

Alcoff, Linda Martín. *Visible Identities, Race, Gender and the Self*. London: Oxford University Press, 2005.

Allen, Paula Gunn. *Off the Reservation: Reflections on Boundary-Busting, Border Crossing Loose Canons*. Boston: Beacon Press, 1998.

Almaguer, Tomás. "Ideological Distortions in Recent Chicano Historiography: The Internal Model and Chicano Historical Interpretation." *Aztlán* 18.1 (1987): 7–28.

Anaya, Rudolfo, and Francisco Lomelí, eds. *Aztlán: Essays on the Chicano Homeland*. Albuquerque, NM: Academia/El Norte Publications, 1989.

Anderson, Arthur. *Florentine Codex: General History of the Things of New Spain. Book 1—The Gods*. Provo: University of Utah Press, 1970.

Anzaldúa, Gloria. "Border *Arte*: *Nepantla, El Lugar de la Frontera*." *La Frontera/The Border: Art About the Mexico/United States Border Experience*. Ed. Natasha Bonilla Martínez. San Diego: Centro Cultural de la Raza, Museum of Contemporary Art, 1993. 113

Anzaldúa, Gloria. *Borderlands/La Frontera: The New Mestiza*. San Francisco: Aunt Lute Books; 3rd ed., 2007.

Apodaca, Maria Linda. "The Chicana Woman: An Historical Materialist Perspective." *Latina/o Thought: Culture, Politics, and Society*. Ed. Francisco Vasquez and Rodolfo Torres. New York: Rowman and Littlefield, 2003. 27–50.

Arteaga, Alfred. *An Other Tongue: Nation and Ethnicity in the Linguistic Borderlands*. Durham: Duke University Press, 1994.

———. *Chicano Poetics: Heterotexts and Hybridities*. Cambridge: Cambridge University Press, 1997.

Arturo Aldama. *Disrupting Savagism: Intersecting Chicana/o, Immigrant, and Native American Struggles for Self-Representation*. Durham: Duke University Press, 2001.

Barber, Michael. *Ethical Hermeneutics: Rationality in Enrique Dussel's Philosophy of Resistance*. New York: Fordham University Press, 1998.

Barber, Russell, Lanny Fields, and Cheryl Riggs, eds. *The Global Past*. Boston: Bedford Books, 1998.

Barron, Nancy. "Dear Saints, Dear Stella: Letters Examining the Messy Lines of Expectations, Stereotypes, and Identity in Higher Education." *College Composition and Communication* 55.1 (September 2003): 11–37.

Bartholomae, David, and Anthony Petrosky, eds. *Ways of Reading: An Anthology for Writers*. 6th ed. Boston/New York: Bedford/St. Martin's, 2002.

Berdan, Frances, and Patricia Rieff Anawalt. *The Essential Codex Mendoza*. Los Angeles: University of California Press, 1997.

Berlin, James A. *Rhetoric and Reality: Writing Instruction in American Colleges, 1900–1985*. Carbondale: Southern Illinois University Press, 1987.

———. *Writing Instruction in Nineteenth-Century American Colleges*. Carbondale: Southern Illinois University Press, 1984.

Bernal, Martin. *Black Athena: The Afroasiatic Roots of Classical Civilization, Vol. I, The Fabrication of Ancient Greece 1787–1987*. New Brunswick: Rutgers University Press, 1987.

Bhabha, Homi. *The Location of Culture*. London: Routledge, 1994.

Bizzell, Patricia, and Bruce Hertzberg. *Negotiating Difference: Cultural Case Studies for Composition*. Boston: Bedford Books, 1996.

———. *The Rhetorical Tradition: Readings from Classical Times to the Present*. 2nd ed. New York: Bedford/St. Martin's, 2001.

Bizzell, Patricia, Bruce Herzberg, and Nedra Reynolds. "A Brief History of Rhetoric and Composition." *The Bedford Bibliography for Teachers of Writing*. 5th ed. New York: Bedford/St. Martin's, 2000.

Bloom, John Porter, ed. *Treaty of Guadalupe Hidalgo, 1848: Papers of the Sesquicentennial Symposium, 1848–1998*. Las Cruces, New Mexico: Doña Ana Historical Society and Yucca Tree Press, 1998.

Boone Hill, Elizabeth. *Cycles of Time and Meaning in the Mexican Books of Fate*. Austin: University of Texas Press, 2007.

———. *Stories in Red and Black: Pictorial Histories of the Aztecs and Mixtecs*. Austin: University of Texas Press, 2000.

Boone Hill, Elizabeth, and Walter Mignolo, eds. *Writing Without Words: Alternative Literacies in Mesoamerica and the Andes*. Durham: Duke University Press, 1994. 3–26.

Booth, Willard C. "Dramatic Aspects of Aztec Rituals." *Educational Theatre Journal* 18 (December 1966): 421–428.

Boquet, Elizabeth H. "'Our Little Secret': A History of Writing Centers, Pre- to Post-Open Admissions." *College Composition and Communication* 50.3 (1999): 463–482.

Brereton, John C. *The Origins of Composition Studies in the American College, 1875–1925: A Documentary History.* Pittsburgh: University of Pittsburgh Press, 1995.

Brotherston, Gordon. *Book of the Fourth World: Reading the Native Americas through Their Literature.* New York: Cambridge University Press, 1992.

Canagarajah, A. Suresh. *A Geopolitics of Academic Writing.* Pittsburgh: University of Pittsburgh Press: 2002.

Carrasco, Davíd. *Mesoamerica's Classic Heritage: From Teotihuacán to the Aztecs.* Boulder: University of Colorado Press, 2000.

———. *Quetzalcoatl and the Irony of Empire,* rev. ed. Boulder: University Press of Colorado, 2001.

———. *Religions of Mesoamerica: Cosmovision and Ceremonial Centers.* San Francisco: Harper and Row, 1990.

Carrasco, David, and Eduardo Matos Moctezuma. *Moctezuma's Mexico: Visions of the Aztec World.* Boulder: University Press of Colorado, 2003.

Carrasco, Davíd, and Scott Sessions. *Cave, City, And Eagle's Nest: An Interpretive Journey through the Mapa de Cuauhtinchan No. 2.* Albuquerque: University of New Mexico Press, 2007.

Castillo, Ana. *Massacre of the Dreamers: Essays on Xicanisma.* Albuquerque: University of New Mexico Press, 1994.

Castillo, Debra, and María Socorro Tabuenca Córdoba. *Border Women: Writing from La Frontera.* Minneapolis: University of Minnesota Press, 2002.

Castro, Juan. *Mestizo Nations: Culture, Race, and Conformity in Latin American Literature.* Tucson: University of Arizona Press, 2002.

Chavero, Alfredo. *Antiguedades Mexicanas publicadas por la Junta Colombina de México en el cuarto centenario del descubrimiento de América.* Mexico City: Oficina Tipográfica de la Secretaría de Fomento, 1892.

Chomsky, Noam. *Cartesian Linguistics: A Chapter in the History of Rationalist Thought.* Lanham, Maryland: University Press of America, 1986.

Cintron, Ralph. *Angels' Town: Chero Ways, Gang Life, and Rhetorics of the Everyday.* Boston: Beacon, 1997.

Connors, Robert. "Dreams and Play: Historical Method and Methodology." *Methods and Methodology in Composition Research.* Ed. Gesa Krisch and Patricia Sullivan. Carbondale: Southern Illinois University Press, 1992. 15–36.

———. "Writing the History of Our Discipline." *An Introduction to Composition Studies.* Ed. Erika Lindemann and Gary Tate. New York: Oxford University Press, 1991. 49–71.

Crabtree, Charlotte, and Gary Nash, eds. *National Standards for United States History: Exploring the American Experience.* Los Angeles: National Center for History in the Schools, 1994.

Crabtree, Charlotte, and Gary Nash, eds. *National Standards for World History: Exploring Paths to the Present.* Los Angeles: National Center for History in the Schools, 1994.

Crapo, Richley, and Bonnie Glass-Coffin, ed. *Anónimo Mexicano.* Logan: Utah State University Press, 2005.

Crowley, Sharon. *The Methodical Memory: Invention in Current-Traditional Rhetoric.* Carbondale: Southern Illinois University Press, 1990.

Diaz, Gisele and Alan Rodgers. *The Codex Borgia: A Full-Color Restoration of the Ancient Mexican Manuscript.* New York: Dover, 1993.

Díaz del Castillo, Bernal. *The Discovery and Conquest of Mexico 1517–1521.* Cambridge, MA: Da Capo Press Publishers, 1996.

Diego Vigil, James. *From Indians to Chicanos: The Dynamics of Mexican-American Culture.* Prospect Heights, IL: Waveland Press, 1998.

Diop, Cheikh Anta. *The African Origin of Civilization: Myth or Reality.* New York: Lawrence Hill Press, 1983.

Dozier. Edward. *The Pueblo Indians of North America.* New York: Holt, Rinehart, and Winston, 1970.

Draher, Patricia, ed. *Chicano Codices: Encountering Art of the Americas.* San Francisco: Mexican Museum, 1992.

Du Bois, W.E.B. *The Souls of Black Folk.* Chicago: A.C. McClurg; Cambridge, MA: University Press John Wilson and Son, 1903, 1999.

Dussel, Enrique. *Ética de la Liberación en la Edad de la Globalización y de la Exclusión.* Madrid: Editorial Trotta, 1998.

———. "Europe, Modernity, and Eurocentrism." *Nepantla: Views from the South* 1.3 (2000): 465–478.

———. *The Invention of the Americas: Eclipse of "the Other" and the Myth of Modernity.* Trans. Michael D. Barber. New York: Continuum, 1995.

Ehrle, Franz, ed. *Il manoscritto messicano caticano 3738, ditto il Códice Ríos, riprodotto in fotocromografia a spese di sua eccellenza il duca di Loubat per cura della Biblioteca Vaticana.* Rome: Stablimento Danesi, 1900.

Fusco, Coco. *The Bodies That Were Not Ours: And Other Writings.* New York: Routledge, 2002.

———. *English Is Broken Here: Notes on Cultural Fusion in the Americas.* New York: New Press, 1995.

Fukuyama, Francis. *The End of History and the Last Man.* New York: Free Press, 1992.

Foster, Thomas. "Cyber-Aztecs and Cholo-Punks: Guillermo Gómez-Peña's Five Worlds Theory." *PMLA* 117.1 (2002): 43–67.

———. *The Great Disruption: Human Nature and the Reconstitution of Social Order.* New York: Free Press, 1999.

Gagnon, Paul. "Why Study History?" *The Atlantic Monthly* November (1988).

Gaspar de Alba, Alicia. *Chicano Art: Inside/Outside the Master's House.* Austin: University of Texas Press, 1998.

George, Diana. "From Analysis to Design: Visual Communication in the Teaching of Writing." *College Composition and Communication* 54.1 (September 2002): 11–39.

Gilyard, Keith, ed. *Race, Rhetoric, and Composition.* Portsmouth, NH: Heinemann-Boynton/Cook, 1999.

Giroux, Henry A. *Border Crossings: Cultural Workers and the Politics of Education.* New York: Routledge, 1992.

Glissant, Eduardo. *The Poetics of Relation.* Trans. Betsy Wing. Ann Arbor: University of Michigan Press, 1997.

Gómez-Peña, Guillermo. Excerpt from Performance Text "The Free Trade Agreement / El Tratado de Libre Cultura." http://www.movingpartspress.com/Text/codexsprd.html. Accessed June 29, 2004.

———. *The New World Border: Prophecies, Poems and Loqueras for the End of the Century.* San Francisco: City Lights Books, 1996.

Gómez-Peña, Guillermo, Enrique Chagoya, and Felicia Rice. *Codex Espangliensis: From Columbus to the Border Patrol.* San Francisco: City Lights Books, 2000.

González, Jennifer. "Review of *Codex Espangliensis: From Columbus to the Border Patrol*, by Guillermo Gómez-Peña, Enrique Chagoya, and Felicia Rice." *Aztlan* 24.1 (Spring 1999): 211–215.

Gordon, Lewis. *Her Majesty's Other Children: Sketches of Racism from a Neocolonial Age.* Lanham, Maryland: Rowman and Littlefield, 1997.

Greenfield, Gerald, and John Buenker, ed. *Those United States: International Perspectives on American History.* Ed. Belmont, CA: Wadsworth, 2000.

Greenfield, Liah. *Nationalism: Five Roads to Modernity.* Cambridge, MA: Harvard University Press, 1992.

Grosfoguel, Ramon, Nelson Maldonado-Torres, and Jose David Saldivar, eds. *Latin@s in the World-System: Decolonization Struggles in the 21st Century U.S. Empire.* Boulder, CO: Paradigm, 2006.

Guarneri, Carl. "Internationalizing the United States Survey Course." *The History Teacher* 36.1 (November 2002): 37–64.

Guerra, Juan C. *Close to Home: Oral and Literate Practices in a Transnational Mexicano Community.* New York: Teachers College Press, 1998.

Gutiérrez, Ramon. *When Jesus Came, the Corn Mothers Went Away: Marriage, Sexuality, and Power in New Mexico, 1500–1846.* Stanford, CA: Stanford University Press, 1991.

Handa, Carolyn, ed. *Visual Rhetoric in a Digital World: A Critical Sourcebook.* Boston: Bedford/St. Martin's, 2004.

Harris, Joseph. "Negotiating the Contact Zone." *Journal of Basic Writing* 14 (1995): 27–42.

Harris, Max. "The Return of Moctezuma: Oaxaca's Danza de la Pluma and New Mexico's Danza de los Matachines." *The Drama Review* 41.1 (Spring 1997): 106–134.

Hartog, Francois. *The Mirror of Heroditus: An Essay on the Representation of the Other.* Berkeley: University of California Press, 1988.

Hernández-Avila, Inés. "The Flowering Word." *American Language Review* 4.3 (May 2000): 1–15.

Herrera-Sobek, Maria, ed. *Santa Barraza: Artist of the Borderlands.* College Station: Texas A & M University Press, 2001.

Hesford, Wendy S. "Writing Identities: The Essence of Difference in Multicultural Classrooms." *Writing in Multicultural Settings.* Ed. Carol Severino, Juan C. Guerra, and Johnnella E. Butler. New York: MLA, 1997. 133–149.

Hocks, Mary. "Understanding Visual Rhetoric in Digital Writing Environments." *College Composition and Communication* 54.4 (June 2003): 629–656.

Ixtlilxóchitl, Fernando de Alva. *Histoire des Chichiméques et des Anciens Rois de Tezcoco.* 2 vols. Paris: A. Bertrand, 1840.

Jansen, Marten and Gabina Aurora Perez Jimenez. *Codex Bodley: A Painted Chronicle from the Mixtec Highlands, Mexico.* London: Bodleian Library, University of Oxford Press, 2005.

Keali'Inohomoku, Joann. "Hopi and Hawaiian Music and Dance: Responses to Cultural Contact." *Musical Repercussions of 1492: Encounters in Text and Performance.* Ed. Carol Robertson. Washington: Smithsonian Institution Press, 1992. 429–450.

Keating, AnnLouise. *Women Reading Women Writing: Self-Invention in Paula Gunn Allen, Gloria Anzaldúa and Audre Lorde.* Philadelphia: Temple University Press, 1996.

Kells, Michelle Hall, Valerie Balester, and Victor Villanueva, eds. *Latino/a Discourses: On Language, Identity and Literacy Education.* Portsmouth, NH: Boynton/Cook, 2004.

Kingston, Maxine Hong. *China Men.* New York: Knopf, 1980.

Kitzhaber, Albert R. *Rhetoric in American Colleges, 1850–1990.* Dallas: Southern Methodist University Press, 1990.

Krampen, Martin, Michael Gotte, and Michael Kneidl. *The World of Signs: Communication by Pictographs.* New York: Avedition, 2007.

Kumar, Amitava. *Passport Photos.* Berkeley: University of California Press, 2000.

Lamadrid, Enrique. *Hermanitos Comanchitos: Indo-Hispano Rituals of Captivity and Redemption.* Albuquerque: University of New Mexico Press, 2003.

Landa, Diego de. *Yucatan Before and After the Conquest.* 1566. Trans. William Gates. New York: Dover, 1978. 2.

Leatham, Miguel. "Indigenista Hermeneutics and the Historical Meaning of Our Lady of Guadalupe of Mexico." *Folklore Forum* 22.1–2 (1989): 27–39.

León-Portilla, Miguel. *Aztec Thought and Culture: A Study of the Ancient Nahuatl Mind.* Norman: University of Oklahoma Press, 1963.

———. *Huehuetlahtolli: Testimonios de la Antigua Palabra.* 2nd ed. Mexico City: Fondo de Cultura Económica, 1992.

———. *Los Antiguos Mexicanos a Traves de Sus C.* Cultura Económica, 1961.

———. *Pre-Columbian Literatures of Mexico.* Norman: University of Oklahoma Press, 1986.

León-Portilla, Miguel, and Earl Shorris, eds. *In the Language of Kings: An Anthology of Mesoamerican Literature, Pre-Columbian to the Present.* New York: W.W. Norton, 2001.

Lewiecki-Wilson, Cynthia, and Jeff Sommers. "Professing at the Fault Lines: Composition at Open Admissions Institutions." *College Composition and Communication* 50 (1999): 438–462.

Lewis, Rand. *The Nazi Legacy: Right-Wing Extremism in Postwar Germany.* New York: Praeger, 1991.

Linebaugh, Peter, and Marcus Rediker. *The Many-Headed Hydra: The Hidden History of the Revolutionary Atlantic.* Boston: Beacon Press, 2000.

Lipson, Carol, and Roberta Binkley, eds. *Rhetoric Before and Beyond the Greeks.* Albany: State University of New York Press, 2004.

Lockhart, James. *The Nahuas After the Conquest: A Social and Cultural History of the Indians of Central Mexico, Sixteenth through Eighteenth Centuries.* Stanford: Stanford University Press, 1992.

Lugones, Maria. "On Borderlands/La Frontera: An Interpretive Essay." *Hypatia* 7 (1992): 31–37.

Lund, Joshua. *The Impure Imagination: Toward a Critical Hybridity in Latin American Writing.* Minneapolis: University of Minnesota Press, 2006.

Lunsford, Andrea. "The Nature of Composition Studies." *An Introduction to Composition Studies.* Ed. Erika Lindemann and Gary Tate. New York: Oxford University Press, 1991.

———. "Toward a Mestiza Rhetoric: Gloria Anzaldúa on Composition and Postcoloniality." *Journal of Advanced Composition* 18.1 (1998): 1–27.

Lyons, Scott Richard. "Rhetorical Sovereignty: What Do American Indians Want from Writing?" *College Composition and Communication* 51.3 (February 2000): 447–468.

Mares, E.A. *The Unicorn Poem & Flowers and Songs of Sorrow.* Albuquerque: West End Press, 1992.

Martí, José. "Autores Aborígenes Americanos." *Obras Completas.* 1884.

Maturana, Umberto, and Francisco Varela. *The Tree of Knowledge: The Biological Roots of Human Understanding.* 1992. Rev. Ed. Boston: Shambhala, 1998.

Menchaca, Martha. *Recovering History, Constructing Race: The Indian, Black, and White Roots of Mexican Americans.* Austin: University of Texas Press, 2001.

Mignolo, Walter. *The Darker Side of the Renaissance: Literacy, Territoriality, and Colonization.* Ann Arbor: University of Michigan Press, 1995.

———. *Local Histories/Global Designs: Coloniality, Subaltern Knowledges, and Border Thinking.* Princeton: Princeton University Press, 2000.

Miller, Richard E. "Composing English Studies: Towards a Social History of the Discipline." CCC 45 (May 1994): 164–179.

Mohanty, Chandra Talpade. *Feminism Without Borders: De-colonizing Theory, Practicing Solidarity.* Durham: Duke University Press, 2003 Montaño, Mary. *Tradiciones Nuevomexicanas: Hispano Arts and Culture of New Mexico.* Albuquerque: University of New Mexico Press, 2001.

Montiel, Miguel, Tomás Atencio, and E. A. Mares. *Resolana for a Dark New Age: A Chicano Dissenting Perspective on Globalization.* University of Arizona Press, forthcoming.

Moraga, Cherríe. "Codex Xeri: El Momento Historico." *The Chicano Codices: Encountering Art of the Americas.* Ed. Patricia Draher. San Francisco: Mexican Museum, 1992.

———. *The Last Generation: Prose and Poetry.* Boston: South End Press, 1993.

Moraga, Cherríe. "Queer Aztlán: The Re-Formation of Chicano Tribe." *Latina/o Thought: Culture, Politics, and Society*. Ed. Francisco Vásquez and Rodolfo Torres. New York: Rowman and Littlefield, 2003. 258–274.

Moreno, Renee. "The Politics of Location: Text as Opposition." *College Composition and Communication* 54.2 (December 2002): 222–241.

Moya, Paula, and Michael Hames-García, eds. *Reclaiming Identity: Realist Theory and the Predicament of Postmodernism*. Berkeley: University of California Press, 2000.

Murphy, James, ed. *A Short History of Writing Instruction: From Ancient Greece to Twentieth Century America*. Davis, CA: Hermagoras Press, 1990.

Murphy, James, and Richard Katula, eds. *A Synoptic History of Classical Rhetoric*. 2nd ed. Davis, CA: Hermagoras Press, 1994.

Nebrija, Antonio de. *Gramática Castellana. Salamanca*. 1517; London: Oxford University Press, 1926.

North, Steven. *Making of Knowledge in Composition: Portrait of an Emerging Field*. Upper Montclair, NJ: Boynton/Cook, 1987.

Nowotny, Karl, George Everett, and Edward Sisson. *Tlacuilolli: Style and Contents of the Mexican Pictorial Manuscripts With a Catalog of the Borgia Group*. Norman: University of Oklahoma Press, 2005.

Nuttall, Zelia, ed. *Codex Nuttall*. New York: Dover, 1975.

Nystrand, Martin, Stuart Greene, and Jeffrey Wiemelt. "Where Did Composition Studies Come From? An Intellectual History." *Written Communication* 10 (July 1993): 267–333.

Ohmann, Richard. *English in America: A Radical View of the Profession*. New York: Oxford University Press, 1976.

Olson, Gary. "Encountering the Other: Postcolonial Theory and Composition Scholarship." *Journal of Advanced Composition* 18.1 (1998): 45–55.

Olson, Gary, and Lynn Worsham. *Race, Rhetoric, and the Postcolonial*. Albany: State University of New York Press, 1999.

Ortiz, Fernando. *Cuban Counterpoint: Tobacco and Sugar*. Trans. Harriet de Onis. New York: Knopf, 1947.

Peña, Milagros. *Latina Activists across Borders: Women's Grassroots Organizing in Mexico in Mexico and Texas*. Durham: Duke University Press, 2007.

Peñafiel, Antonio. *Códice Mixteco: Lienzo de Zacatepec*. Mexico City: Secretaría de Fomento, 1900.

Pérez, Emma. *The Decolonial Imaginary*. Bloomington: Indiana University Press, 1999.

Pérez, Laura. *Chicana Art: The Politics of Spiritual and Aesthetic Altarities*. Durham: Duke University Press, 2007.

Powell, Malea. "Blood and Scholarship: One Mixed-Blood's Dilemma." *Race, Rhetoric, and Composition*. Ed. Keith Gilyard. Portsmouth, NH: Heinemann-Boynton/Cook, 1999.

Pratt, Mary Louise. "Arts of the Contact Zone." *Profession* 91 (1991): 33–40.

Quiñones Keber, Eloise. *Codex Telleriano-Remensis: Ritual, Divination, and History in a Pictorial Aztec Manuscript*. Austin: University of Texas Press, 1995.

Rabasa, José. *Writing Violence on the Northern Frontier: The Historiography of Sixteenth-Century New Mexico and Florida and the Legacy of Conquest.* Durham: Duke University Press, 2000.

Rama, Angel. *The Lettered City.* Trans. John Charles Chasteen. Durham: Duke University Press, 1996.

Ramos, Juanita. "Gloria E. Anzaldúa." *Contemporary Lesbian Writers of the United States: A Bio-Bibliographical Sourcebook.* Ed. Sandra Pollack and Denise D. Knight. Westport: Greenwood Press, 1993. 19–25.

Richardson, Elaine, and Ronald Jackson II, eds. *African American Rhetoric(s): Interdisciplinary Perspectives.* Carbondale: Southern Illinois University Press, 2004.

Ríos-Bustamante, Antonio. "A General Survey of Chicano/a Historiography." *Voices of a New Chicana/o History.* Ed. Refugio Rochín and Dennis Valdés. East Lansing: Michigan State University Press, 2000. 245–293.

Rodgers, Daniel. "An Age of Social Politics." *Rethinking American History in a Global Age.* Ed. Thomas Bender. Berkeley: University of California Press, 2002. 250–252.

Rodríguez, Ileana. "Introduction." *Latin American Subaltern Studies Reader.* Ed. Ileana Rodríguez. Durham: Duke University Press, 2001.

Rodríguez, Sylvia. *The Matachines Dance: Ritual Symbolism and Inter Ethnic Relations in the Upper Rio Grande Valley.* New Mexico: University of New Mexico Press, 1996.

Romano, Susan. "Tlaltelolco: The Grammatical-Rhetorical *Indios* of Colonial Mexico." *College English* January (2004): 9–29.

Rosales, F. Arturo. *Chicano! The History of Mexican American Civil Rights.* Houston: Arte Público Press, 1996.

Saenz, Benjamin Alire. "In the Borderlands of Chicano Identity, There Are Only Fragments." *Border Theory: The Limits of Cultural Politics.* Ed. David E. Johnson and Scott Michaelsen. Minneapolis: University of Minnesota Press, 1997. 68–96.

Sahagún, Bernardino de. *Florentine Codex: General History of the Things of New Spain.* Trans. with notes and illus. by Charles Dibble and Arthur J.O. Anderson. Santa Fe, NM: School of American Research, 1963.

Saldívar-Hull, Sonia. *Feminism on the Border: Chicana Gender Politics and Literature.* Berkeley: University of California Press, 2000.

Sánchez, Rosaura. *Chicano Discourse: Socio-Historic Perspectives.* Houston: Arte Público Press, 1994.

Sanchez-Tranquilino, Marcos. "Introduction." *The Chicano Codices: Encountering Art of the Americas.* Ed. Patricia Draher. San Francisco: Mexican Museum, 1992.

Santiago, Deborah, and Sarita Brown. *Federal Policy and Latinos in Higher Education.* Washington, DC: Pew Hispanic Center, 2004.

Sassen Saskia. *Globalization and Its Discontents: Essays on the New Mobility of People and Money.* New York: New Press, 1998.

Schroeder, Susan, Stephanie Wood, and Robert Haskett. *Indian Women of Early Mexico.* Norman: University of Oklahoma Press, 1999.

Scott, James. *Domination and the Arts of Resistance.* New Haven, CT: Yale University Press, 1990.

Segura, Denise and Patricia Zavella, eds. *Women and Migration in the U.S. Mexico Borderlands: A Reader.* Durham: Duke University Press, 2007.

Shaughnessy, Mina. *Errors and Expectations: A Guide for the Teaching of Basic Writing.* New York: Oxford University Press, 1977.

Simmons, Marc. "New Mexico's Colonial Agriculture." *El Palacio* 89.1 (Spring 1983): 3–10.

Swearingen, C. Jan. "Rhetoric, the Polis, and the Global Village. *Rhetoric, the Polis, and the Global Village: Selected Papers from the 1998 Thirteenth Anniversary Rhetoric Society of America Conference.* Ed. C. Jan Swearingen and Dave Pruett. Mahwah, NJ: Lawrence Erlbaum Associates, 1999. 3–6.

Takaki, Ronald. *From Different Shores: Perspectives on Race and Ethnicity in America.* New York: Oxford University Press, 1994.

Tedlock, Dennis, ed. *Popul Vuh: The Mayan Book of the Dawn of Life.* Charmichael, CA: Touchstone Books, 1996.

Tremblay, Gaëtan. "Is Quebec Culture Doomed to Become American?" *Canadian Journal of Communication* 17.2 (1992): 134–138.

Trovar, Juan, ed. *Codice Ramirez.* Mexico City: Editorial Leyenda, 1944.

Todorov, Tzvetan. *The Conquest of America: The Question of the Other.* New York: Harper and Row, 1982.

Vasconcelos, Jose, *The Cosmic Race: La Raza Cósmica.* 1945. Trans. Didier Jaén. Baltimore: Johns Hopkins University Press, 1997.

Vélez-Ibáñez, Carlos G. *Border Visions: Mexican Cultures of the Southwest United States.* Tucson: University of Arizona Press, 1996.

Wade, Peter. *Race and Ethnicity in Latin America.* London: Pluto Press, 1997.

Wallerstein, Emmanuel. *The Modern World System: Capitalist Agriculture and the Origins of the European World Economy in the Sixteenth Century.* New York: Academic Press, 1974.

Water Information Network. "Protecting Water and People on the Border." *The New Environmental Activists: Fighting Pollution, Poverty and Racism by Building Natural Assets.* Ed. Miriam Zoll and James Boyce. Amherst: University of Massachusetts, 2003. 54–55.

Winter, Marcus. *Oaxaca: The Archeological Record.* México: Minutiae Mexicana, 1989.

Yancey, Kathleen Blake. "Looking Back as We Look Forward: Historicizing Writing Assessment." *CCC* 50.3 (1999): 483–503.

Yarbro-Bejarano, Yvonne. "Gloria Anzaldúa's Borderlands/La Frontera: Cultural Studies, 'Difference,' and the Non-unitary Subject." *Cultural Critique* 28 (1994): 5–28.

Young, Morris. "Standard English and Student Bodies: Institutionalizing Race and Literacy in Hawai'i." *College English* 64.4 (March 2002): 405–431.

Zermeno, Sergio. "State, Society and Dependent Neoliberalism in Mexico: The Case of the Chiapas Uprising." *Politics, Social Change and Economic Restructuring in Latin America.* Ed. William Smith and Roberto Korzeniewicz. Miami: North-South Press, 1997. 123–147.

Reading and Discussion Guide

Those who communicate easily with others are likely to participate more frequently during discussion, while those who are timid or introverted may not speak at all. Therefore, it is helpful when those who talk regularly are attentive to their quiet neighbors by seeking opportunities to respectfully draw them into discussion. Telling others what you already think and know does not constitute dialogue; the most fruitful discussions are inquisitive, inclusive, and fully collaborative. Consider the following questions in small or large groups.

Questions

- How are Indigenous and Mestiz@ peoples represented on national or local news?
- What are the latest representations of Indigenous and Mestiz@ peoples on film or television?
- Who are today's most prominent Mestiz@ spokespersons? What do they have to say?
- If you have access to a Composition Textbook or Literature Reader, note how many times Mestiz@ writers are represented. Is there a satisfactory explanation of those writers' historical and present-day context? What do these Mestiz@s have to say?
- If you are a student or teacher, can you identify how, when, and under what circumstances Mestiz@s appear in your curriculum? If you are working and/or have graduated from school or college, answer the same question by recalling the last time you were in a conventional classroom or educational setting.
- Do you agree with the author's use of the term "Mestiz@," or would you propose other, more appropriate identifiers?
- As part of an ancient Mediterranean interterritorial system, early Greeks certainly did not self-identify as European. Moreover, African, Asian, Phoenician, and other cultures significantly influenced ancient Greek society. Today, however, early Greece is typically represented as an ancient European civilization. At what point in history did ancient Greeks become identified as European, and what did/does this accomplish?

- Territories and borders—both real and imagined—play a significant role in *Mestiz@ Scripts*. In what other instances do borders appear and what do they represent?
- Are "borderlands" metaphors a distraction from the material realities and lived experiences of migrants crossing the Mexico/U.S. border?
- In *Borderlands/La Frontera: The New Mestiza*, Gloria Anzaldúa does not offer a direct solution to the North American Free Trade Agreement, nor does she offer solutions for the struggles of undocumented workers in the United States. Should Anzaldúa have offered a solution?
- Does Gloria Anzaldúa reject Judeo-Christianity? Does Judeo-Christianity reject Anzaldúa?
- Anzaldúa's "new mestiza consciousness," in part, is a perpetual transgression across the symbolic borders of identity and subjectivity (cultural, economic, linguistic, gendered, erotic). Yet, Anzaldúa grounds herself in the "soil and soul" of Chicana feminist lived experiences. Since we are not all "new mestizas" any more than we are all "Aztecs," what is the cultural and intellectual relevance of "new mestiza consciousness?"
- What elements of Mesoamerican and Mestiz@ histories surprised you the most?
- One of the earliest definitions of "writing" in the Western Hemisphere is *Tlaquilolitztli*: "the spreading of color on hard surfaces." How does this complicate fashionable scholarship in visual literacy, digital literacy, and multimodal literacy studies?
- If you embraced *Tlaquilolitztli* as a point of origin, would your relationship with "writing" change? What role might "writing" play in your life?
- On what indigenous land is your institution or building located? Which indigenous nations fall within and around your region's borders? What are the present-day interests and struggles of these indigenous nations?

Index

Abbot, Don Paul, 9, 76
Abuelo, 113–14
Acoma, 44
Acuña, Rodolfo, 49
Adorno, Rolena, 135
Afghanistan, 140
African Slavery, 42, 43, 140, 160
Afro-Mestizos, 43, 120
Alarcón, Norma, 16, 82, 110
Aldama, Arturo, 34
Almaguer, Tomás, 43
Alternative Rhetoric, 32
Alvarado, Pedro, 33, 41
American Indian Movement, 55
Amoxoaque, 74, 84
Amoxtli, *see* Codex
Anahuac, 81
Anzaldúa, Gloria, 1, 5, 10, 15, 17, 54, 82, 113, 120, 122, 130
Arismendi, Yareli, 44
Arteaga, Alfred, 13, 153
Aryan-Germanic Enlightenment, 120, 137, 141
Assimilation, 5–6, 14, 20, 30
Atencio, Tomás, 58
Autohistoria, 15
Aztec/Culhua-Mexica, 36
Aztlán, 37, 83, 138, 149

Bacon, Francis, 129
Barron, Nancy, 8
Bartholomae, David, 22
Berlin, James, 152
Bernal, Martin, 150
Bhabha, Homi, 90
Binkley, Roberta, 151
Bizzell, Patricia, 22, 122
Black Panthers, 55
Blood-quantum Identity Politics, 16
Boon-Hill, Elizabeth, 77–8, 139
Brown Berets, 55
Brujaria, 28
Burciaga, José Antonio, 156–7

Calaveras, 80
Calmecac, 26, 27, 70, 73, 110
Campbell, George, 129
Carrasco, Davíd, 85
Cascajal block, 35
Caso, Alfonso, 77
Castillo, Debra, 21
Catolicos Por La Raza, 55
Chagoya, Enrique, 64, 80
Champe, Flavia, 104
Chavero, Alfredo, 76
Chavez, Cesar, 54, 130
Chicano Movement, 54–6, 74
Chicano Spanish, 28
Chingada, 17
Cholula, 41
Choreography, 1
Christianization, 9, 18, 25–6, 29, 42, 66, 74, 79, 81, 85
Cicero, 129
Cintron, Ralph, 8
Coatlicue, 17, 148

Codex/Book/Amoxtli, 1, 26, 63, 68–75
Comparative Rhetoric, 31
Connors, Robert, 119, 147
Conversion, 6
Cortéz, Hernán, 17, 40, 73, 81, 84
Culture
  defined, 4
Curanderismo, 28

Díaz del Castillo, Bernal, 40, 43
Diego Vigil, James, 54
Difrasismo, 70
Digital Cultures, 7
Diop, Cheikh Anta, 150
Douglass, Frederick, 129
Dozier, Edward, 102
Dussel, Enrique, 13, 142–5, 162

Ehrle, Franz, 76
Encomenderos, 42
Erasmus, Desiderius, 129

Fukuyama, Francis, 153

García, Alma, 57
Geertz, Clifford, 2–3
Gilyard, Keith, 151
Globalization, 5, 21, 26, 42, 64
Gómez-Peña, Guillermo, 44, 64, 81
Gordon, Lewis, 139
Grimké, Sarah, 129
Guadalupe/Coatlaxopeuh, 17, 66, 86–7, 108
Guaraní, 145
Guarneri, Carl, 141
Guerra, Juan, 8

Haas, Angela, 7
Hames-Garcia, Michael, 21
Hayles, N. Katherine, 7
Hemispheric Plurality, 13
Hernández-Avila, Inés, 27, 84
Herzberg, Bruce, 22, 122
Hidalgo y Costilla, Miguel, 47
Historiography, 14
Huehuetlahtolli, 4, 9, 26–7, 70–1, 145
Huerta, Dolores, 54
Huitzilopochtli/Mexitli, 37, 38
Hume, David, 129

In tlilli in tlapalli, 25, 69
In xochitl in cuicatl, 70
Indo-Hispano, 97, 101
Inka Khipu, 35
Iraq, 140
Invention, 5, 14, 16, 28
Itzcóatl, 38

Keali'Inohomoku, Joann, 3–4
Kurath, Gertrude, 104

Lake Texcoco, 36
League of Latin American Citizens, 53
Leatham, Miguel, 108
Lemon Grove Grammar School, 52
León-Portilla, Miguel, 26, 78, 84, 139, 150
Lipson, Carol, 151
Locke, John, 129
Lunsford, Andrea, 24
Lyons, Scott, 141

Malcolm X, 130
Malinche/Malintzin Tenepal, 107–13, 148
Marcus, Joyce, 77
Mares, E.A., 1, 6, 14, 58, 59
Marianismo, 86–7
Martí, José, 119, 149
Mejía, Jaime Armín, 8
Menchaca, Martha, 43
Mestizaje, 2
Mexican Revolution, 75
Mexitli/Mexica/Mexicatl, 54
Mignolo, Walter, 13, 27, 31, 91, 135
Moctezuma, 39, 107

Montiel, Miguel, 58
Montoya, Delilah, 80
Moraga, Cherrie, 57, 63, 64, 80
Moreno, Renee, 8
Movimiento Estudiantil Chicano de Aztlán (MeCha), 55
Mural Art/Writing, 74, 79

National Hispanic Cultural Center Foundation, 118
Navajo-Dine, 20
Nebrija, Antonio, 29
Nepantla, 25, 107, 111
new mestiza consciousness, 1, 5, 10, 13–14, 16, 18–25
Nezahualcoyotl, 65
North American Free Trade Agreement, 64, 89
Nuttall, Zelia, 76
Nyanga, Gaspar, 43

O'ke Owinge, 59–60
Olmec, 34, 69
Oñate, Don Juan, 44–5
Ortiz, Fernando, 123

Pedagogy, 22, 30
Peñafiel, Antonio, 76
Pérez, Laura, 106
Petrosky, Anthony, 22
Plato, 4
Pohl, John, 77
Popé, 45, 59, 61
Popul Vuh, 33
Posada Aguilar, José Guadalupe, 80
Powell, Malea, 141
Pratt, Mary Louise, 24, 122, 124
Proposition 187, 56
Pueblo Revolt, 44–5, 59, 116
Puerto Rican Young Lords, 55

Quetzalcoatl, 40, 65, 71, 80, 84, 112
Quiche Maya, 36
Quintilian, 129

Radin, Paul, 76
Reynoso, Diego, 33
Rhetoric and Composition Studies, 3, 5, 8–9, 22
Rice, Felicia, 64, 81
Ríos-Bustamante, Antonio, 148
Rivera, Diego, 98
Robb, John, 104
Robertson, Donald, 77
Rodríguez, Sylvia, 105
Romano, Susan, 9–10
Rosales, Arturo, 53

Saenz, Benjamin Alire, 19
Sahagún, Bernadino, 9, 31
San Ysidro Labrador, 116–17
Sánchez, Rosaura, 28
Sanchez-Tranquilino, Marcos, 79
Semasiography, 69
Sephardic Crypto-Jews, 43
September 11th, 140, 162
Sleepy Lagoon Murder Trial, 53
Snake Woman, 17
Spanglish, 64
Spanish-American war, 140
Steward, Maria, 129
Swearingen, C. Jan, 119

Tahurumaran Ancestry, 20
Techialoyan, 74
Tenochtitlan, 26, 36–8, 61, 73, 81, 84
Teotihuacán, 69
Tijerina Alianza, 54
Tlacuiloliztli, 29, 70, 99
Tlacuiloque, 27, 70, 78
Tlaloc, 37
Tlaltelolco, 9, 73
Tlamatinime, 27, 70, 78
Todorov, Tzvetan, 56
Toltec, 37, 84
Trail of Tears, 161
Transculturación, 123
Transmodernity, 145

Treaty of Guadalupe Hidalgo, 51–3, 55, 74, 132
Triple Alliance, 109, 138
Tulum, 95

United Farm Workers Union, 54
Urton, Gary, 35

Vargas, Don Diego, 45
Vasconcelos, Jose, 16, 17
Vélez-Ibáñez, Carlos, 56–7
Vigil, Frederico, 95, 96–9, 117
Villanueva, Victor, 9

Wallerstein, Immanuel, 145
Water Information Network, 115
Williams, Raymond, 3
World War II, 148
Writing Systems, 7

Xi, *see* Olmec
Ximénez, Francisco, 33
Xochiquetzal, 112

Yancuic Tlahtolli, 27, 78, 84, 87
Yaqui, 20

Zootsuit Riots, 53

CPSIA information can be obtained at www.ICGtesting.com
Printed in the USA
LVOW082203240512

283242LV00003B/33/P